Chapter 1. The Begi

We all have our very own story to tell, we.. would like to introduce myself. My name is Justin, and I was born on Mother's Day in Plymouth, Devon. I have a clear and definite recollection of a day in January, when I was about four years old. Looking out of the window I could see that there had been a heavy snowfall which had fallen overnight. Snow had piled up to a considerable depth on both the tarmac and the grass verges. My Gran and Grandad were going to look after me for the day

My Dad told me to put my trainers on as soon as possible since he had a football game. We walked from our house to make our way to my Grandparent's house. At the bottom of a very steep hill, my father offered me a piggyback ride on his shoulder. Dad had only taken a few steps, and he slipped, I flew above his head and landed on the treacherous ground below me landing on my head. Blood was pouring, dripping down my face into my eyes, I could barely see my head was thumping with a massive headache. My Dad ran into a house nearby and called for an ambulance, an ambulance arrived and rushed me to the nearest hospital's emergency department, where I eventually received thirteen stitches to my head. I was unable to see my Gran and Grandad at their home, that day. My Grandparents worked at the same building in Bath, Somerset, which served as one of our country's Military and Defence headquarters. They had their first meeting there, they both lived in Bath at that time. My Grandad was born in Devonport. He was such a soft gentle soul, always smartly dressed, he loved cars before he married, he had a red sports car. My Grandparents had my Mum after a few years of being married.

My Mum was born in Bath. My Mum is quite small with strawberry blonde hair, she is very much like her dad, very softly spoken and despising any form of conflict. My Gran held an administrative job with James Murray Widdecombe during her career, James was the Minister in parliament for the Ministry of Defence. Ann Widdecombe was his daughter, Gran used to babysit for her in Bath. She loved to talk about this to me, especially if Ann was on television. Gran used to say this with the greatest of pride. My Gran was an extraordinary woman who was constantly full of energy. She was so enthusiastic about her work. It was forbidden for her to disclose any details of her work in the Civil Service due to its extremely sensitive nature. Obviously, she never discussed anything with me, I was aware that, besides working for the Government, she was a Red Cross volunteer throughout the war. My Gran grew up in Somerset, where her family had a confectionery store which was part of the house. She had four sisters and one brother; my Great Grandma ran the shop.

My Great Grandfather's surname was Sperring, none of the girls carried on the family name, he worked in the coal mines. My Gran was devoted to her sisters, they lost their only younger brother at the age of ten. He was riding on the back of a bicycle with his friend which crashed into a lorry on a notorious hill, remarkably close to their family home. His friend died too the lorry driver never ever drove again. My Gran would tell me this story with tears in her eyes. She did not allow my Mum to have a bicycle, but she did allow her son eventually. My Gran's Uncle was the chairman of Bristol Rovers, Gran was a significant blues enthusiast. My Great-grandfather Charlie was a remarkable man, used to wear a top hat and a suit with a one eye lens with a chain he looked the part. His family owned a dairy shop in Dartmouth, Devon, where they sold and made various dairy products. The whole family worked there. The house is still standing in Dartmouth to this very day. The shop was in an ideal location, just a stone's throw from the sea, with a stunning view of a massive river going towards the sea. It was a blessing to visit my Great Grandfather when I was a child, he lived close by to my Grandparents. He belonged to the Freemasons and held a high rank. He had the rank of Grandmaster. My Gran drove my Great Grandfather plus myself to church every Sunday, my Grandad never attended a church. My Grandad described it as "an old pile of garbage." My Grandfather took us as a family unit with my Great Grandfather to obtain his Maundy Money from Queen Elizabeth at Exeter Cathedral. He was so proud to receive this accolade which was for his service to the church. I had the greatest day with a smile from the Queen which I will always remember.

My Great Grandfather lived near the home Park stadium, where Plymouth Argyle played. He used to tell me remarkable stories about the team. Johnny Hore, a Plymouth Argyle player, later a manager, lived behind my great-grandfather's back garden. He would frequently talk to him across the wall that separated the back gardens. My Great Grandfather loved working in his garden whenever he could. He grew all kinds of vegetables and fruit, although I did not like gooseberries. Great Grandad one day fell from his apple tree when he was ninety years old, this caused his health to deteriorate, which led him to move into a residential care home. He unfortunately passed the day before his ninety fifth birthday, it was a huge loss to our family. I was so fortunate to have spent excellent quality time with him.

My other Grandma, my Father's Mum, had an affair with an Apache Indian man who was in the United States Army. This was considered a felony at the time his mum went to Manchester from Plymouth to have to give birth to my dad. My Dad remained deeply upset that he never had the opportunity to meet his birth, Father although my Dad's Stepfather, Ken was a great role model to the family, a navy man and a knowledgeable, kind man. He was brilliant to my dad, very friendly and kind, Dad told me lots of pleasant things about Ken and Dad felt he could not have asked for a nicer Stepfather.

The horror stories he told me when he was child about his Mum were horrific. Parts of Keyham in Plymouth were notorious for being rough, people got brought up hard, rough, and ready. My Dad had to do his siblings' washing by hand and clean the house. His Mum would beat him black and blue the other kids did not see this he was deemed the black sheep of the family. My Dad had three younger sisters, and three younger brothers and his Mum adopted another boy and girl. So, there were nine kids to feed. Ken was the dad of the other brothers and sisters. Ken had a brother named Ron, he was my Great Uncle, he was a kind man, although at times he lived with one of his sisters, he also liked to live in a tramp style of living.

Ron often had a rat in his pocket, he was often seen in the streets of Plymouth with a shopping cart filled with clothing and snacks for the homeless. I saw Ron several times as he pushed his trolley up and down Royal Parade, he wore a blazer, giving him the appearance of an elderly character, of Grandad from the TV program "Only Fools and Horses." Ron was well known in Plymouth for his charity work, he never touched a drink. I spoke to lots of tramps who loved Ron, and he was painted by local artists. Boxing was extremely popular in my father's family, particularly among his younger siblings.

My Dad's favourite sport was football. My Dad had skills like Diego Maradona. He had trials with Plymouth Argyle, which was against my grandma's wishes for him to play. She told him that he was not allowed to play. One day she hid his football boots, and he could not find them anywhere. My Dad had to sneak out of the window and walk up to Home Park with his friends to get trials. Dad had to play with his trainers on, he was playing for about twenty minutes before his friends saw his Mum coming up to the bank. His friends shouted at my dad, but he did not hear them. His Mum ran onto the pitch shouting 'you little bastard' then she struck him over the head with metal-studded football boots. The blood was dripping down his head, Dad ran home.

Dad eventually ran away from his home when he was sixteen. He could not stay with his Mum anymore, he always wanted to be a footballer, but his Mum ruined his dreams. Dad had helped with gardening for Avis and Reg, his friend's parents, in exchange for some extra pocket money. Eventually they provided a place for my father to stay, it was just a couple of houses away from his family home. Dad looked up to them both as his parents, Avis, especially as if she were his mother. Dad worked in the Royal Naval Armament Depot, he was able to play and enjoy football. He played semi-professional for Falmouth but later for the civil service and he frequented played with his friends.

The Falcon pub was a few streets away from where he lived. My Mum worked in The Falcon evenings, although she was not old enough. She worked all day as well but really wanted to save to buy her first car. Mum was seventeen, Dad was slightly older, that is where they first met. They got engaged, soon after they got married. They lived in rented accommodation extremely close to my Grandparents and decided to return to Mum's parents' house to save eventually for their own home. Fourteen months later my sister Rachel was born.

Mum became the housekeeper for the household as everybody worked. The house was in Beacon Park at the posher end, well-known Swilly was at the other end. Despite Swilly being rundown and tough in parts the locality it remains the same to this very day. There are still some originals who have remained there and their relatives who would not live anywhere else. I was born two years and a few months after my sister, we remained at my Grandparent's house until we moved to our very first three bedroomed house in St Budeaux.

The house in St Budeaux had old floorboards which made screeching noises. My Dad made a Ouija board in the house. It seemed like there was a dark presence when I went to bed. I could always hear a noise getting closer, like a screeching sound always happening in bed late at night. One day when I was at play school, there was a thunderstorm; lightning struck the house next door causing a fire. Although we were extremely grateful to have our own home it was not the best area to live. Eventually we were transferred to a brand, new house on a new estate in Thornbury. It was a lovely area with plenty of fields and open space with horses, cows, and a farm nearby. It still is a lovely part of Plymouth, but of course there have been many changes made which were inevitable. I loved the new house. We had a beautiful long garden, woods facing the back garden, it had three bedrooms and a driveway. I thought everything was simply fine with family, although you do not see or understand what really goes on at the tender age of four years old.

Mum worked evenings to help to support us. But one day unexpectedly my Mum met another man named Trevor. He also worked in the Dockyard, he eventually left there and started running his own business and become a taxi driver and a landlord. Mum left us children and went off with Trevor, although I could not understand at that time why.

My Dad took good care of us, and Mum's parents were amazing they were always there for me and my sister they spoilt us rotten so it more than made up for Mums absence. They spoiled us with the best food, day trips and love. I often asked for crisps, Gran would say 'yes just take one packet' so I went in the cupboard and always took two or even three whilst hiding them and then going to hide upstairs to eat them. Gran was soft and would give us most things we asked for.

Grandad, well he was the opposite, he loved to save every penny he needed to, as my nan would spend money like water. Gran spoke with a posh Bristol accent, while Grandad spoke poshly with a very gentle voice. He loved to listen to the radio and his records. He would listen to his music whenever he could, driving everyone else potty. I would try to help with jobs, with a knife cutting out weeds in the grass, cutting the grass, washing his car, and cleaning the windows with vinegar. I hated the smell of vinegar. He would give me money to go to the shops at Ham Green.

I used to take their dog for a walk called Becky, a beautiful golden retriever whom I spent so much time with. She was a lovely natured dog full of love. Gran always said that 'manners do not cost anything 'I would always say 'Good Morning' to most people especially, my elders as Gran said, 'you should always respect your elders and help people that are less fortunate than yourself.' She also said 'you do not need to swear' but I could not help swearing sometimes, she would say that she would have to wash my mouth out with soap. She was so funny and made me laugh so much. She had, such an enthusiastic sense of humour.

I stayed at my Grandparents house at least three times a week, especially weekends. Me and my sister had two different houses to live in when we were children.

I used to be so nervous. On my first day at school, it was so scary, but after lunchtime I realized that there was nothing to fear at all. I met new friends who lived in the same street and others not too far from away. The new friends that I met arranged to play football after tea, so I felt great about going to school. On my third day at school, I had an accident and pooped myself. My friend's mother worked in the school cafeteria, so she cleaned me up. It was so embarrassing. They phoned my Grandparents, and they had to come and pick me up as Dad was working.

Nick M was a friend of mine, simply mad with his monkey hairstyle. He was a bad boy, but a funny boy, who tried to be the ringleader, he was very boisterous. In the first week, he informed the girls on the opposite side of the table that the boys would show their manhood if they showed us their bits under the table. My friends and I then exchanged nude flashes. Mark and I pulled our pants up quickly. Nick M had not yet put his little pecker away. The teacher completed her cigarette and returned to the classroom. She asked, 'Nick M what are you doing?' The whole class burst into laughter. Nick M was so humiliated and legged it home he did not live far but he was gone in a flash. We played all sorts of games in the playground, there was a metal airplane, we all pretended to be flying this metal plane. We would skip and play football, my childhood was a happy one, especially at school. I loved playing games at break time, but I did not enjoy schoolwork. I was just rubbish at writing, reading and math's.

Dad found a lady nearby who was our child minder. She kept an eye on us so that Dad was able to work. Once the lady cooked us dinner it was faggots which was just like meatballs. I was not too fond of faggots, the smell, the taste was utterly disgusting, I told her I was not eating that shit. The unpleasant woman told me to wash my mouth out with a bar of soap. She shoved it in my mouth, I was feeling sick. I told her to get fucked and that she was not my Mum. I ran away but my sister chased me, we waited outside our house till my dad got home. We only lived up the road from the evil lady. Our father came home from work and said he would find another babysitter to look after us. Time passed and Dad was on the bus one day and met a nice woman named Pamela. Mum applied to the courts to have her children back, Dad had done his best, but she was granted custody.

Mum returned to our home, while Dad moved in with Pamela as she had her own home. Pamela had two older sons who worked but were still living at home. My Father was good to me, he taught me all the fundamental football skills I needed to know. He took me up a country lane about a five-minute walk away where there was a junior school with a football pitch. He would unleash a barrage of shots at me, from his goal to my goal. I would smack them back. My Dad taught me to kick the ball at the bottom of the ball to make the ball go high in the air and to keep the ball low to put your head down and kick the ball in the middle. This helped tremendously. The pitch was tiny, exactly right for me to learn, I played with my football boots on. As a result, I became a brilliant goalkeeper, and I excelled at long shots. I was good at playing out of goal as well, my all-round game was good. After playing the game with my dad, Pamela was kind to me. She grilled the best burgers with onions and brown sauce, they were the best burgers and tasted delicious. I would then help my dad with gardening, he had an allotment right next to where he lived. After a roast dinner I caught the bus back to Mums on my own. Back then, being a kid was a lot safer than it is now. It made me street wise and independent. One-week Dad took my sister and me on the bus into town so we could have a Wimpy. Dad made us get off the bus as he had seen Trevor washing his car with a bright red bucket. He told us to be quiet as we crept up and my sister and I had to hide behind a car. Dad was on his tip toes whilst he approached Trevor quietly from behind. He grabbed the red bucket Trevor was washing the car window he did not see Dad. Dad placed the bucket over his head, the water was dripping down his neck, the red bucket was stuck on top of Trevor's head. My father took a few steps back and punched the bucket so hard with a punch. Trevor went to the floor knocked out cold. He lay there motionless for a short while with the bucket still on his head, before getting up from the pavement. Dad then took us on to town for a haircut and a Wimpy which was my favourite burger place.

Amy and Jason were my cousins they both looked Spanish with their very dark features. Amy was pretty she loved to play football with me and Jason who was a natural all-round sportsman. For a young girl she played football well. We always had our football games on Sundays, at my Grandparents' house, either in the garden or in the drive, up against the bright red garage door at the back of their driveway, our pretend goal. We also used to play hide seek; were one of us would hide and the other two would have to find the person my Grandparents had a quite large house so there was plenty of places to hide away. We always followed our games with a delicious roast dinner and salad for afternoon tea. Some weekends we would park at the Tamar Bridge and just watch as trains passed through from Devon to Cornwall. Grandad loved to watch the trains go past. He would sometimes get ice cream from the ice cream van afterwards.

There were other times Grandad would drive us over the Tamer Bridge and a few miles down country lanes to pick primroses. Gran loved picking primroses in this lane, it was like a secret spot with thousands of primroses in the hedge. I always remember the scarecrow that stood in a field, I loved Wurzel Gummidge the TV program as a kid. The scarecrow in the field reminded me of him. My Auntie Kay and Uncle Robert had a chalet in Whitsands Bay in Cornwall, it was nestled in the cliffs. Me and my sister would play with our cousins Stewart and Michael, swing ball, tennis, football, and swimming. We went every summer holiday as kids with Mum, our Grandparents and Kay's Mum, Aunty Dot she was related to Grandad. Mum loved it there, so did I, it has many beaches, long walks which are down steep cliffs to the beaches, a stunning place to visit. I would play football every day with friends from school. We would also play football at the school; we would jump over the fence to play when we should not have been there. I played with older lads too, over at Biggie Park with the Pollard and Chapman's family. Me and my friend Matt also went to Marjon's, a sports college, where we played with older lads from my sisters' year group. The pitch was amazing, it was a perfect likeness to the pitch at Wembley with the nets up on the goal. We played with so many diverse groups of boys who enjoyed playing football. I managed to play some sort of football each day, I loved it, it was my life. When I was ten, I played for the school football team. We had a tournament at Staddiscombe, Plymstock on a full-size football pitch. I was good in any position, but I played as goalkeeper. Dad taught me as a child it made it easy for me to save kids' shots easier as his shots were much harder to save. We did have talented players and Matt had amazing skills like Gazza. Mrs. Hatherley was the school's football manager, it was quite unusual for a woman to be in charge, back then, but we had a big football competition. She knew exactly how to coach us and was an exceptionally good coach. Most of the lads knew each other's game as we had played football together from the age of five upwards, growing up together as a team.

Nick had the appearance of a bulldog, he played like one and always told us all that he was a bulldog, and that no one would ever get past him easily, if they did, he would kick them. Nick was the naughtiest kid out of all of us, he even smoked when he was only ten years old. He loved to have fights; he was just so boisterous. Leighton was also in our team he took his spot in the middle of the defence, he was tall, a brilliant defender who could pass the ball well. Paul, well he was loud, he boiled with rage and went red in the face when he shouted. He had a short fuse, but was a brilliant player, he was not to be messed with as he was hard as nails, not the tallest but of firm build, he played right back. He reminded me of madman Francis Franco Begbie from the film Trainspotting, no one in their right mind would upset Paul. Carl was so mouthy he acted like he was a hard, but he would not hurt a fly. Carl had good skills, he was the joker out of the pack, he was a good laugh, Carl played on the right side of midfield.

Matt's skills were amazing, we were always messing around in the playground. When Matt had his trainers on it was almost impossible to get the ball off him. He had the same abilities as Gazza did. However, he was always the best when he played with trainers on for some reason. Matt was easily our best outfield player, but he just was not perfect when he had football boots on. He could not master the spins and drag backs that he often played when he had his trainers on. He was one of the best players in Plymouth for his age.

Daniel was like Ryan Giggs with his left foot. He lived in a nearby expensive house but a very down to earth lad he did not act like he was better than any of us. Most of the team came from the council estate. Whereas Daniel came from the posh houses that were situated at the top of the road near the airport. The airport is no longer there, Daniel was a kind boy he was a good laugh too he loved Manchester United, he was a left winger. Neil H was another player from a nice area, he lived near Daniel he was a strong centre forward. He was of big build; he could hold the ball up nicely and could score a goal or two. Ian was such a fast-little skinny skinhead with a bit of a temper for someone so small. He was so fast, but he was not scared of anyone, he was a centre forward, but he could chase the other players like a little whippet.

Tyron was a good, steady midfield player. He reminded me of Jamie Redknapp with his smart looks. Scott was a reserve, a cute blonde boy always with a big smile, a skilful player, he had great skills even though he was a substitute.

We competed in a football tournament hosted in Plymstock. It was all the primary schools in Plymouth with one big knockout competition like the FA cup. The prize if we got through the competition the final game was being played at Plymouth Argyle's ground Home Park. I wanted so much to get through and take part in the final. A dream of mine was to play in front of the

Argyle fans before a league match at Home Park. So, we played the first game and won easily, I cannot recall what school it was against. My joy was uncontrollable. We breezed through the other two games. We were in the quarter final, and we should have won as our school team was far better at football than their school.

It was the last minute of the game, and someone ran through, and Nick recklessly chopped their player with one of the dirtiest fouls and conceded a late penalty. I really wanted to win as we were so close to getting to the semi-final our big chance to play at Home Park. The goal was so big for me only being ten years old, a boy ran up and smashed the ball into the left top corner. This side was my weakest side to dive for the ball, but I managed to lunge and dive so high and tip the ball, over the bar, it was the best dive I ever did. All the team jumped on me, it felt good just as if I was a hero. Very soon after we were playing again, the ball came to me, I picked it up and booted it to the other end of the pitch. The ball went over the defence to Scott, who had just come on as a substitute, he ran through and lobbed the ball past the keeper. It was a great goal, we all dived on top of him, and we were through to the semi-final. The semi-final was beginning to feel as if it were the final, as the prize was to win our last match and then we would be playing at home Park, the home of Plymouth Argyle.

It was a nail-biter right throughout the game, it was so close, we were the better team, however we lost 3-2. We all went home muddy and miserable; I got over it after a while I felt so gutted. Then Mrs. Hatherley called us for a meeting we did not have a clue what the meeting was about. We could not believe that the other team was going on a school holiday. We all jumped up out of our seats, screaming with joy. My ambition was to compete and play at Home Park. It was going to happen, what a brilliant feeling, I had butterflies for an exceptionally long time before we played the game.

We were to be playing Woolwell primary school. They were posh boys from a posh estate, we thought that we had a great chance of winning. Ian Calvert, a DJ from the local radio station, was the referee of the game. I do not know why it was called the Police Cup. There were about sixteen thousand fans waiting to watch Plymouth Argyle play. I was so nervous in front of so many people, the butterflies killed me on this day. My legs were shaking, the pitch looked so massive. The game kicked off, one of their players after five minutes came clean through, I raced out, he took a shot to my left side. I tipped the ball around the post, the crowd were cheering, I got the chills right through my body. It felt so good, I thought at the time, I could one day play here as a professional, this was my dream. I was making some unbelievable saves, every time I did the crowd seemed to be on my side. From the beginning of the match every save I made I would get the biggest of cheers, it was an amazing feeling. The game ended in a 0-0 draw. It went to penalties and their first penalty a boy stepped up with glasses on they must have been steamed up he took a huge run up and shot at me, it hit the left corner flag. Both teams had five penalties each, it was sudden death, the tallest boy on the pitch stepped up for them he blasted it past me, we lost we were gutted. I had a momentous day even though we lost, it was a great memory to get to play on the pitch of my dream, my favourite football team, I was football crazy back then.

On Saturdays, I played for Elm United, they were in the Devon Junior Minor league. I played in goal. It was mostly lads from school and some from nearby neighbourhoods, we played in orange tops. We jelled as a team, we all hung around with each other playing in the streets getting up to mischief, we played football with each other all the time. I was an amazing goalkeeper, but it was annoying me as I knew I was good enough to play out of goal.

Chapter 2. Shadows of Innocents

 My first day at Grange Hill, some called it at the time, just like the TV program the people were a little mad, to say the least. It was called Estover Secondary school. The first thing we had to do was get into our tutor groups for registration for twenty minutes. Then we had to go to assembly and sing songs and pray, it was like going to church for twenty minutes. I was absolutely rubbish at schoolwork, but when the teacher handed out the timetable for lessons, there were a lot of sports to do. This was my favourite thing to do, I was a sports freak.

We had green jumpers with a green and yellow tie, I wore Farah trousers, they were fashionable back then. I knew what it was like at school as my sister went there, she was crazy too, fighting boys, she broke one of the hardest boys' noses. I loved break times, they sold the best chocolate biscuits, they were massive, the biggest I have ever seen, we used to run to the restaurant, in case they sold out. The school free meals were the best hot meals, I used to steal a big French stick and put it up my jumper sometimes, I was greedy but skinny at that age. We had such a laugh in school, I never did much schoolwork, we would all just play pranks on each other. The most common prank was when someone was standing up, someone would sneak behind them and go on the floor in a little ball, someone in front of them would push them and they would fall over backwards on the person on the floor, that was just one prank out of many pulled. Also, another prank was when someone went to sit on their chair, we would pull it away.

One day, I pulled away the chair from a girl called Kerry, she smacked her head badly on the table, she ran out of the room screaming and crying. I felt so bad, but I could not apologies, she went and told a teacher then she got sent home, I got detention. She lived behind us, I do not know why at the time she really annoyed me, for some reason she just got on my nerves.

I used to play football every day after school with Paul, Ryan, and Matt, Ryan lived opposite, Paul Croke lived right outside the football courts. We played our usual games of heads, volleys, and Wembley was pitch black as we always played until we could not see any daylight. I was walking up the hill, towards my home which was halfway up the hill. The entrance to the Fursdon Leisure Centre had a huge hedge around it, this man jumped out on me. It was Kerry's Dad, he was a huge and chubby man, he was carrying a baseball bat which he swung at me. I ducked and dodged him and ran quickly home to ring my dad to tell him what had happened. Dad told me he would not be long, he left immediately on his push bike. Dad was at my house in no time, he told me to hide behind a fence and stay put. I could not help but look around the fence. My Dad then knocked on the front door of the house.

The big man answered the door. They were standing on the front doorstep, my father lent back, all I saw was my dad punch him right on the jaw. Dad taught me how to fight, he always said the best place to punch is on the jaw. Dad did that, the man was knocked unconscious, he just lay not moving, out for the count on his doorstep. I thanked Dad for coming so quickly, he told me you should not get in any trouble from now on and if you do phone me straight away. I never had any grief from him ever again, I bumped into him a week later. I apologized for what I had done to his daughter. He said it was not a problem, he was always nice to me after that.

My sister and I were always close, she always looked out for me, she was kind, she used to pay me to go to the shops. I did not mind it was crisps and sweets for me.

The best class at school to mess around was the English lesson, I used to sit down with Mike and Neil, we entertained ourselves by playing American football with a two-pence piece. We just flicked the two-pence piece with our fingers and the two pence would normally slide off the table but sometimes it would land right on the edge of the table. We then had to flick our middle finger from where the two pence were hanging on the edge of the table, then we had to catch the two-pence piece in our hand. The other player had to make a goal with their hands like an American goal post. Then you had to put it in between your thumbs, to flick the coin over the hand goal for an extra point.

I could hardly see anything on the projector board. I did not know I needed glasses as a child until later in life. There were not many opticians around in those days, I thought it was normal not to see too far away I did not know, I thought that was the way it was. I was put in a group of students who had special needs who had learning difficulties.

We did not have the knowledge they have these days with mental illnesses, we just got called the dunce group, away from the others. I just messed around in school and just thought I was going to be a footballer, so I did not try at school.

I participated in sports and excelled, performing at an elevated level in any sport. I was in the rugby, cricket, and football teams, I was brilliant at tennis, running and any sports with a ball. But Mr. T, a sports teacher, loathed me. I did not give him a reason to not like me, it was that he singled me out and hated me. On one occasion the school's cricket team played John Kitto. I played football against Duncan, and despite our rivalry, when we played against each other at football we were good friends in the football world. Mr. T was the empire at the time, I chucked the ball behind Mr. T, but the throw was illegal, I did not do the normal over arm; I threw the ball full pelt. It hit Duncan's pads hard. Even Duncan laughed at Mr. T did not find it amusing at all, he went red in the face, Mr. T then picked up the ball and tossed it squarely at my head. Thank goodness I ducked; he was well known for having a short fuse. I really wanted to smack him. I returned the ball to him by throwing it back towards his head, but I missed by miles. He informed me I needed to take an early shower, most kids thought he was watching them while they were in the shower, they referred to him as a pervert. He did not play by the rules,

I was one the best Players out of the whole of Plymouth, at least I thought I was. As a centre back no one could pass me, I also played midfield. I had skills like Gazza but when I played in defence I would go where the ball was to play a free role. As soon as the other team got the ball, I would rush back in defence and go back into a sweeper role. This tactic worked for every team I played with; it gave an extra player in midfield. I was good as a winger and even brilliant at playing as a centre forward. I could play anywhere to a high standard, my first season with Elm in goal we won the league.

The second season the A team goalkeeper joined us Phillip, he was an amazing goalkeeper, his dad was a remarkable manager he took over the club and changed the name to Estover. He made me the captain; I loved that role. That year we won the league again and I won the players player trophy.

We won the next season as well and I won the players player and managers player of the year, which is rare as they normally let another kid get a trophy. We won the league out of all the teams in Plymouth. The fact that I won both trophies just proved that Mr. T was not playing by the rules, making me sub for the A team. I was the goalkeeper for the B team just to keep me happy, but I was not happy while he picked his favourites, who were not the best players it was very annoying, it did not do much for my confidence. As a result of his acts, my trust in him diminished.

When I was in the B team as goalkeeper, which was the reserve team, I took a goal kick while I was in my penalty box. The wind picked up, I kicked the ball, and it flew above the goalkeeper's head. The ball went right in the goal without bouncing, I had the biggest kick in Plymouth for my age. People could not believe how far I could kick the ball, as it was unusual for someone of my age to kick the ball that far. Sometimes when I was goalkeeper, I would take on all eleven players and dribble around the field, to score goals without passing the ball, it was all in good humour.

At break time and lunch times we would play football. Neil was an excellent goalkeeper. Chris, a ginger-haired young man, a clever lad but for a posh boy he enjoyed a good laugh. Steve and Chris were classified as nerds, but Steve loved football too, he was a good friend at school. Andrew was the most intelligent person in our year, he was a genius, but his breath stunk. I do not think he ever cleaned his teeth, but he was a pleasant lad with his short curly dark hair. Steve was another example of a geek, but he was an admirable player, Steve was in the B team. Ollie, who was a real nerd, had older parents than ours. At the time, the couple were in their late fifties, Ollie was a major source of amusement. In pursuit of the ball, he would run after it, he was a dirty clumsy player. He was rubbish but was a clever lad with his schoolwork.

Then Nathan, a ginger lad, was rubbish simply nuts, he was a menace in class always getting into trouble. Neil was a goalkeeper, a good keeper but there were lots of good goalkeepers at that school, but he should have been in the goal for the B Team. This Ginger lad, Gary would play was good despite being a geek, he always had a smile on his face, he was from the rich estate, and in most of my classes. Michael D was obsessed with cars. He played football even though he was not interested in it. Then as his name suggests, Lofty with blonde hair was a very tall centre-forward for the B squad. He was musically gifted and should have at least been a sub for the A Team. But Mr. T was not a fair teacher.

Every break time and dinner time we would put our bags to make our own goals up. We had a fun time playing football every single day.

I socialized with people from all levels of society, from the insane to the geeks whose situation I would pity. We would stick drawing pins on the chairs of teachers and particularly the girls. So, it was no surprise that the girls had a grudge against us. To say the teachers went insane would be an understatement. We had to do woodwork lessons.

Mr. H was a woodwork teacher, he absolutely adored his prized guitar. He had to go to the toilet, so he left a bunch of naughty kids in the room. Jodie, who had white hair was the maddest in the room and one of the nuttiest in the year. He glued the teacher's briefcase which was next to the guitar to the guitar. Mr. H returned to the room. The room went silent, he picked up his briefcase, all the guitar's strings snapped, his pride and joy. Mr. H absolutely lost his head, despite his reputation as a meek Christian, Mr. H went mental. He screamed, "Who has done this to me?" We all yelled that it was Ollie's fault, Mr. H picked Ollie up by gripping his ears. Ollie was sent home, but Ollie was back the next day laughing about it. Mr. T had a little tiny Fiat Uno car, some Boys from our year had pushed it out of the parking lot. The hand brake had never worked correctly. Mr. T's car was pushed onto the main road. The entire academic year all had to make their way to the headmaster's room. Everyone lined up and one by one were investigated to determine who was to blame. Mr. T assumed I was involved in the situation, although I was not even present, I was aware of who was to blame, but Mr. T was hated by most kids.

Neil used to make me act like Chris B, he had the most wicked dirty laugh going. Every time we were in the same class, Neil would nudge me in the side say, he would say do his laugh, while the class was going on, then I would impersonate his dirty laugh Neil would be crying on the floor. While Chris would turn around, bright red in the face, looking at me from a few rows down the classroom.

Chris despised me, he knew that I was better at football than him. He was the Captain of the A-team, I believe I should have been Captain, but I imitated his dirty laugh out of respect for Neil. He thought he was better at everything than anyone, looked like Boris Becker the tennis player apart from being a lot taller, we never failed to share a good laugh.

Mr. V was an amazing sports teacher but most of all a wonderful person. He was the best teacher in the world, faultless. Everyone cared about him, he was an excellent teacher, particularly in rugby, tennis, and golf. He thought I was the most talented football player. He advised Mr. T that I should have started for the A team rather than being a substitute, he was going to have a word with Mr. T.

Uncle John, my Mum's brother used to take me to Aggie Weston's (sailor's rest), it was a sports centre for the Dockyard and the Royal Navy but there were some weird rules. The hall had pillars everywhere coming out of the walls. It was excellent for three aside football if you have ever heard of that, the game consisted of three players against three. There were some exceptional players and some who were less than stellar. Joe, who was in his seventies at the time, was participating in the game, he was a true gentleman. Joe was also responsible for bringing out the first aid kit if someone got injured. Pete, with legs like tree trunks, would play in his Liverpool top, he had some amazing skills, and it was hard to get the ball off him easily the best player down there.

Mike, the goalkeeper, would scream all night if he did not get his way. He was a rush goalkeeper, he would charge out of his goal aggressively, as it was with a rush goalkeeper, he would not pass the ball much but take shots and miss, Mike was a devoted Christian. I must have been about twelve years old at the time, I would spin with a Ronaldo spin, then put the ball right between John's legs, John would then always kick me in the leg. He was a lovely man but a dubious character when he played football. I always tried to take the ball past him as I tried to use every trick in the book, to get the upper hand on him.

Jason John's son was full of tricks. He was about eight years old when he first played down at Aggies. He was extremely good at football and could play against men, he was so clever with tricks, he scored lots of goals. Then you had this clumsy man playing Colin, Colin's legs would be all over the place, constantly fouling everybody, his elbows would hit us in the face. He was just a filthy player; he was prone to getting hurt on a regular basis. Steve would play the role of a defender, he was like a pit bull, but he was an excellent defender. Lesley was the name of a regular visitor who came by on the first of every month. He ended up hurting himself every time he came. Pete once hit the ball; the ball hit Lesley in the face, it shattered his glasses, but also the ball's impact was enough to knock him out cold. Joe dashed to the locker room, where he found his first aid kit. As Jason was so fast, he went to tell a kind Irish man called Ivor who worked in reception, who requested an ambulance. Even though he was frequently injured, everyone assumed he was playing on it. Lesley was taken to the hospital by ambulance, we could not believe it when he showed up the next week to continue playing. When he was playing football, he reminded me of Mr. Bean; he was seeking sympathy. I went for many years to this unique place.

I also had to play football on Saturdays for Estover in the Devon junior minor league. My leg became stiff after playing the night before, but the stiffness in my legs completely disappeared after I played a bit of the game. We hardly ever lost a match, one or two in the whole season. I would travel with Nick M and Mathew G, Nick's Dad, gave us a lift in his black taxicab. My father would ride his bicycle to the football match to watch me play, I do not think that he ever missed a game.

We all decided to leave Estover after two years. It was a hard choice, but we always stuck together. Nick and Matt were both assigned to the team's reserves bench, although I got the players trophy again. I joined Plymouth Colts, with Matt and Nick who were currently third in the league. Anthony C played centre forward for the team and was the fastest player in Plymouth for our age group. We played nice football, and we came second to Estover that season.

I was with Gary who I played with as a kid. We were passing the football to each other, Gary hated football. Glenn S was a hard lad he looked like Kane Dingle, he lived across the road from the Fursdon, he shouted down to us I will go in goal boys. Gary passed the ball; I smashed the ball so hard it hit the crossbar and Glenn's finger at the same time. Glenn's middle finger had flown off, blood was everywhere, he was okay till he looked at his hands, and realized his finger had come off. Glenn shouted and screamed all the way home; his parents made a phone call for an ambulance. The ambulance came and the paramedics asked us to help find his finger as quickly as possible so he could have it stitched back on. I yelled that I had found it. 'Here its is' I said, I was not picking the finger up it looked absolutely disgusting. Glenn was taken to the hospital. I did feel guilty so when I went down to his house the next day to see if he was okay, they had managed to stitch the finger back on.

I used to go to Plymouth Hoe. It is the most beautiful place to visit in Plymouth for its breath-taking views where you can see Drakes Island. We used to go on the diving boards which were so high, the top board was such a big jump. There were five different heights to jump, it was free and fun. Mathew Yeoman was the nuttiest kid around a year older than me and Irish. He guided each of us up on the Hoe, there was a strong breeze as you climbed the steps to the top board. It was so dangerous on a windy day, as the wind felt so strong it used to shake the diving boards, so that your legs shook too.

Matt was insane, he did somersaults off the top diving board. Once I did a belly flop, off the top board it was like hitting a brick wall. When I surfaced, I swallowed water, and nearly swallowed a tampon floating on the surface. I was vomiting when we returned to our towels. Paul Croke and Clint Obrion was a funny blonde surfer who would wrestle with Croke all time play fighting doing mad summersaults of the top diving boards he would do anything to make us laugh like jump from the road into a tiny pool you got to be insane to do it, and Croke was not far behind him one wrong move and there dead. Ryan G lived across the road he was mad, we always went on a regular basis, such a laugh always doing mad dives and piggybacks off the diving boards. Mathew R always brought his fishing rod, any remaining fish, usually mackerel, he would use for bait. We used to catch the bus as we lived on the other side of Plymouth near the moors about six miles away from the city centre.

We would throw fish at random people walking past the bus from upstairs on the bus. Mathew Yeoman the Irish lad attended St. Boniface School, a Catholic school for boys only. He dated my sister when they were much younger. He was a year older, tougher, always getting into trouble, I never had any problems with him, he was always nice to me.

Charlie was Francis's father, and he was a real character. He had considerable power over Francis, as well as his brothers and sisters. He would beat his kids up for nothing and was extremely strict, he hated me with passion. They were a large family, with five girls and four boys. His mother was of Polish origin, Francis was good at sports and loved it when he was allowed out to play with us.

Yeoman chose two separate groups; there were about twelve of us that day. We were standing on the side of Blunts Lane, an incredibly old road that weaved through the woods and forest. The goal of the game was for one team to avoid being a stone while running through the lane, fortunately, Matt chose me to be on his team. Our team was at the top of the bank, they were required to throw stones at the other team's head when the other team made their way up the lane. However, Matt being Matt, he picked up the rocks, I was able to grab a sizable one while Frank was running through. I hit him square in the head, he went to the ground crying, blood dripping down his face, Frank got up and ran home crying. His Dad was soon knocking on the door wanting to speak to my Mum.

I never got into trouble or grounded like Frank Dad treated his children. Frank was only allowed out one or two days during the week. Mum let me out all the time, I had a brilliant childhood. Yeoman was wild, only he could think of a mad dangerous game to play, but he was fun to be around. He led us into the woods, the army used to train there, when Seaton Barracks was there in Crownhill. Yeoman instructed us to throw stones at the army as they ran through the forest. We would hide behind the trees throwing stones at the army whilst they were carrying out their training exercises.

As a result, we would sneak into the military ground when no one was around. I was rubbish at the monkey bars, I just could not do them, something I could never do. There were lots of underground tunnels, nets to climb up high, then underneath there were nets to crawl through with muddy water, we had to get on to our bellies. Matt Y thought he was a general ordering us all around, he thought he was in the army.

Shaun Norman walked up to that location, he was just another mad teenager he would pop out of nowhere and walk in the woods. Shaun would always knock on the door for me, no matter how many times I told him not to knock, although he was my best friend, Mum hated people knocking on the door. Shaun knocked on my door when he was little in his nappies and asked to be my friend.

Shaun went all around the estate begging for a cigarette or a smoke of hash, which I did not do at the time. Nick M gave Shaun a head fuck then Shaun would eat spiders. He was willing to go to any length for a few head fucks. The bottle they would cut a plastic bottle and then get tape, and the bag should then be taped to the bottom of the plastic bottle. Aluminium foil was around the top of the bottle, then a drawing pin was used to put holes in the foil, then cannabis could then be burned at the top of the bottle while the bag was being pulled.

Shaun would then suck the bottle; the bag would fly up with smoke, Shaun would hack up his insides after inhaling the smoke. Shaun would turn into Incredible Hulk or Bruce Lee as he studied his moves and would practice all the time and mastered Bruce Lee to a fine art if, he had consumed cannabis.

Shaun had eaten a deadly fly agaric mushroom when he was fourteen and was tripping permanently, he was sent to a mental hospital at an incredibly early age. He could make anyone laugh by singing Elvis's songs, but he was especially adept at making the girls laugh. He would show off more to the girls, everyone liked him as he was so very polite, despite his madness and would do anything for anyone. Shaun was a brilliant climber; he could climb trees with ease; he could climb trees with no branches by wrapping his legs and arms around the tree. He climbed a Conker tree to the top on this day, like a monkey in the middle of the forest and yelled "conkers!" galore. No, it was not conkers, it was a massive poo on the head of Croke and Leanne who screamed. Croke went mad no that was not the word, berserk, telling Shaun to get down immediately, Croke covered in poo all over his head and clothes. He ran home shouting 'Shaun, I will get you for this.'

Croke was a boxer and was hard for his age, Shaun was nuts but hard too, he was afraid of me and Croke. At Christmas me and Shaun would go out carol singing well to tell the truth I used to get Shaun to do the singing, and I would hang around the corner. We did this every year he was good at singing, we made a lot of money, especially in the posh areas, on the local council estate we knocked on more doors than the post man ever delivered letters. We knocked on four different estates, which involved thousands of houses, we made a tiny little fortune.

One day we were at Keswick on the council estate, I was fourteen and Shaun was twelve. Shaun knocked on an angry man's door, the man pushed Shaun, and he flew on the floor. I ran up, smacked the bloke right on the jaw, he collapsed, cold out on his doorstep. Each year we did this as the money was so good. We used to go into Shaun's house when his parents were not in and watch porn movies. We also would have boxing matches.

Shaun, Wayne who was a good friend who I grew up with, as a toddler lived opposite me was present and with just one glove on and the other hand just a bare knuckle. Shaun would push the seats back and the front room became the boxing ring. It was good, we boxed each other, we played the winner stays on. Not being big headed but I won the tournament. I should have gone boxing like many lads around the area, but I did not as I was mostly playing football.

Mum carried on seeing Trevor, but not in front of us. My Mum got pregnant, and I could not tell you how excited I was for her. The arrival of Mathew, my angelic brother, was a true blessing, it was the only good thing to happen with her getting with Trevor who was a useless father, whom had nothing to do with Mathew especially as time went on, Trevor got married to someone else, but he was a sneaky player with the lady's. Mathew reminded me of the young boy in the movie "Home Alone". My younger brother used to stand on the side of the road and show the middle finger to my friends. Mathew did this for many years, people laughed at him. He was only five, he is a wonderful younger brother, I was twelve years old when my brother was born. His Dad was a right idiot, Mum found out he was having affair, as he met someone else, although continued seeing Mum.

Then one-night Trevor came around when match of the day was on, my second favourite team, it was a mid-week game. I loved Spurs the same as Argyle back then especially Glen Hoddle he was my idol. Mum told me to go to bed, I told her no, I am watching football. Trevor shook his head in disgust, I ran up to him and booted him in his balls. He went running as I chased him up the steps and jumped in his car and drove off, he was a useless father a wimp he didn't put up no fight to see my brother, so I did try to take care of my brother as best I could.

Next day I played for the rugby team. We played all the schools in Plymouth. This day we played against Eggbuckland, I performed admirably, particularly against the toughest competitor in Plymouth for our age group. He was supposed to be the hardest in Plymouth, we kept a close eye on him as he raced down the sideline. He was so fast, I delivered a right hook to the side of his head, he went down to the ground, he then challenged me to a fight. Some of my Estover teammates also jumped him, he had no chance. Big Paul and Stewart Harchom were the props in the scrum, the two biggest lads out of our year, they were so big and strong anything in their way, would have no chance they just steamed into him he had no chance against Stewart and Paul M. The hard lad from the other team was hurt and taken off the field holding his ribs; after that I do not think he was the toughest in Plymouth for our age.

We had some big lads in our team, we won on the day we had an excellent team; I could kick conversions or penalties from anywhere on the pitch. Mr. Vav was an excellent rugby coach, but he always looked out for me, everything about Mr. T was a vendetta against me. Mr. Vav stated that he would speak with Mr. T, but he was not aware that Mr. T had chosen most of his players from his tutorial group; he did pay attention to Mr. Vav. He assured me he had spoken with him, after that I was centre half, I was reintroduced to the first team line-up.

I took part in the game alongside Chris, the other centre half, no one could get past us. The A team went undefeated for the entire season, I would continue to play in goal for the B team. The boys on the opposing team from the other schools would complain that I was in the A team as I played with them or against them on Saturdays following that, I was no longer permitted to play for the B team.

Sports was something I was deeply enthusiastic about, but it was a lot of fun getting into mischief at school too. I went to the local Youth Club with Paul, Mark, Carl, and Leighton, we played snooker and pool, I was good at that too! My Dad bought me a pool table at an incredibly early age, so I won most games as I was able to practice.

After going to the Youth Club on the way home, we would go around knocking on random people's doors. It was called cherry knocking, we used to knock on doors then run away. We would knock on this end house on our way back from the park, the man was completely mad. We always got a big chase from this mad man's house, he tried to catch us every time. But we were too fast, and he could never catch us, I made friends with a diverse group of children my age.

An older experienced group, as well as younger boys, I also made friends with children that lived near my Grans. I made friends with many Swilly lads, bonfire night was crazy in Swilly, on a field they had the biggest bonfire around. The whole estate chipped in with wood and all sorts for the fire, it was massive. Stolen cars were put into the massive bonfire with police turning up, it turned into a riot. I loved staying out at Grans and hanging around the lads in that area, as a result, I was acquainted with many people.

We shuffled the football teams once more. Mathew and Nick were leaving, so we all joined the SV Locomotive team. Anthony Ginter's Dad was the Manager, Anthony also played for Torquay United youth team. I was about thirteen years old when I first started playing SV Locomotive. Paul Croke was present. He came to watch as it was near my estate, when I scored three goals, one of which came from a corner kick, I scored two incredible free kicks to advance our new team in this game. The game ended with a score of three goals to two.

It was not all that long after that game that Gordon, Nicks' father arrived home from work as a taxi driver, it was about four o'clock in the morning. He discovered his oldest son, Jason, dead on the floor, next to an aerosol can that he had inhaled. Nick and his entire family were shocked; Nick was a brazen young man. However, after that he deteriorated, whereas his other brother Jamie, who was more sensible and capable of looking after himself, was the complete opposite.

Nick was not spending as much time as he used to playing football, he became friends with people with whom I had difficulty getting on with. Gary was an absolute bully and Jason would walk around the neighbourhood brandishing a samurai sword, he used to be a psychopath when we were younger. Following that, Simon also had it in for me for some inexcusable reason, these three young men had a thing for me, and we never got along. They pursued me as I walked home from the shop one time, and I had to run to avoid them. Gary, despite being a few years older, was never going to catch me, but I had not realized Simon would be waiting for me down the alley way, he punched me in the nose, and broke my nose. I should have informed my father, or my sister I was too scared to tell anyone, otherwise my street credit would have been ruined. It is something that makes us feel very lousy about ourselves getting bullied. As a result, I kept trying to avoid colliding with them, I really wish I had just fought them back.

The following day, My Uncle John took me was the game against Bristol Rovers and Plymouth got promotion on that day. I was given permission to run on the field by Uncle John. When the boys were attempting to break the goal post, I jumped up onto the crossbar, it was hilarious to me, when the goal post nearly snapped. I got a taste of what it was like to be a hooligan. We all sang songs on the pitch, the Captain of Plymouth Argyle emerged from the room, clutching a massive trophy, I really loved the atmosphere.

My Uncle was beaming with delight as he watched us all sing, he had a soft spot for Argyle. He always got autographs after the game was over, he collected autographs from every player that visited Home Park. Uncle John went to Liverpool and pretended to be a steward to gain access to the changing room. He met several famous people, including John Barnes. Ian Rush and Kenny Daglish were all delighted to sign autographs for Uncle John. He was willing to go to great lengths to obtain famous names.

My Father also took me Argyle, I went by myself when I did not have a match to play, I went to the craziest part of Lyndhurst stand. It was more exciting; it was not too far from my Grandparents' house. My Gran spoilt me by feeding me an abundance of food. Grandad was always reading the newspapers and playing records or listening to the radio.

My Gran took pleasure in spoiling both my sister and I, in every way imaginable. I spent an equal amount of time there, we technically had two homes. I used to like going to the Ham shops to get sweets and crisps. I thought it was fantastic that we had such wonderful Grandparents, Amy, Jason, and I played hide and seek games and football at their house. I would also go to John's and Aunty Lynn's house, where she would make us a delicious roast to eat while we played football around the back, we would play heads and volleys with Jason's friends.

Chapter 3. The Tragic Innocents

One day my cousin Amy had to go into hospital, which was such a terrible thing. Following a walk with the school to Plymbridge, according to the doctors she picked up a bug, she was extremely ill. The doctor said she would be ok, but over the following month things went tragically wrong. She died so young she was close to being seven years old, leaving my Grandparents and my Mum heartbroken. Having lost both my cousin and best friend, it was a terrible experience, being in my teens, it was the worst day of my life. God only knows what Lynn, John and Jason went through. It caught me very off guard. She loved dancing as a ballet dancer, she will always be an angel, she will always be in my mind for eternity.

My Gran said 'not again' as her brother had died when he was only ten years old. She never ever got over the death of Amy, Grandad was the same, Amy was a beautiful, sweet little innocent soul. One year after Amy died my sister had a daughter called Rebecca on Amy's birthday, she is dark like Amy which was very strange.

I was adamant about reaching my goal of playing professional football, I was thirteen years old at the time. In addition, I played rugby for Plymouth Albion, I had the potential to reach the pinnacle of the rugby world. This was yet another area where I excelled, but I could only choose one sport to play. Sundays were set aside for rugby, I played lots of games for Plymouth Albion Juniors, even though it was too much for me. Football being my favourite sport, a football manager at the bottom of the hill was having trouble finding enough players for his team. He recognized my talent and asked if I would play under a different name because I was too young to play for Buckfastleigh, a semi-pro team.

I was about to compete in the Cup final in my junior team, it was against Estover. I could not tell anyone I was playing for another team. On the other hand, I did not pass up the opportunity to play semi-professional. I was thirteen years old the Manager told me a name to remember, it was the name of an injured player. As a result, I was probably the youngest semi-professional in the country at that time. I played an absolute blinder; more specifically, I played midfield. I passed the ball around and I did not mess up once every ball I kicked went to the other player. I was flawless I played the ball through the gaps where Steve D was, so fast, he did profit setting him up five goals in this match. They asked me to play once more, it gave me a massive confidence boost that I played well. I had to pretend to be ill on the junior team because I wanted to play for them in the final that was coming up.

The following game was against Newton Abbot, I was outstanding; I adjusted easily to the environment; and I competed successfully against men. I was constantly passing the ball around the pitch, like David Beckham. I went through players like Gazza would, weaving in and out of the game, and I discovered that I could easily play at this standard, I had so much time on the ball. I was raised to never back down from a challenge, so I gave it my all against another player. We both kicked the ball at the same time in mid-air; we both hit the deck; my foot was hurting so much, because of the pain. The physio sprayed some magical spray on my right foot, I only had my left foot to play with and was hopping around the pitch. I used my head to pass the ball, I felt excruciating pain as soon as I put weight on my foot, I was told to carry on until half time, but there were no plans to remove me from the game.

At halftime, I told the manager that I could not play because I could not put any pressure on my foot. The manager suggested I should give it a couple of days to see if it got better. I knew he was more worried he would be in trouble as I was playing illegally, I went home, but the next day I was in terrible discomfort. The pain was unbearable, so I had to go to the hospital. I had discovered that my right foot had suffered three separate fractures, I asked the doctor how long it would take to heal as I had a cup final to play for my junior team. He told me it would be a long time before I could get back to playing again.

I was desperate to play again, but the final was five weeks away, even though I was in a lot of pain and had a big brown boot on my foot, I was still hoping to play in the cup final, even though it seemed most unlikely. I played golf in the big park with Paul Croke to pass the time during the long days. I could hit the ball far but one day while playing I sliced the ball and all we heard was a big loud smash where I smashed someone's window who lived on the edge of the park.

The weeks went slowly by, after four weeks they took the bandaging off and the big brown boots. I ran it hurt so bad but as the week went on, I could run but with a limp I really wanted to play. It was cup final day, the manager was aware of my injury with Buckfastleigh, my entire family were in attendance. Uncle John had approached me to get my autograph when we were warming up. The manager after the warmup said I was unfit, I could not believe it, when he did not start me in the game it was the first time, I was the substitute my foot was not ready, he was right, but I went mad, like a spoilt brat. I told the manager to fuck off and jumped over the fence and stood with my family in the Mayflower End. I told Dad and Mum; they both told me to apologize for my inappropriate behaviour. I told them I was so sorry, the manager said I will be playing in the second half which made me feel a little better. We were one zero down with half an hour to go, Matt G had been removed from the game. I was brought on to play midfield. I was hobbling around, but I kept on playing, my foot was still hurting. Following that, I made a terrific tackle that had everyone in the Mayflower stand applauding and cheering, but I was playing terribly, and we lost one zero.

The following week my dad took me to Newcastle, where Pamela's family lived at the time. We took the train there, her cousin Tom, who was blind in one eye picked us up with his wife Irene. Tom was a postal worker they were both genuinely nice to me and made me feel most welcome. They were beautiful people, I loved the accent, we all went to a pub on the first night, it was quiz night. I had a pint and a half of lager instead of a pint, the glass was much larger than the one in Plymouth. A man in the pub, who was banned from driving, had had his license revoked, he told me stories and made me laugh. He then said he had a tractor in the car park as he told me he never got stopped by the police. I did not believe him, he told me he had to go and began driving his tractor as I glared out of the window.

We went to the Metro Centre the next day, which had many more innovative attractions, such as a miniature roller coaster that weaved its way through the shop. I had never seen anything like it. I paid two pounds for a haircut and three pounds for some Gordie jeans, everything was significantly less priced than Plymouth. My Dad and I went to watch Newcastle football team, when Dad saw Gazza signing autographs, he told me to grab a picture and an autograph from him. I was standing next to him, I replied negatively and indicated that he was useless. My Dad told me that he was something special, Gazza was about eighteen years old then. It was such an incredible stadium, Newcastle were 4-0 up, Gazza then sat on the ball, before performing a role in which he tossed the ball into the air, over Neil Foster head, Foster then punched Gazza in head. Foster got a red card and was sent off. Gazza played amazing the tricks he pulled off was something out of this world. I had the feeling that I was seeing the best player in the world, Newcastle won 5-0. My father asked, "Do you consider him crap now?" I replied, 'he is the best player I have ever seen.' I conveyed my disappointment that I did not obtain a photo with him.

After that day, my opinion of him as a player dramatically changed, he was my favourite player, Gazza was something special. We ended up watching Sunderland play in a night match, they were only playing Luton, Luton were not a wonderful team, I wish it had been Spurs or Manchester United. The atmosphere was amazing, Sunderland won, but I cannot remember the score.

We travelled to Whitley Bay and found a bar in a cave, there were stories of it being haunted. The cave's entrance was built into the rocks, the lift would take you down to a bar where there was a massive glass window looking out, under the sea. I had a fantastic time in Newcastle, it was by far the best place I had ever visited.

A few weeks later I went to Portsmouth with Uncle John, and the lads whom I played with at Aggie Weston, it was my first ever away trip with Plymouth Argyle to watch the battle of the ports. We travelled in a minibus that we had hired, I had problems falling asleep the night before I was so excited, I hardly slept a wink. I cannot remember the game apart from remembering we lost. It kicked off outside the ground the police were causing trouble as they arrested a young lad for nothing and was getting heavy handed with the Plymouth supporters what I could see. We stopped off at Southampton and went to some pubs and spent a few hours there. I just did not like a place not like Plymouth, I could not wait to get home. We had an enjoyable day out at Portsmouth, it was a wonderful experience, the atmosphere was electric. I got the bug for it; it was not long before my Mum trusted me to go away by myself.

The first game that I could go to by myself was the mighty Hammers West Ham in a FA cup. Again, ` I could not sleep, I was lucky enough to run into a boy from school who was in the same year as my sister, I sat next to him on our coach. Noddy was also on our coach, a famous Argyle fan who enjoyed singing even if it was by himself. The entire ride from Plymouth to London, he sang constantly. Noddy was in his sixties but when he was younger, he got beat up in a pub. He was unable to hear or speak properly because of his brain injury, during home games, he could be heard singing by himself in the Mayflower End. However, he had everyone singing the chorus of his famous song to the bulk of the games, which was "ah oh Noddy, Noddy hay oh" this was repeated about ten times, Noddy would sing the chorus none stop, this was the tune we would all sing to him while riding in the coach. He sat at the front of the coach, he thought it was fantastic, we had a terrific time laughing on the way up. Pranks were far too interesting to fall asleep to, you would just not want to fall asleep.

A poor exhausted boy who was asleep, had his shoelaces tied to his other trainer one of many pranks, when he went to the toilet, he fell tripping up with his trainers tied together banging his head on the floor. We finally got there, the police boarded and searched the coach, we were directed to go one mile to the stadium without a police escort.

West Ham was such a frightening area, we did not walk far, a few boys younger than me emerged hastily from the pub. The Central Element, a well-known football firm based in Plymouth, was in front of us. These boys fled back to the pub, The Inner-city Firm came flying out of the pub and pursued us, I was running just behind the Central Element to the ground. It was lucky I was fast, we managed to flee without being caught, I was glad that I was quick. In the football ground a big pillar blocked my view of the game, I was able to make my way to a position where I had a pleasant view of the game. It was an amazing game, but we were defeated 3-2 nonetheless, David Byrne scored an incredible goal, I caught the bug, and I could not wait to go away again.

A few weeks later my sister when I was fourteen years old took me to the Dance Academy, before we went out, we met two of her other pals at Agnes place which was a shared house who was Frank's sister was my age I knew her well, the other girl was very pretty who lived next door I fancied her she was 21, but I do not remember her name. The pretty girl stayed home. My first drug experience came in the form of Pink Floyd. I was against drug use, but I took the acid tab, after spinning out for an hour getting lost in hidden rooms climbing stairways leading to different balconies what just went higher and higher this place was a mad it was huge.

There were tales of it being haunted. The very top of the building was a room as people said that's why door was boarded up. It was certainly a spooky destination but breath-taking I was lost then the police came running as someone was armed and attempted to steal people's money in the rave. The police came and told everyone to leave the building, I returned to her friends' house, thinking my sister would return, as I lost her in Dance

Academy. The pretty girl answered the door as it was a shared house, she told me my sister and Agnes had not returned home yet. I felt insecure and vulnerable after taking that acid tab, she told me to come into her room. I ended up in her bed where she was giving me a cuddle. It felt so good, I really fancied her, she was so pretty.

My sister arrived home quite late, at four o'clock in the morning, I was gutted as the cuddle was over. For laughs, they all thought it would be funny to shave my hair, it was a long bob which took me ages to grow. They also gave me Valium; they had shaved my head into a skinhead and shaved the name acid on the back of my skull. I went to school a few days later with acid written on the back of my head, as a result, I was sent home and instructed to get my hair shaved off and get rid of the name of acid on my head. The fact that acid was written on my head, I kept reminding myself how much I despised narcotics. I will never take it again, well that was my immediate thought.

Time passed, we had a school holiday, a water adventure camp for a week at Bude. Which is a place in North Devon, next to Cornwall with lovely beaches, to do water sports. We arrived and students from a Kent school were there, they had a union jack and shouted "you wankers" that was the wrong school to say that to as we were insane. We all went to our shared rooms with bunk beds, some of the lads in our group went to the beach and placed stones in their pillowcases. I was not interested in weapons. The way I liked to fight was with my hands or feet, the boys from Kent were upstairs and we all made our way up. We knocked on the doors where they were staying, there were seven rooms upstairs, we knocked on all the doors at the same time. They dashed out of the room, the lads from my school who were carrying stones in pillowcases thrashed them mercilessly over their heads, as we stormed their rooms. It was total carnage with one lad trying to run away, I tripped him, he got up and smacked me hard on the jaw. I grabbed his arms and kneed him in his privates, he squealed, then I gave him a Swilly head butt in his nose, which split open with blood dripping he ran down the stairs, screaming. They were a year older than our year group we later discovered, but we easily won this massive fight. It was twenty to thirty on each side, the ambush caught them off guard. We were all compelled to attend a meeting the next day after breakfast. The teachers were not happy, and an instructor told us that our school was the worst to ever attend the adventure water sports hostel, in history. The instructor and our teachers told us all that we would all be sent home the next day; we had one more day here. They said "there will be no refund as we had caused so much damage to the rooms" we were all thinking that our parents who had paid, would be livid.

The next morning, they woke us up around five o'clock, they said "we had better start behaving ourselves and told us we could stay, but one wrong move by any of us and we will all be sent home. They shouted at us like we were in the army, we had to get down to the outdoor swimming pool which was filled with sea water. We were forced to jump into ice-cold water, we all came out moaning then we were told we had to run for a mile on the beach in one huge circle. We did as we were told and then went back to face our rubbish breakfast of cornflakes and toast. The instructors advised us that we would need to walk thirty miles, set up camp and stay out for the night as they were splitting us up from the lads from Kent, as they were going home the next day.

Along the way to stay at the facility, Ian C expressed a desire to go home, despite being high on cannabis, he continued to stroll. We pitched our tents up for the night, not me, but most of the other lads were high. I never smoked even when I was younger even though I did take an acid tab. I wanted to be a professional footballer, so I was not smoking although the cannabis did smell nice though. We had to walk another fifteen miles the next day to get back to Bude along some of the most beautiful coastline.

We made it back to Bude safely and it was teatime, it had taken twenty-four hours to walk thirty miles. They kept repeating that we were the worst school that had ever been there. Every morning, we were compelled to enter the pool first thing in the morning, in addition to windsurfing, we went canoeing, kayaking, surfing, but it was a brilliant experience. We all enjoyed the prison camp we all called it.

It was the last day of school for the year above. It was a tradition throughout the school's history that the pupils kick in, the year below every year, when that year group leaves school for good. We were all aware of this, there were fourteen of us on the field to play our usual game of football what we did every day. There was nobody on the field, it was a strange feeling, nobody from our year group or anyone's year group was out that dinner time. Normally the fields were packed full of kids, playing football, smoking, or doing something. Then unexpectedly, there were about one hundred lads from the year above, all standing on the other side of the field. They charged at us, sprinting from one side of the field to the other, my friends ran and jumped over the fence and out of the school grounds. I stood alone and took all of them on for a fight they all piled on me, punches coming from everywhere.

They ripped my school shirt to shreds, I saw blood and got some strength, I pulled loads of them off me punching them back, I was doing well as there were so many. I gave one lad, the most nerd looking one out of them, a kick in his face and broke his glasses. I roared like a lion, then chased them all back across the field, a teacher was present, I was unaware he was there. He grabbed me and gave me a good telling off, I said "they all jumped me it's not my fault," eventually he understood that they attacked me first, I put it all behind me, and thought it was just a tradition.

I went skiing in the South of France with the school on a skiing holiday. We trained on the dry slopes in Plymouth which were so hard, I was rubbish on the dry slopes. We left the school with all our parents waving embarrassingly at us as we left. It took us twenty-four hours to get there on a double decker coach, the drivers were scousers, it seemed like they were drinking and driving. That is what the rumour was going around, about them, but kids will be kids, we went across on the ferry at Dover.

The boat was rocking badly; it was like a fairground ride, we were going to stay in a top-class hotel, it was lovely and hot at the bottom of the slope. The view of the mountain was breath taking in the French Alps, we arrived late, I could not wait till the next day to go skiing. We had to get to the top of the mountain, we travelled up in a cable car, I feared heights. Some of the boys thought it was funny to rock it and it came to a sudden halt, we were stuck in the car cable, the wind was blowing strongly, we were rocking on a piece of string. I hated every minute as the lads kept on rocking until I went mad. I absolutely thought that we were stuck forever, it was such a relief when it started moving again after a very tense hour.

The first day of our skiing venture the skiing instructor taught us the basics, how to turn and how to stop, I enjoyed how straightforward it was to grasp on the snow. It was only my first day, I left my wallet in the pillowcase in my room, so I did not lose my money. When I came back to look for it, I could not find it, I think the cleaner had pinched it, or one of my room mates. I was sure that no one saw me hide it as I was the last one to leave my room that morning. I had to phone my Mum and ask her to put some money through the bank.

The next day we done bobsledding down the slopes. That evening we went to a nearby indoor swimming pool; I opened a locker to put my clothes in and there bang in front of me was a wallet that contained a substantial sum of money, I kept it, it was amazing to find the wallet after losing mine. The next day, after we were on the slopes again it was so hot, most of us had a nice tan which I did not expect, going somewhere with mountains full of snow. Even though we were always supposed to be with the instructor, a few of us disregarded the rule and went our separate ways. We sneaked off knowing we would be in trouble later, but me, Scott, and a lad whose nickname was Dolly crossed into Italy on skis. The slopes had assorted colours on posts to show the slopes' difficulty. I remember yellow was an easy slope, but the slope we decided to go down was a black slope, the worst, the most dangerous slope.

For the entire day, we were totally lost it was getting dark. A nice Italian man took us back to where we were staying, on skis and many different cable cars to eventually get back to where we were staying, it was a massive adventure. The next day, we had descended a slope next to a massive cliff, one wrong move and it would be curtains. The slope had a tight turn with the cliff top close by and the whole group went down in single file. Rob came down alongside me, with extraordinarily little space between us and the cliff, I did not have time to wait for him to pass. He hit my skis and was on the edge of mounting a huge drop, he went flying off the cliff, I stopped, I looked over the cliff. The whole class I was with disappeared down the bottom of the slope, I saw Mr. Vav down the bottom of the slope, I informed him of what happened to Rob and when I told everybody we all presumed that he was dead.

A search party was set up, but he was not found until the helicopter found him the next day. He came in laughing and told us that he had hit a tree on top of the cliff. He said he thought the branch on the tree would snap, he could not believe he was even telling us the story. I blamed myself as if I had just stopped, he would have passed me, but I was so relieved that he was back.

Rob was a year younger, a tall lad with a menacing face, a bad boy, although his dad was a police officer, it did not stop Rob being a wheeler dealer but a loveable character. It was such a fantastic holiday, to get to go to the Alps, which is heaven on earth, the most beautiful experience I could ever have even imagined.

It was back for a friendly game for the SV Locomotive team, we played against Torquay, Anthony Ginter was fast and a skilful player who played for both teams, but Anthony played for Torquay on this day. Darren Moore played to a high standard and eventually played in the Premier League. Darren Moore was the centre half for West Bromwich Albion. But on this day my management instructed me to remove him from the game, so I did that. He played centre-forward on this day. He could not get past me not once, I man marked him out of the game, I was too strong for him. He was so tall, they played lots of balls into the air. I was good in the air and managed to beat him on every header. He was six foot three and I was five foot eleven. I was playing a blinder. We went on to win against them three two, and I scored a spectacular free kick that helped us win.

I was offered to play in a trial match for Torquay, I went to a trial game, I played well, and the coach asked me if I would like to join Torquay. I honestly thought they were rubbish. I had higher ambitions of one day playing for Plymouth Argyle that was the team I wanted to play for, so I never returned.

My dad got me trials with Bugle FC. My dad worked with colin and Glyn building nuclear missiles. I passed the trials and was playing against men in the Jewson southwestern league. I found it easy. I played for Bugle FC when I was fourteen, one of youngest semi-professional players in the country. My school team had an important match, we performed well enough to make it to the national school semi-finals. We had never lost a match in the whole entire time since we started from the first year up to the last game. The game was just outside Exeter, I have no memory of the other school's name, which was many miles away. We had never lost a game since the beginning of the school year. However, we suffered one loss on that day, we were the better team. We just could not hit the net like we normally do, and we lost by one goal. We decided to celebrate our first ever loss by letting the rival school's coach tire down. The other teacher told Mr. T what we had done just as we were leaving, he shouted at us, we all laughed at him. We were singing in the minibus on the way back home, "Mr. T is a wanker, Lalla," repeated we sang, until he abruptly slammed on the handbrake, sliding on the motorway, sending some of the boys flying across the minibus. We kept singing the same song, ten minutes later he pulled at the handbrake again, but this time someone flew from the back seat, all the way to the front of the minibus, smacking his head on the roof. Mr. T was on the edge of exploding, we all laughed heartily at his expense. He was so violent, especially with his words, swearing and raging, his face was burning red, it looked like he was on fire, but he was always like this, a ticking time bomb. He informed us that we would all be detained for detention. We all laughed at him, he said "we were the worst kids that he had ever taught in his teaching history."

When we returned to the school, he told us that we all had to go to detention in the sports hall. It was late at night, so all the lads just jumped out of the minibus and ran home. It was the last week of school for our year, but we did not continue the tradition of kicking in the year below. School was a brilliant laugh, I was sad to leave but I have such fond memories, but I could not tell you everything as there were too many things.

One thing I do know though my Mum was the best she let me live my childhood the right way, yes, I got up to mischief, but I never stayed in. I never did a piece of homework; I got an A+ for sports and the rest of my results were not great. I had to think about what I was going to do after I left school, as I ever wanted to be a footballer

Chapter 4. The Shadows of Dreams

I played a season with Bugle FC. I enjoyed the training. I played brilliantly the last season coming on as a substitute, but was so young they were breaking me in. I was hoping to be in the first team this season. Then we were back for preseason; every player in the football team was from Plymouth, as a result, they trained anywhere throughout Plymouth. We were practicing pre-season in Estover, next to factories one day, we had to jog down to Plymbridge with its huge stunning forests and beautiful rivers, it was an eight-mile run. It was all downhill to start with, running down a steep lane which took us to Plymbridge, we ran across the forest to the moors, we then had to jog back.

We had to conquer the biggest hill to get back to the football pitch, I was normally no good at long distance running, I was more of a sprinter, but I made a point of returning before everybody else, to make a favourable impression. After that, we had done some ball work, Colin B mentioned that I would be taking the free kicks and corners, as a result, he told me where I should cross the ball. I followed his instructions, and I kicked the ball straight to Paddy C on his head, he headed the ball straight into the net.

I had assisted a goal directly from a corner to show them what I could do. They indicated that a friendly game was coming up, the game was against Ivybridge. I started off being one of the reserves, as usual, I really thought I should start. They decided to bring me on with thirty minutes left in the match. Someone took a free kick just in front of the halfway line, the ball hit my boot and went in the goal. It was a fluke, but they did not know that, following that, I executed a spectacular free kick the wind took it to the top right-hand corner. I managed to get the man of the match and only played for half an hour. I felt so confident that I could play easily at this level. I could not have been happier that it happened during the pre-season.

After that, I took part in a league match against Launceston. I was a reserve, I came on for the second half, I was wearing my boxer shorts at the time. It was just incredible, however, my adulthood had dropped out of my shorts down the inside of my leg, as I was running fast down the wing. The ground had a little stand which had lots of people watching, as I was right next to the home supporters, I successfully managed to return the snake to its proper spot, before passing the ball to Paddy C. With his header, he guided the ball into the goal, my name on the sports page of the newspaper, where it said that I had an unfathomable football talent.

Following that, I went to a training session. Colin B believed that I was far too talented for this team. He said do I want trials for Exeter city, I responded affirmatively, indicating that I would appreciate the chance to try out for Exeter City. Even though Plymouth hate Exeter, our local rivals. My stepbrother David drove me there the first time, they wanted me to return every week. My uncle continued to take me there every week, out of the hundreds of youngsters that tried, eventually, only a goalkeeper and I was left to play for Exeter city. I could not refuse they played nice football, and I fitted into the group well. The youth set up was amazing, their style of football suited me.

 I met Alan Ball, who was Exeter City manager at the time the English world cup winner. I was playing for the scum as Plymouth hated Exeter. I needed to play with a professional team, and it was not that far from home, I used to go training twice a week, I loved the style of football, the way that they passed and moved it, suited my style of play and I found it easy, in the youth set up. Once while I was in the changing room, my uncle filled the boot of his car with footballs with writing of "Exeter City " on each ball. He had a massive autograph collection I had no idea he was also a ball collector. I was there for about two months.

Alan Ball was departing to take over as Manager for Southampton, he approached me and asked if I would like to go with him, to complete an apprenticeship. He told me to think about it, I was so excited. I phoned my dad straight away, Dad said "go it is a brilliant place to play football" but I just did not want to leave my family. Exeter's youth coach, Peter Dustin, paid me a visit at Mum's house.

Peter Dustin had a new job he was the new head coach for the Plymouth Argyle youth team. He asked if I would be his first signing. I wanted to hear my dad's opinion, so I called him, Dad advised me not to and said "you are stupid if you sign for Plymouth" but I did not want to leave my family. Despite this, I stated that I had a long-time ambition to play for Plymouth Argyle. "Do not" Dad said, "you are being ridiculous" Southampton are far better I did not know what to do, but he reminded me that it was my life and my choice. I told Dad that I would sign for Plymouth. Dad said, "but you are making a massive mistake." Pete informed me that if I joined the club, I would be his first signed player there, he told me that I could not let him down and he was optimistic that I would do well at Argyle. I signed on the dotted line.

Southampton did not appeal to me as it was so far away, I did not like the place, I had been there when Plymouth played Portsmouth with my uncle. So as a result, I went to the first training session at Plymouth Argyle, I had to get new football boots. Dad bought me the Gola football boots for me, but I wanted a pair of Puma King boots. I had no choice, he had delivered them precisely just before my training session, everybody had Puma King football boots.

Shane was a young man a year older who lived around the corner from Mums, he disliked me with a passion, I do not know why. When I was about eleven, I passed him in the street and said "ok" he just glared back with an evil stare of hate, he was a year older at school. Shane might have been aware of my footwear; at some point I walked out of the room and into the toilet. My boots were nowhere to be seen, when I returned to the lounge it was just unbelievable to me, my boots were perched on top the trophy cabinet. They were all laughing at the situation, I could not get to them, Martin Edworthy got my boots for me, he was in the first team who was two years older. Peter then suggested that Andy Morrison would show me around, I had to accompany him to the dressing room, I had to clean his boots, so I did just that. He then directed me to comb his hair, he did not have any hair, he was a skinhead. Unfortunately, it was too late, the whole team were laughing at me.

I wished I had listened to my dad, and not joined Plymouth Argyle, I lost all my confidence straight away. The lads of my age were jealous of me since they had been attempting to sign up for a long time. I signed on without even kicking a ball, I never felt like an outsider in any of my prior football teams, my initial workout was nothing like the Exeter youth setup, which was far better training. David Kemp was the manager his style of football was the long ball game. I was picked for the reserves to play Yelverton away, Plymouth was too good for them, I assumed that I would be given the opportunity to play, with a 7-0 lead with twenty minutes to go, I thought I would be making my debut, Michael Evans scored four goals. At first because he was slow in training, I found it easy playing against him, I thought he was a donkey, he went on to be a successful footballer with a good career.

 I never got on the field which seemed unfair, I had to hand out bottles of drinks to the players. Shane yelled at me to "fuck off" when I offered him a bottle of drink, he was trying to make me feel uncomfortable which he did, he was like a bully. I should have just smacked him in the jaw, I could easily have beaten him up if I had wanted to, but I did not want to get booted out of the youth team. I assumed that giving up at this time would have been easy, just for me to walk out. Regardless, I did not give up and did not allow the bully to win.

 David Kemp informed me that I would be participating in a game for the reserves, the game was at Harper Park, the training pitch for Plymouth Argyle. The game was against Camborne, David Kemp informed me that I could only use my left foot, my left foot was terrible at any time. He shifted me to the centre of midfield. I could not help but feel like I was on the other team. My left foot had no purpose for me, it was superfluous for me to use my left foot. In the game, only Diego Maradona, the best footballer in the world, could only use his left foot. I would estimate I played for ten to fifteen minutes altogether, after the ball was booted out of play, to the left side of the field, it went out for a corner kick, I resolved to show what I was capable of with my right foot. As a result, I knew the goalkeeper was already off his line, so I decided to try to score straight from the corner, I curled it into the top corner of the goal. I was feeling good about myself after scoring my first goal for the club, until I observed David Kemp telling me I was being substituted. He was mad with me, as if I had just committed a terrible crime. He told me I was only allowed to use my left foot, and that was the reason for my early exit off the field. I was completely shocked; the incident completely damaged my self-esteem. He was the worst manager I had ever encountered; he should have told me to work on my left foot in training, I just wanted to walk home.

Following that, the training was a complete flop, I could kick the ball for miles, which was great for the style of football they played. I preferred to play football in the South American way, which was what I enjoyed.

Exeter played nice football; I could not believe what I was hearing on Tuesday, because I was still a fan of the first team, I watched. Then before the game, I noticed all the young people were signing up for the club, they all took to the pitch when their names were being called out. I could not understand why I was not called out, I felt left out and hurt, I forgot that I had already signed but at the time my head was all over the place. I was better than everyone else my age and older. At that moment, I understood that my window of opportunity was closing. I was there for a few months, the training was terrible, it was not enjoyable like it should be when you play football. I am sure Shane thought I was going to take his place, and worried that he would be relegated because of not making the grade. He was so jealous of me, but I could not understand why.

David Kemp was rubbish, it seemed like he had it in for me too. We went out with the first team for a night out, to the city's nightclub and we all got drunk. Spencer B and I shared a cigarette that evening, on the Monday after training me and Spencer was called into the dressing room, we assumed we would be selected for the reserve team with a match, which was coming up. We did, however, get into trouble, in front of everyone for smoking cigarettes.

Shane was out that night and saw us smoking, I knew it was him as he hated me being there, so me and Spencer were not wasting our time anymore, we walked out. I walked home leaving the club, we never wanted to go back, we had had enough of the others, so envious, and against us, we had no chance, we were just wasting our time, my dream was over.

I wished I listened to Dad but that is something I had to live with. The set up was terrible, just like Dad had said, but I did not know this until after I had joined, I had to learn the hard way not listening to Dad. I could not believe how much other players made such fun of me, and that infuriated me. Shane was never going to make it as a professional, with one or two exceptions, everyone was completely wasting their time. I was fully aware that I was acting irresponsibly, especially given that I should have spoken with Alan Ball at Southampton that would have been my ticket to being a star or I wished I went back to Exeter, but the moment I took my first drag, on a cigarette everything changed. They were entirely unaware that my dad was completely correct. I still went to watch Plymouth Argyle despite the way I was treated. I still supported the first team as all those players were good towards me, I had no trouble from them. It was painful watching my team play, as I was always thinking what could have been.

Chapter 5. Tug of Temptation

Matt R who lived across the road handed me a cigarette, at the time, he was only thirteen years old, it was a major blunder. I was sixteen and I found that once I started, I could not stop. It was Saturday night I always had a beer Mathew G we done this most Saturdays but, on this night, we took acid with Jim Maiden Mathew became romantically involved with a lamppost. James suggested we visit the big park, which is what we called it, it was near where we lived. Mathew refused to leave the lamppost, he exclaimed about how gorgeous it was and how much he adored it. Jim pulled Mathew who had wrapped his arms and legs around the pole. I ran to see how fast I could run up the hill; I ran so fast the acid tab made me faster than before. It seemed like I would beat the 100-meter world record on this acid tab, it seemed like I had a turbo engine in my trainers. Jim said he had observed how fast I had been running, he said, you were like a bullet, laughing whilst he laid on the grass, looking up to the sky, at the stars in the distance. He was able to see things that I could not, he was saying how beautiful the stars were.

Mathew began strolling down the hill toward the lamppost, which he had previously visited. Jim remained at the park, lying on the ground, rather than leaving, he did not want to leave. I pulled him up and told him we were leaving, Matt continued to love the same lamppost, at some point, we all went home, and the refrigerator began talking to me. I could not get to sleep, I was worried Mum would see my eyes were massive, like alien's eyes.

I did take a lot of acid tabs that year to tell the truth, losing my football career had a massive effect on my mental state of mind. I was drinking heavily and started smoking hash. I joined a youth training scheme through my local job Centre, we were in a group till we found a placement of work. We only got paid twenty-nine pounds and fifty pence; I could have chosen any sort of work. The advisor said to me would you be interested in becoming a career, after spending so much time with my grandparents, one thing I had was respect for my elders. I got a place in a residential home, called Manor House for the elderly.

The care home with lovely, and the staff were great, and the residents and I had so much fun, playing music bingo and all sorts. I was a great listener, and they enjoyed telling me their stories. I felt like it was so rewarding.

Neil lived nearby. I spent my spare time with Neil, it was good hanging around at his place, playing football and tennis most days. Neils' parents who had a lovely house treated me with profound respect they were always kind, even though my eyes were bloodshot from smoking cannabis. We spent a great deal of time at the George Pub drinking underage, eventually Neil introduced me to Christian. He was originally from Gillingham, he moved to Plymouth with his parents from Kent, he had a London accent, he lived just around the corner from Neil.

Then I met Tristan Rutherford with his friend mad Reg, who was ginger but a skin head, they were both from Southway. Tristan had brown hair, he was tall and about 6ft 3. We played football behind where Tristan lived with his parents. Reg, who rambled on and on about the IRA, spoke so fast in an Irish accent, we had lots of beers I got on great with them. We all arranged to meet the next week and decided to go watch Argyle, we went in a little group to watch Plymouth v Birmingham, it was a Tuesday night match.

Following the game, the Zulu gang, the Birmingham fans, roaring their famous scary chant, as they left the stadium in a terrifying manner. On this specific day, the core of The Central Element had about fifty boys older than us. In Plymouth we call each other boys even if they are men. When a popular man named Lenox asked us whether we wanted to join The Central Element, a football gang from Plymouth, we all said Yes. I have always wanted to be a part of this firm. Then, as the Zulus were outside the football ground, an older man with a beard and long hair, about forty years old, no one knew who he was then he said the words "fuck it" and took a huge run-up from one end of a big car park to the other, he dived into the Zulus as they stood outside the ground, he knocked one of them unconscious, an ambulance came and so did the Zulus.

The top boy, I cannot mention his name, told everyone to join their arms together and make a chain. Neil was nowhere to be seen, he had run to the pub. After only a few moments, Reg, Tristian, and Christian joined the chain. I was in front of the chain, the Zulu warriors were running through the parking lot. I dodged in and out of them as they ran into the chain of the Plymouth boys. I then got chased by the meatheads, I noticed a bus approaching, I ran to board it. When I looked back, from the bus window it was kicking off in the car park everywhere. Even though I fled the scene, I got the buzz for it.

The following week, The Central Element invited us to the Barbican for a drink, I was not telling them about the nature of my work, as I think they would have taken the mickey out of me. Christian, mad Reg and Tristan we all had a couple of cans of lager before meeting in the Dolphin pub, on the Barbican a beautiful part of Plymouth. The Central Element was outnumbered by a gang, known as the Efford boot boys from a neighbourhood in Plymouth. The tattoo dots on their knuckles helped them identify as an Efford boy. On this day, around forty Efford boys and fifteen TCE lads all older than ourselves and the leaders of the firm were present. So, I thought I would show them who I truly am after eluding them the previous week. I could sense the atmosphere was becoming strained as whispers began to shift around, I could tell we were coming near to a battle. As a result, I drank three quarters of my pint. "Come on, then let's fucking have it," I yelled, as I smashed the pint over my own head, sending glass flying in all directions with glass stuck in my head, blood dripping down my head.

The Efford lads who were much older than me all took off running, I was not even old enough to drink. We continued to the next pub, each of the leading men of The Central Element ran his own business. One was a financial advisor, another owned a large construction company, another an estate agent I got a massive buzz this day being part of the TCE.

I sold hash as well, at an early age because I could get it so cheap from a good friend even though I worked as a care assistant it did not affect my work.

The Central Element originated in 1986, I will just not say his name, but a well-known gangster in Plymouth originated the firm, and brought lots of hard nuts together. The firm stood in the middle of the Lyndhurst end of the football ground, at Home Park, which is where the name The Central Element came from. It brought lots of lads together from all diverse levels of society.

Nicholas, an original member from the start, was in the Royal Navy when he joined who told me the history about the firm, he still loves it till this day. Then you had your lads with their own businesses and whether they were posh boys or not, they wanted to be bad boys. You had people in the services, also there were drug dealers, drug users, drinkers, and people who were on benefits, even thieves, people from all walks of life, even a solicitor. Unbelievable several of the boys were in care homes abused, raped with terrible childhoods. The TCE is where they felt safe, as the Element's lads took these lads under their wings and they never felt safer, it was one big family who looked out for each other.

The TCE had lots of numbers of lads. One lad was brilliant at stealing, he would go into the designer shops nicking the designer clothes for the lads. He stood out in the crowd with his blonde hair, he is still going to this day. They spent time together in town, and everybody knew them, there were lots of fights in pubs back then. They ran the city with drugs and the underground economy, the firm was well known, but looked out for one another. There were fights with rival gangs in Plymouth as well, as the football rivals, my sister even hung around with these hard nuts at a noticeably youthful age.

My employment required me to care for the elderly, I had to bathe adults, I just had to get on with it and try my best as someone had to do it. The Matron was nice, and she was good to me, I was on the Youth training scheme, I only got twenty-nine pounds, but the Matron paid me a little more for my efforts, which took it to sixty pounds, which I did so much appreciate. I had a terrific time doing that, but it had to stop after six months. That was the end of the contract, I learnt so much at that time that I was there, and it was something I wanted to do, to work in the care industry.

I then discovered a pub called the Wellington pub in Greenbank near to town. It was an excellent place; it was possible to get cannabis and smoke joints in this pub. I was already acquainted with a handful of the guys that hung out in this pub, so I knew what to anticipate. Gary was the name of one of them, well he called himself Gary but really it was Gerry as he was a dealer and if anyone grassed him up, they would be grassing up someone else. He had a boxing background, he presented himself as Gary, I will not reveal his genuine identity, especially his surname. He demonstrated an elevated level of intelligence and was sound as a pound!

The main people at the pub were the Aquila. A well-known Plymouth motorcycle gang, I went up to someone going by the nickname of "chopper" he was a much older fat man with a moustache. I asked him if I could buy hash, he did not seem to like me, he told me to get lost, he was the only person who made me feel uncomfortable.

I spent a significant amount of time at the Wellington pub, I became quite friendly with this gang. Local police did conduct searches and seized drugs at the place on several occasions, despite this, people continued to skin up joints in this pub.

Popeye was the nickname of the man I was friends with, he was easily twenty years older than me, he looked like something out of the mad Max films with a skin head and a ponytail. He would travel to Wales or outside of Devon to steal Harley Davidson motorcycles, then return to Plymouth, disassemble them, and rebuild them into his own motorcycles, which he would then resell for a big profit. Additionally, he sold acid tabs so cheap to me, I was on acid every weekend back then, I got them for my friends too after being his friend for six months I got to know him well. He told me that he had enough with his life, he informed me he was going to kill himself on his motorcycle. He was walking his dog with me up the park, he told me he would take twenty acids, drive along the motorway at such a high speed, and crash that was how he was going to commit suicide. It was clear that he adored his pet dog whilst playing with his staff dog in the local park, it was difficult for me to think that he would commit suicide after having such fun with his dog. Hearing that he had committed suicide was a severe blow to me, he made it to the M5, where he went into a truck and wrecked his bike, travelling well over the speed limit. He gave Gary his dog just before leaving Plymouth, knowing Gary loved dogs, he was the right person to take care of his dog.

I then got myself a training job at the Manadon Day Centre, with disabled people, it was like a school for the disabled people to go to and learn different activities. Michael T was a character, he was never able to stay out of mischief. He got into fights with others, he had serious disabilities, yet was known for his outspokenness. He loved to sing the Wurzels songs, a famous band from Somerset, who my Mum loved, Dad also sang these songs to me. We got along great; part of my job was to accompany him on the bus into town so we could go for coffee and a pastie. We did this every other day when I worked there, it was always enjoyable to go with Michael and a capable lady with learning difficulties, to a café in the city centre.

Working at Manadon was a fantastic learning experience for me, I learnt sign language and became fluent in it. I had the honour of working with some of the world's most generous and compassionate people. Avon and Richard tried to be a loving couple if they could have their own way. Avon was lovely; she had Down syndrome. Richard had Down syndrome as well. If she did not, get her own way she would go crazy. but she had a massive heart. Avon would like everyone to be her boyfriend, she used to fight other ladies over her boyfriends, one of the jobs I used to have to do was break up lots of fights quite often.

I travelled to Bristol City with the TCE, I could not sleep the night before, I was familiar with Bristol because some of my Mum's relatives lived there, I did visit Bristol lots of times growing up. I was aware that we would certainly be outnumbered, I knew Bristol had a massive firm, we ended up taking up about five hundred up. When we arrived, the boys were high up on the tree branches, watching us, they had mobile phones and transmitting our whereabouts to the rest of their crew. I have never seen anything like it before. The police almost right away apprehended us, on their horses and on foot, they had us between horses and marched us to the ground, there was no escape. We sang our well-known song, we are The Central Element, this was one song I loved to sing. We did not win the game, and we all left before the final whistle.

The police ordered us to leave the Bristol area. Our leader received a phone call from their top lad in Bristol. The top lad knew all the other hooligans from all over the country, by going to the England games he was well known. When you go to England games, everyone is on the same side, but when it is a club match the friendship goes out the window. Fists up was the rule, sometimes it got dirty with bottles and sometimes weapons, most hooligans would use their fist only, but sometimes you get one or two idiots.

Our minibus pulled over in a car park outside Bristol, we had a phone call from the top boy from Bristol, they asked how many boys we had and who was up for a fight. The head man of the TCE told the Bristol lads we had about seventy, but we were too far away to turn around, they said they would match seventy for a fight. There would have had a lot more lads than that, I was relieved when the top lad told us that they would have many more lads, and they would be setting us up. So, we went to Exeter instead on the way back to pay them a visit, some of the lads made phone calls to other lads to meet at Exeter. We came to a halt in Exeter, and some of our group recognized four individuals heading up the road, one of them was a well-known England hooligan supposed to be their top boy.

I was with a lad called Dave who was one of the original members he looked Italian. We chased four of them up a steep hill, and a man supposed to be a top England hooligan from Exeter. I was so fast I got close enough to kick his rear end, I booted him three times, he said "ouch" every time I booted him. I ran out of steam, and they managed to get away, Dave and I were laughing all the way back down the hill.

Everyone headed to the same pub, where the sly crew drank, that is what their crew was called. There were about seventy Plymouth hooligans in Exeter on this specific day, we drank in their pub, which is generally where they spend time together, but they were not present when we arrived. We had an enjoyable time at the pub, especially when one of the girls behind the bar flashed us her boobs. The girl flirted with me and Dave, after an hour everyone started to leave. Me and Dave wanted to stay as we were chatting with the bartender. Suddenly all we could hear was a massive roar coming from outside. An Exeter lad had charged into our mob, and he got the biggest kicking to his head, as people ran past some gave him a boot. I just ran past him as I could see he was in a bad way. We heard that there was thirty-odd sly crew scum in a pub close by, so we went to the pub and stormed it. We battered them, they did not expect us to jump them, after the brawl which we easily won, we legged it back to the minibus. The lad who got booted on the floor Wayne believed he had killed him. We could see him moving as we made our way back to the vehicle.

There was a police helicopter in the air, not long after we drove off. Wayne straight away thought the helicopter was for him he went into a state of paranoia, he said "he was going to prison," he was not really the fighting type of person although he was quite a tall lad. There was not a single flaw in Wayne's body, he insisted that he was in some type of trouble. We kept assuring them that he would be all right, he was not so much a hooligan as he was a supporter, he wore his Plymouth Argyle top to most games apart from this day, he had his casual clothes on.

Hooligans like to wear stone island mainly or something casual, he had no intention of causing anyone harm. He worked at what is today known as The Range, he was so ill as he was waiting for a kidney transplant. Some of his organs were missing and the odds of survival were quite slim, but he tried to enjoy life to the best that he could.

I used to go drinking a lot back then, especially in Union Street, where all the nightclubs were in Plymouth, was my favourite place to go. I was on a night out with my sister, a navy man was dancing with her. He was all over her trying to kiss her, she pulled away, but he would not leave her alone. He was groping her, so I planted him with a punch to his nose. His nose split open, all what was left was the sight of his bones in his nose, it was not a pretty site.

I then had a fight with the bouncers, my sister and I were fighting with the bouncers till they chucked me out, but I lost my sister outside the club. I made my way over to a club called Boobs, it was so cheap, before twelve o'clock, fifty pence for a tequila. I ended up bumping into someone from work, she was a secretary at the Manadon day centre, we were dancing before I knew it, she had started kissing me.

Vicky lived in North Prospect, us locals call it Swilly, I was staying at my Grans which was just up the road. We were making out behind a dustbin shed in Swilly, I asked her if she wanted to watch Plymouth Argyle and go clubbing after. She said that her dad used to take her to Argyle, she would love to come with me, she was a man's dream girl to have. I was well happy at that time, I arranged to meet her outside the stadium at the Devonport End, but she was not there when I arrived. As a result, I gave Argyle a miss and headed downtown to go Boobs night club, the easiest place to pull a bird, this is Plymouth talk up we call girls birds. I pulled a bird, she was a big girl pretty, so I thought but I had had too many shots of tequila. and went back to her place which was near Home Park. I stayed there for the night; she did not look so pretty the next day.

I was introduced to some hard nuts next door to her place, I cannot say their names, but they are two brothers, I started hanging about with three other brothers who were not related to the other brothers, but extremely dangerous, although they treated me ok at the time. The brothers asked me whether I was up for taxing punters, taxing means robbing people as they were pimps who looked after the prostitutes, in our city. I said "yes," they gave me Valium and told me the plan. I had to pretend to be the prostitute's boyfriend and catch her in bed with a punter who was a judge. I walked in and said, "what are you doing with my girlfriend" while the two brothers stormed in saying "give us cash else everyone will find out what you have been up to." They drove the judge to a cash point machine, and he had to pay a lot of money, I got paid a bit of cash and lots of Valium, temazepam. I got addicted to drugs easily. Then they took me out collecting money and taxing drug dealers, as the drug dealers could not phone the police. I was sixteen years old, young, and stupid; my family were worried sick about me as they were looking for me and reported me as a missing person. I Just did not get in touch as I was goofing on the pills. I was living at my grandparents' house at the time, but I should have let them know, that I was ok.

All my family were searching for me on the nearby beaches and rivers, I was close to all my family members, so it was unusual for me to go missing. I also had a job so it would have worried them like mad, but those three weeks seemed like a week, whilst floating on those pills.

I fell asleep during the day, as the Valium and temazepam would knock me out. We would go out taxing punters with the prostitutes at night, I stayed with Sam, but I did not fancy her, she was more of a friend, I was next door more than being with her. I did not really like her after a while, I think she might have been a prostitute as she was shifty.

Then one night we went out robbing someone's drugs there were six of us and I had to knock on the dealer's house, I was told to knock on the door and ask for some heroin. The other five stood on the side of the house, I knew the lads were with me he would not have had a chance. I knocked on the door. This man who looked like a meathead, answered the door, he asked me "what I wanted" I said, "twenty pounds worth of heroin please". He told me that he did not know what I was talking about and to go away. They bundled him to the floor and put a knife to his throat and made him hand over all the drugs and money, that he had. That was the only time I got paid well, as they made thousands just on this one hit.

The three brothers, not the two brothers, took me to one of the brothers' flats near Swilly. I cannot mention names as they are not nice people. I could not believe what they showed me, they had a little operation going on, he opened his cupboard. It was full to the brim with little bugs, from tiny cameras that were so small to watch people and to listen to people. They told me they sold them before this sort of technology was on the market, I was shocked to say the least. I thought they were big scum bags. They said you can watch people when they go out, we can even put them inside TVs, and could even sell them, one of the brothers said whilst laughing.

Also, another dirty trick of theirs was to put bugs in the speakers of stereos, sell the stereos then break into houses when they knew the people were out, they would target drug dealers. To tell the truth I thought these three brothers were scum, I did like the brothers at first as they did look out for me, they were up front with me, but they were horrible nasty people who were just using me, the three brothers were just nasty smack heads. It was a wakeup call that these brothers were just utter scumbags, I could not wait to get out of the situation that I was in.

It was time to escape, the lads were all asleep, it was early in the morning, I had the worst dry mouth. I decided to walk to my grandparents, a twenty-minute walk, they were not in when I arrived, the Mencap centre was not far away from where I was, so I walked there. The person that I worked with suggested I should call my family since they were worried sick about me. I phoned Mum to say I was ok, she came to fetch me, she told me that they thought I was dead as they were looking for me on beaches and rivers as they just thought the worst.

I got the sack from my placement at the Mencap Centre and the Manadon day centre, I had worked in both places as part of my placement, I was able to comprehend the logic behind my dismissal.

I attended a football game at home against Bristol City, there were a lot of us, about two hundred- maybe three hundred, we were waiting for Bristol City to come outside, the football ground on the edge of central Park there were loads of police, Bristol City were making their way over. The police were outside the ground with horses and dogs, the police let the dogs off their leads.

We were all running with dogs chasing us, it was a sight to see, so many men running across the field. A man standing next to me was being mauled by a dog, the dog had his legs locked in the jaw of the dog's mouth, I was right next to him. The man got the dog legs and ripped them apart with blood exploding everywhere, it was not a pleasant sight, I do not think that was in conformity with the rules. As I ran, a police officer was pursuing me, he was an arm length behind me, as he tried to grab me. I ran across the road and jumped the barrier in the middle of the road. Unfortunately, out of all the cars in Plymouth, one in a million, it was my dad's car that I rolled onto the car's bonnet. Dad and Pam looked horrified stunned to see it was me who had rolled over the car's bonnet. I kept running as the police officer would not give up the chase, he pursued me all the way to the train station, I was lucky to be a fast runner which helped in these situations.

After we crossed the railway track, after pursuing me for a mile or two, I eventually lost him. I walked back into town to the Newmarket pub, I saw some of the central element, but I did not know these lads as there were so many in the TCE. I just kept to the ones I knew but we are all on the same side, one of them received a phone call that Bristol hooligans were in the Colin Campbell car park. So about thirty of us made our way down there. We got to the minibus, and they all jumped out, they looked huge, and much older than us they looked like marines. I ran in, I looked behind, I was fighting fifteen of them by myself as the others had run away.

They stopped fighting me and after a couple of minutes they said, fair play. I got beat up badly, but they respected me for it as I was just a kid. I felt older and thought I was a man I did not look at myself as a kid. I went to the bus stop with a battered face, with my clothes covered in blood and my best top ruined.

On the same evening, Jason and Gary assaulted and beat up Ian C he unfortunately died. He and I were the same age, Gary was three years older, and Jason was four years older. Ian was irrational, but not aggressive, he was thin, and wore spectacles.

I initially blamed them, but it turned out he had overdosed on medication, even his mother thought the punches to his head were enough to kill him. She thought they had gotten away with murder. They enraged me, I could not wait to get my own back one day with Gary. I hated him, I was hard enough to take care of him now, as he had tried to bully me when I was young, but if he crossed my path, I was ready, for him.

My sister and I went down to Union Street, I went out with her a lot back then. Darren King was my sister's friend, but I became friends with him too. He told me so many stories on how hard he was, he was a joker a funny man but also could be sly ripping people off, with fake clothes, fake drugs, and bad copies of DVD's. Darren was knocked down by a bus, spoke with a lisp and was blind in one eye. I spent a significant amount of time with him. He claimed to be the hardest person in Plymouth, which was false, he was the epitome of a liar.

There was also another person called Darren King who lived in Plymouth, he took advantage of his same name, as the other Darren King was a giant of a man, he was enormous and was a hard nut. He was clearly attracted to my sister, which made me laugh. He was spending time together with Scottish Mike and Mark Duffy with brown hair always would wear a hat little in size smart funny but a hard little character both from Scotland, Mark lived in Plymouth at the time. Mike came all the way from Scotland for his holiday with Mark, he loved Plymouth so much he stayed.

My sister told Scottish Mike about my experiences with Gary, Mr. Sweets was the night club we were in, Scottish Mike gave Gary a massive kicking. I observed as he went down like a ton of bricks, then whilst pleading with him to stop, punching him whilst crying like a baby girl. I could not help but lay a boot in his face and knocked the big nose bully for six, he was dazed for a minute or two. Other TCE lads jumped in beating him too, he was out for the count and that was what he deserved. I was glad to see he got a good kicking; it made my evening a great one.

I went away with TCE to watch Bristol Rovers away; we drew the match 0-0, then were hounded by a swarm of meathead, they had about a hundred, we only had fifty. This big fat man took a right hook at me, but I ducked and hit him right on the chin, then I legged it. I had loads of them chasing me through their town, I saw a friend from Plymouth on the team coach who played for Rovers. He was in the reserves but on their team coach waving at me from the back window, I went back and luckily for me the minibus waited for me, the lads thought I was nuts.

I went to Swindon, away, I did not always go with the TCE, sometimes I went with friends from my area. Swindon and Plymouth we hate each other, as they killed one of our TCE lads a few years before the match in a mass brawl. I will not mention any names, as I do not want to get into trouble. They ran onto the pitch for promotion, so we ripped the chairs up and hurled them with chairs as they ran onto the pitch.

I went to Everton, away in the FA cup replay I bought myself a hat as a souvenir. It was full of Argyle fans; I went by myself. Someone had pinched the hat whilst I walked through the crowd, I was not too pleased.

Cardiff, at home was one to remember, there were a lot of lads present on that day, we all marched up from the pub. Soul crew were on the football field just next to the stadium, we challenged them with the Zulu chant before engaging in combat. A hundred verses, one hundred, we got the better of them. I was on top form on that day. Christian was on form knocking one to the ground, Tristan with a sweet headbutt knocking a lad out cold on the floor.

Tristan was tall with a heart of gold always laughing, we were so young, but we were on such a high buzz, battling with the sheep shaggers, but we lost the game. We followed the Cardiff mob to the train station, after the game, I grabbed a brick in my hand. A young man from Cardiff was by himself when he became trapped by a wall near the train station. He had nowhere to go, nowhere to hide or flee. I aimed the brick at his head and threw it at him, it flew full pelt towards his head. I was grateful that he ducked, and he avoided the brick, I think it would have killed him, as it was a house brick. As the police were closing in on us, we could see them in the distance, we saw lots of Cardiff fans getting on to the train, so we chucked stones at the train. The police chased us, but we were miles in front of them, then we ran to the hide in the pub.

I did not go away as I planned too but the boys went away to Cardiff, and it all kicked off but the of minibuses cars all got smashed they all came home freezing from having no windows on the vehicles from Cardiff to Plymouth there was always a rivalry between the clubs.

 The following week I was in trouble with the police, I went out with my sister and her boyfriend. At that time down union street my sister was arguing with the police as I said what is going on to the police. Me and her ex-boyfriend got into a fight with the police. I ended up in Charles Cross police station. I often ended up in there after a night out.

The next day, I sat in the waiting room of the police station waiting for Mum to pick me up. There were booklets on drugs with pictures of different acid tabs that were on the market. Each page displayed a different type making it look authentic. I took every booklet that had pictures of the acids, I showed Paul, he thought it was a brilliant idea. We picked the page what had pictures of strawberries were very mild trips not ever strong and then people would fall for it even more.

There was writing on the back of each picture, so we got Tippex and carefully painted over the writing. Then it was up to me to sell them to all the local riffraff, which I did for five pounds each, I sold about forty of them.

One lad called Graham bought one, he was a dozy kind of a person he often tried to scab free cannabis always asking for a bong from me or Paul all the time. It was unusual for him to have any money, but he did get money for the acid as he never done one before. After twenty minutes whilst pulling bongs, he started freaking out saying he was seeing things he really believed he was tripping, me and Paul we are gigging and thought this swindle was good. But then a large lad my age produced a baseball bat, demanding his money back. I was sly and said, "look I have been ripped off and lost more money than you." He was going mad I said look I have been ripped after he asked for the address of the person who I got the acid off I said look I have lost money but here you are and gave him twenty-five pounds back. All the estate wanted their money back, but I repeated the same story.

I did real acid the following week, with the younger lads around where I lived. I was able to obtain a powerful acid tab from the Wellington Pub, called crystal maze. We all climbed into the woods, then we walked about a couple of miles through a cow field. We had the most fantastic views because we could see as far as Dartmoor. The hallucinations were amazing, I had shivers with my hair standing up on my neck. With that the cow manure was breathing fast, it was alive with a face and a mouth. We were all staring at it, and I said "boys can you see that shit breathing and the face and mouth" they all said "yes" with a burst of laughter. The trees moved around and exchanged positions across the field, which again I asked if they were seeing the same things I was seeing, again, it was a "yes."

The world was spinning faster than it normally did, there were flying firework missiles, pure white in colour, flying at us, we all saw fireworks coming at us, one just missed my head. It was the best acid I took in my life, but acid tabs do not normally agree with me, it would usually end up with me going on a bad one. I was looking for my cigarette box and cannabis. I took a knife from my pocket; I never carried a knife normally. I do not know why I had it, I pointed it at each one of them, and said "give me my fucking fags back and my hash back, I know you have stolen it," whilst holding the knife in my hands. They all thought I had gone insane, which I clearly had, they all chucked their cigarettes on the floor, whilst fleeing. I picked up all the different cigarette boxes, they all ran apart from Paul. I ran up to him and gave him a leg breaking kick. He said, "what the fuck did you do that for," crying he limped off in agony. Left standing by myself in a field spinning around. There were big snakes in the trees, I was walking and running through the forest, which had little rivers.

I could understand why they called this acid crystal maze, as I was stuck lost in a maze going around in circles. I looked up to the magical sky, it was a dark red sky, with the moon that looked like a giant crystal. I was looking at the trees that had changed the way they looked, with white glowing crystals in the leaves of the trees. My hands grew ten times bigger; I knew every part of these woods growing up in them as a kid, but on this trip, I did not have a clue where I was going. About four hours had passed since the boys had left me. I went completely the wrong way; I ended up in Crownhill when I was supposed to be in Estover. I eventually started to get my bearings, I walked the road home, I was not going back to the jungle no way not with those snakes, I was thinking at the time. It took me an hour to get back, the road was moving up and down with cars that looked like they were flying off the ground. I honestly thought I was going to die as the trip was so intense, I eventually got back to Estover. I knocked on the door of Paul's house, where he lived with his mother and father. At the time, Paul was tripping badly, I apologized for kicking him. He was trembling with fear in his eyes, it was blatant to see. I asked for his help in locating my items which I had lost earlier. He said, "you promise you will not hurt me," I made myself vow I would not beat him again. I guided him back along the path we had taken before we went to the woods earlier, where I thought I had lost my hash, we could not find it, so we made our way back to Paul's house. He was convinced that I was going to beat him up when we were out walking in the dark. He said to me "I thought you were going to kill me." I explained the acid took over me, I told him he had no worries.

After that, I was back to feeling normal, we walked into his room and discovered everything I had lost was behind his bed, I profusely apologized for kicking him so brutally. Because the acid was so concentrated, neither of us could remember putting it in his room. I felt bad about kicking him earlier and apologized, the acid had entirely overpowered me. This acid gave brilliant visuals, but it was a very horrible experience for me. I apologized to all the lads that I took acid with, but they did not forgive me easily, after a while they understood it was not really me that night, the acid overtook my real personality.

I was fortunate to find work in Plympton, at a meat factory where we made pies and pasties, I kept falling because the floor was so greasy. I decided to leave my new job after just two hours, it was too much for me. I found it so hard my sweat was going into the pastry and so was other people's, what I saw, I swore I was not ever going to eat their pasties or pies again. I went to get my old coat from where we had to leave our coats, which was in a café in the factory. I did the lowest of the lows, I took an Adidas jacket that was identical to the one that the Liverpool manager was wearing. I walked to a car boot sale my Mum was doing at Central Park, it took me over an hour and a half to walk. I wanted to sell the jacket, but I did not arrive until it was too late, she was already getting ready to leave, as a result, I kept the jacket.

After I had a smoke with Paul, I was walking up the hill, I bumped into an old friend outside where I lived, I had not seen him in a long time. He hit his girlfriend; I cannot mention his name because it would be unjust. He did not tell me that he had hit his girlfriend, he asked me to walk over to Leigham, the estate right next to Estover. When we got to Leigham, a substantial number of males arrived, including so-called school friends and other boys, whom I did not really like.

There were forty to fifty of them, they came at us from all directions, I had no chance, someone had a baseball ball bat punching us from the left, right, and centre. My stolen jacket was covered in blood, and the sight of blood all over my jacket drove me nuts, as a result, I charged them while roaring like a lion. Then we headed to the Windmill Pub, where the bartender told us that she would call an ambulance, following that, I went to the toilet. I looked in the mirror, blood was everywhere, I could not open one of my eyes.

My face was in such a bad state, an ambulance arrived and transported me to the nearest hospital immediately. The hospital sent another ambulance to get me to the eye infirmary, I had to spend the night there. When I awoke, there was a young man next to me who had been drinking on his birthday night out. He had lost his eye because of a drunken person glassing him in the eye, as a result, he was blind in one eye.

The police arrived and questioned who was to blame for what had occurred to me. They told me that if I gave information on the main suspects, I would be compensated a substantial amount of money for my injury. I told the police two of the names of those whom I thought had done the worst damage. They were both put in prison, I had lost thirty percent of my vision in one of my eyes. When I blew my nose, it would completely shut my eye, I could not open one of my eyes for the best part of two months.

Mum had an idea for me to work at Butlins, to get away from everything and everyone. She really wanted me to change my life around, I applied but I did not want to leave my family.

Chapter 6. Crossroads of Redemption

A neighbour named Fred lived next to my mother's house, one of his nephews was Welsh and a player for Plymouth Argyle. Fred was seeking a charity game, Plymouth Argyle new and old players versus the Estover teachers.

We played a training session, I was worlds better than they were, and even the Welsh internationals could not get the ball off me. They told me I was one of the best player's they had ever seen, that was a pleasant thing to say, coming from Argyle first team, players. From one end of the football field to the other, I dribbled the ball past the entire team; in terms of ability, I was light years ahead of them. They could not believe that Argyle let me go and the way David Kemp treated me.

We played the teachers, and we won 16-0. When I looked over, I noticed my mother standing on the sidelines, she told me that I had been successful, and I had been offered a job at Butlins in Minehead. I was hesitant to leave, I applied for a job there, but I did not think I would be hired. I told my Mum "No, I am not taking it" She said, "it is in the fairground you will have so much fun." I also needed a fresh start because I had a bad habit of getting into mischief, I thought I would try it and give it a go.

My grandparents drove to Minehead in their car, I was dreading having to leave them. It was difficult for me to leave my family, especially my younger brother, I had a little tear running down my face as they said their goodbyes at Butlins. Not long after that, I met a friend called Neil, he was going to be a great housemate, as he admitted to smoking marijuana, my symptoms improved almost immediately. We got on well, we had a smoke and a good laugh that day, I felt very much at home. I was quite excited to be there.

Marcus, another housemate, was gay, he did not like us smoking weed. Lee was another man in the place where I was staying, I got on well with Lee, he lived near Plymouth in Saltash, a big lad always laughing with a nice spirit. He did not smoke weed, but did not care if we did, he was so laid back.

I had a job in the fairground where people played games and won prizes, basketball was one of the games and darts was another game. I became friends with Ian, from Hull, he taught me early on how to steal money and keep the change for myself. If someone wanted two goes on the game, they gave us a five-pound note, I would give them three pounds change in exchange to keep two pounds. That was the only way we could make money then pretend to put it in the money flute.

There was one game which was impossible to win, it cost one pound for three hoops, the hoops were little in size, but very heavy that is why they would bounce off the glass bottles. People would normally chuck one hoop at a time, it would just bounce off it was impossible to win unless you chucked three hoops at once, one might get stuck on the bottle was the only way to win. People would often ask if we could sell them a ted for their kids, we would tell them not to tell a soul, if you give us ten pounds, we will pretend you have won. Then to make it look good we shouted we got a winner over here, that trick worked a treat.

Neil had the most disgusting plan for Marcus, Neil went to his room and pooped in his bed, I was giggling childishly as Marcus came in from work, Marcus made his way to his room for a rest. He got into his bed then began to start shouting, who has pooped in my bed, screaming, and going crazy, running around whilst being sick. He knew it was Neil, whilst chasing him Neil ran away, Marcus had gone to asked to be moved as he really didn't get on with any of us, but they moved Neil for doing that to Marcus even though I didn't get on with Marcus' I thought Neil was sick doing that to him.

I had to show this Australian girl around as it was her first day, I got on well with her after our shift. I asked her if she smoked hash, she said yes but she said she preferred to smoke weed. She said that she could build the best joints, I said, "build a joint," as we sat in a field inside Butlins. I bought a quarter of the hash; I was upset when she put the whole quarter of the hash in a joint. I said you did not use all the hash for one joint. She said that is how we smoke it where she came from, I had to buy more, I would normally get about twenty-five joints out of a quarter. I asked the Australian girl on a date, and she said yes, I told her I would take her out. She said next week when she got paid, I told her I would take her clubbing that night with Ian, but she said, enjoy yourself and that she would prefer next week, as she was feeling ill with a bad cold.

Marcus had a friend who would come to our place to walk with him to work, she was called Paula. She was speaking to me before she went to work, and I was laughing and joking with her. I could not help but fancy her. Lee said she had a horrific experience with a security officer, and he got done for rape. Lee said many have asked her out on a date, but she said no to all of them. He told me I had no chance; I could not get Paula out of my head; I saw her every day when she came for Marcus to walk to work.

Ian knew a lad who sold weed, we went around to get it, the lad let us in his room there were about five other lads there. We smoked the red cannabis, called Durban poison, which was being grown in the camp, a lad from London was growing it. We all took a few puffs and one by one, they were all falling asleep. Me and Ian were still wide awake, we would walk up to this store every night in Minehead, a few miles up the road just outside the camp. They had several variations of the drink called 20-20 strawberry and orange kiwi apple that we frequently bought. We found it to be more cost effective to get drunk at home before going out, so we drank a bottle or two before we hit the clubs.

 I was at Paula's nightclub, where she and Marcus worked, he was a chef as food was served there as well. Ian and I had both had too much to drink, so I decided to go ahead and ask her out on a date because I had nothing to lose. She was born in the Welsh village of Merthyr Tydfil; she was about three years older. I was convinced that there was no hope for me, I pleaded with Ian to ask her out for me, I did not have the bottle. I could not believe it when he came back, and said, yes. I went over, she said are you going to walk me home after she had finished work. I walked her back to her accommodation which was far better than the place where we were living. I felt bad for the Australian girl, I told her the truth, but she was so mellow about it.

It was convenient for Paula that Ian and I were always out until 3 o'clock, because she worked until then, I always went to her place after the clubs shut. I was always doing the same thing repeatedly. As a result of my constant use of marijuana and drinking with Ian, and only having a few hours' sleep, I was never able to fully open my eyes at work. Even though the most difficult part was staying awake at work and constantly pushing through the fatigue stage, I had a fun time every day and night. For three months I have been doing the same thing with just two hours sleep every night.

I was told to go work at a kiosk; I was shown how to use the cash register. I was not listening properly, and the supervisor then said will I be ok with using the till, I said yes without having a clue. I bought two packs of Royal Rotherham's cigarettes before going to work. Ian approached me and informed me that they had hidden their cigarettes beneath the newspapers. Ian, who spoke with a strong northern accent, mentioned that they did not count cigarettes.

We dressed in red jackets, on the fairgrounds' grounds, Ian kept coming back telling me to pinch the fags. Then being gullible I started stuffing cigarettes into the pockets of my red jacket, my boxer shorts, down my top, I was just stuffing, myself with fags. The supervisor came in and told me to empty my pockets, my cheeks were flushed, matching the colour of my red jacket. I lifted my top and about one hundred packets fell to the floor. I was ordered to stay in the place where I was staying and was not allowed to leave.

When it came to Paula, I was at a loss for words, even though I was certain I would be fired; I had no choice but to wait until the morning, I then had an interview at the office in the morning. They had a security van driving around to check that I was staying in my accommodation, I waited until it was completely dark outside before going to see Paula. I knew I was going to lose my job, so I might as well stay with my girlfriend for one more night, I knew the outcome would be going back to Plymouth the next day.

I explained to Paula that Ian had told me to pinch the cigarettes, it was the only justification of which I could think. I asked if she would still be my girlfriend, once I was back in Plymouth. I said I will come up and see her now and again and I will ring most days.

She said we are still a couple; I was so relieved as I thought she would not want to know me anymore. I spent the night in her place that night, I sneaked around the back of our accommodation to climb through the window. When I returned to my apartment, security was waiting for me to pick me up and drive me to the office. They got me in the van and took me to the office to be interviewed.

I was met by the manager of Butlins, he was very stern and did not look incredibly pleased with me. The man was so strict that the guy who interrogated me, with the supervisor, warned me that if I did not tell them who else was stealing from the carnival booths, they would call the police. I said straight away it was Ian who was the main person, and it was him what made me pinch the fags. I did not want to grass him up because I spent most of my time with him, but it was his fault that I took the fags, so I did not care if he got in trouble as I was not going to see him ever again.

I thought it is better to snitch on him up than be taken away by the police. They claimed that there were more people stealing than I mentioned, they wanted more names. I honestly did not know of any other people stealing, so I said Matt as another because he was an absolute idiot. He was not a thief, but he was a control freak, always telling me what to do. I just did not like him, they wanted another name, else the police were coming, so that is why I named Mathew, another thief.

As the manager said there are more thieves, and I want more names, he was getting ready to call the police, I responded by saying, "That's all the people I know." He told me at the time that I would never ever be allowed to enter Butlins ever again, and I was banned for life. He told me he would be in touch with the Benefits Office to tell them that my job at Butlins had ended, because I had been stealing from the company. Paula was waiting outside the office, we agreed to stay connected, I told her I would come to see her because I did not want our relationship to end.

I ran into Ian while walking up to the town centre for an inexplicable reason. He stated that I had grassed him up, I said to him he had to take my word for it, I told him he was my friend, and I would never snitch him up. I explained I grassed Mathew up instead, so I did not get taken away by the police, I was the only one in the office, so I knew for certain that he was unaware of the situation. He insisted that I had grassed him up, I maintained my composure in the end, he had faith in what I said, I said farewell to Ian with a hug.

My grandparents turned up to drive me back to Plymouth and let me stay with them. I called Paula on the phone every day, I told Paula if I moved to Minehead, would she mind. She told me to do that if that is what I wanted to do, it was ok with her. My Dad thought I was being dumb young and stupid, did I listen? No, I rendered myself homeless and went to Minehead, on the train. I spent the weekend at a bed & breakfast, the people who ran the bed & breakfast were originally from Italy. The Italian guy informed me that I needed to be back at the house by midnight, not a minute later he was extremely strict. Paula did not finish working until 3:00 am, so I climbed out of the window, I was successful in avoiding being caught. Several hours were spent by us conversing as we sat by the water. I managed to snuggle her into the bed and breakfast the next night, he knew that I sneaked her in, afterwards he was done with me and kicked me out of the bed and breakfast.

Following that I went to the Social Services office, they told me that I could go into Stonham, which was a place for the homeless, but she explained that it was all ex-prisoners in this place, on a rehabilitation order. Would I mind staying there till they found me somewhere else? I said, "yes please." I did not care if I could see Paula, the only reason I was there. The lady explained during the day there was always a staff member on duty to help with my housing needs. The former prisoners made up most of the rooms, I had to share a bathroom, my small space contained everything I needed. There was a strict rule stating I was not allowed any guests to stay, that really annoyed me, but rules are rules sometimes, made to be broken. I had pleasant encounters there with a few ex-prisoners. Everyone went inside Matts' room to smoke, Mathew was so laid back, kind and generous he certainly did not act like a criminal. He had the best room in the house, it was massive, compared to my little room. He had a bong and invited all the lads in for a smoke in his place, he invited Lee, another housemate, Lee was a new age traveller from Minehead. His Mum lived down the road from where we were staying, he sold the best hash and weed. Peter was tall with blonde hair; he looked a shifty sort of character but made me feel very welcome.

Mathew was much older than I was in his early thirties, I was eighteen, Mathew told me that he often had a smoke with Mike, a prohibition worker who worked in the building. Mike's wrongdoing was intended to remain a secret from me, I was not supposed to not know or say anything. I promised Matt I would not tell a soul, he pleaded with me not to tell anyone. I would meet Paula most nights around 3 o'clock, she would meet me at the gates of Butlins, we just used to look out and watch the ocean that separates England and Wales. We spent a couple of hours together before we went our separate ways.

I managed to sneak in over the fence one night, I got inside the building of Butlins undercover, and then later, I got drunk with her in a club wearing a baseball cap, so no one recognized me. It was not very often that she drank, but on this night, we spent the night making love, this was the first time we made love in three months. I was a total gentleman, I wanted to make love before, but I understood her previous experience of being raped, so that is why I took it slow, as I did.

The next day I sneaked out of the entrance of the fairground, it was the easiest way out. I asked Paula to stay at mine that evening, I sneaked her in, and we got drunk again, I only had a small room with a single bed, but it was a night of passion again, I had the biggest hangover ever. I prepared a full English breakfast to surprise Paula as she was still asleep, I thought I would just shut my eyes for a few minutes, but I fell asleep. When I woke up, the smoke alarm was going off, because the cooker had ignited, staff members were knocking on my door, I advised Paula to take refuge beneath the covers of the bed. When I opened the door to the staff they poured buckets of water over the cooker. When the fire crew turned up, we had to get out of the room, the staff did not seem to be pleased with me. Paula was hacking up a lung, full of smoke, they were successful in putting the fire out. The walls were covered in black smoke, they cleaned my room out and painted the walls. They also purchased a new cooker for me, it was a stroke of fate that I was not chucked out of the building.

I found myself in Matt's bedroom as usual, Lee was peddling the finest acid tabs that he could find after attending the Glastonbury festival. In Matt's room, along with Lee and Peter we all took an acid called the penny farthing, the visuals straight away were amazing, I could see red rain pouring down in his room, which turned into being inside a boat.

I was experiencing the most beautiful colours, Peter was saying his acid was rubbish and it did not affect him, he told Lee he wanted another one. It was not long before he had started tripping badly, he kept saying that he wished he had not taken two of them. He felt that half of his body was missing, we kept reassuring that his body was there, and he was just freaking out. We reassured him that he would be fine. He hated the bad trip he was on, he kept being sick all the time and he was white as a ghost, constantly thinking he was going to die. It is me that normally thinks like that when I took them in the past, he had taken one too many.

Mathew's apartment was breathtakingly beautiful on this acid tab, his apartment had round windows on both sides of his room, it resembled being in a boat. It was raining red constantly, we went outside Matt's room into the hall, we climbed to the top of the stairs which was so high. The lads jumped through the spiral stairway sometimes for a laugh, I watched them do it so many times, but I never had the bottle to do it until now, smashed on this acid. The fall was dangerously high leg breaking, I jumped and hit the floor so hard my legs gave way, and I smacked my head on the wall behind me. My head was killing, I was seeing stars, I got back to Mathew's room, the room felt like it was rocking like a boat, he was playing music, The Doors, we had some bongs, we got so hungry, so we strolled up to the garage station. I had to pay for my items, I had a load of change of money in my pocket, and the pound coins were stuck to my hand. I was attempting to pay the woman, but the money was stuck in my palms. I tried tossing my hand at her, but still the money was stuck, I used all my force to toss the money out of my hand. Eventually, the cash spilled out of my hand and onto the floor, it went everywhere; after having a good chuckle, we all left the garage.

I could not sleep all night; I saw it rain red in the building. It went on all night, it was a nice floating feeling, it was the best trip, I did not go on a bad one, which was rare.

Peter engaged in the illegal activity of stealing from telephone boxes with his country bumpkins, in the countryside. He also skilfully made crop circles with his friends in Somerset, the police station was miles away. He was always trying to trick people; he even made it into the newspapers, he showed me all the newspaper clippings. Peter banned out of all the arcades in the area, he used a magnet placed underneath the fruit machine. The machine would think it was full up, he was successful all the time. He showed me how to cheat the machine, I triumphed so many times and managed to make money, till I got caught and was banned myself.

My Gran would give me money as I was receiving a decrease in the amount of benefit, after getting fired from my previous job at Butlins. I only gained ten pounds a week on benefits. I made roll-ups out of flag butts, from the floor in the town centre to feed my habit. I always did the same thing, every day I high with the other guys, and then found time to hang out with Paula when she finished work.

There was this one occasion when we went on the craziest camping trip. The probation officer took us to a mystery destination, he was a brilliant man. He was going to surprise us with where we were going, so we treated the probation officer like one of our own. Mike was about forty years old; it was a delightful surprise, he took us to the location where they were filming Maid Marian and his merry men, the children's series. Lee brought us acid tabs called Strawberry, we all took two each, as these trips were very mild. We all had sworn in our lives that we would keep it a secret Mike for taking acid with us, and smoking weed and hash. We made our way through the film set, which had a lot of wood stacked up for the biggest bonfire I have ever seen. We were in the forest, which seemed like the middle of nowhere, set up camp for the night. Next to the film set, a field and trees separated us, it was a television show geared for younger audiences. We all dropped a couple acid tabs; a beautiful grey horse ridden by Robin Hood whirled by our tent, at that same moment, we started to come up on the acid. It had started to turn dark, suddenly there was a massive fire, and a big roar. There was a lot of commotion, and they began filming. We watched the huge fire whilst smoking a spliff. After about an hour while they were filming, we all crept up through the woods while making sounds like we were birds and monkeys. Matt expressed his confusion, and he kept shouting, "Where am I and what the fuck is going on, while constantly falling over. As I was getting closer to the film set, the bell rang, I was standing right next to it. Tony Robinson, who also played in Black Adder seemed amazing, but he immediately began to chase after me. I narrowly avoided him as he tried to grab me, but he fell over a tree log. We did the same thing after we returned to our tents to smoke weed. To ruin their filming, we all did the Zulu chant, running through the film set, they all looked shocked, then all the people who played in the series began to chase me, but I managed to get away. We had no sleep all night as we were ruining their filming, it was the best adventure.

The next day, the film crew returned to our tent and handed us money so that we could move on. They said we are ruining their filming. We were going home anyway, but we accepted their payment and divided it among us. Since there was no cost associated with camping, we all had fifty pounds each. As a result, the fact that we were paid for our performance brought us boundless joy. It was an experience to recall being pursued by celebs off the television set, therefore, we had breakfast in a cafe that we stopped in on the way back home.

Mike was a very smart guy; he discussed his plans to make me play football once again. He assured me that Minehead would hire me if I were in shape, and that he would assist me in getting back to being in decent shape again.

I continued to use bongs despite having nothing to lose, so I answered in the affirmative yes. On the first day of my training, he had me jogging down the seashore with him, he would then have me sprint from one lamppost, and then have me walk to the next lamppost. We did this exercise for a good hour walking and sprinting every lamppost in sight. This is something Mike did with me every other day, as getting me in shape was his primary focus, I did not participate in any ball work. He performed an outstanding job, and at the end, I was fitter than I had been for a long time. After a month of getting fit with Mike, he got me a trial with Minehead FC, the team that was playing in the Great Mills League at the time, one league away from the football league.

Mike said that he had connections inside the Taunton football club, who were one of the best in their league. He suggested that I give Minehead a go, even though they were towards the bottom of the league. I played my trial game with trainers, luckily the ground was hard. I did ok, but not my best. They informed me that they were interested in signing me to a contract, even though I needed to work on my ball work and fitness. There was a former member of the Northern Ireland International team who was the left back of Minehead at that time. I did not think he was particularly good to be honest. The Manager was so friendly to me, he accompanied me to a sports shop in the town Centre, so he could get me new football boots. He told me he was rich; he did have a nice sports car, and I could choose whatever boots I wanted to have. I said you cannot do that, but he insisted, I chose Puma King boots, a pair that I always wanted to own.

The Manager had previously served on the management staff of Bristol City, and to begin with, he assured me that I would get one hundred pounds every game. After that, he put me through some one-on-one training to help me regain my ball abilities. I was following closely after him as we made our way to the locker room, he let four hundred pounds fall out of his back pockets. I was not the most angelic, and I should not have taken the money that he dropped, as he was so kind to me, but I did since I was so short on cash at the time. He did not seem to realize that he dropped the money, he carried on to the training pitch, he was so polite, I felt so bad.

His son was there while taking a vacation from Tottenham, he was a member of the Spurs reserves, he instructed his son to treat me to a drink in town.

After taking the money, I felt even worse about my decision, I got intoxicated while hanging out with his son in the main square of the town.

The following day, his son joined me doing ball exercises, he had the sweetest left foot. I could understand why he played for the Spurs. He had massive potential; he was 21 years old. Even though he believed I was too good for his father's squad, I played my first game. I was not in the best of shape, for the first half I did not look great. After halftime, I performed much better. I started getting my confidence and magic touch back. I was like Gazza, weaving in and out, playing lovely balls through for the centre forward to run onto. I played six games for Minehead, I was getting back into it and played well for the rest of the season, when the season ended, they wanted me to play another season, but Mike got me a trial with Taunton.

The conclusion of the new season was getting quite close, he assured me that he would get me an opportunity to try out for the Taunton football club. They paid each player two hundred pounds, in most cases more money, depending on how skilled you were.

Even though I was still consuming weed, hash, and cigarettes towards the conclusion of the season, which was what led to my demise, I decided to go through with my trial, nevertheless. The Training was strenuous, we had to give each other a piggyback ride all the way across the field, then the other person would swap, we did this for thirty minutes. We then had to run around the football field for a further thirty minutes, followed by press ups, sit ups and stretching, which finished with sprinting, we trained for two hours every Tuesday. I was in no way physically fit, their training was really challenging, I left before I even ever kicked a ball.

During that season, they went all the way to Wembley and ended up winning the non-league cup, if only I had not left, since I always knew I could hold my own. Those silly bongs did me no good or smoking. I was a letdown to Mike, but at least he was good about it, he was upset but remarked that it was my life.

Paula and the rest of her family were going on vacation together, she was aware that I smoked, but not that I smoked cannabis, I did that behind her back from the start. I had spoken to a girl who was from Exeter, I happened to run into her in one of Minehead's pubs. I did not say I had a girlfriend; she was all over me, she came back to my place. She had blonde hair and was stunning, a year younger than myself, I would rate her ten out of ten. It was in the middle of the night; we snuggled up in bed kissing and talking all night. She had a serious crush on me, I had one on her too, she told me she loved me, Paula did not pursue me relentlessly like this girl did. She would not stop kissing me the whole time we were with each other. Even though I got on with her far better than I did with Paula, I could not help but feel awful about Paula. We did not do anything but kiss and hold each other, she returned to Butlins.

It was her last day before she was returning home to Exeter with her parents, she told me she would come and say goodbye before she left to go home.

Later that day she returned, and for an hour she was crying telling me how much she loved me. She told me she would phone and write letters; my greatest fear was that Paula would discover the truth. She kept on calling me every day, it was time for Paula to return from her vacation, I was trying to devise a strategy to get rid of the Exeter girl because, based on the letters she sent me, she was hopelessly in love with me.

I became friends with Sam, who lived in the apartment on the top floor, I asked her to phone the girl up from Exeter. She did that, I gave her hash as well, the poor girl sobbed when Sam called her, and told her to leave her boyfriend alone. Sam informed me that she would no longer call or contact you in any other way. It is unfortunate that she stated she sounded so distressed, I felt sympathy for her situation, but I was relieved that Paula would not find out.

After three days of not hearing from Paula, I bumped into an acquaintance called Ben who worked on one of the rides in the fairground. He informed me that Paula was seeing another guy, Ben said to her do not you go out with Justin anymore, after he saw her kissing another man. She told Ben that she had no ring on her finger and that she could do whatever she wanted to do. I was so gutted, I had gotten rid of the girl from Exeter, which was close to Plymouth, it was just my rotten luck that I got Sam to call her.

I returned to my apartment after that, I went to get my football trophies, every year I was named player of the year and sometimes manager's player of the year, I had a massive trophy collection. I ended up breaking them all, throwing them against the wall as well as the window that I smashed. I had blown it, and I was made to leave, but winter was approaching, I was glad to be out of there, they made me promise I would pay for the window.

Chapter 7. Homecoming Shadows

I was eager to return to Plymouth because I had such fond memories of my time there. I missed Plymouth and couldn't wait to return I wished that I didn't get Sam to phone the girl from Exeter but that is what happens when you try to outwit karma; I got what I deserved. My grandparents travelled all the way up to pick me up, even though I had a fantastic time in Minehead, it was time for me to return to Plymouth, which had always been my true home.

I stayed with my grandparents and hung around with Neil, during which time I frequented the George pub with him and his friends, we had such good laughs, it did not matter how much money I took. I sometimes took thirty, sometimes one hundred, it did not matter. I used to put it all in the fruit machine, I never won once. I used to always go down to Union Street on weekends, I used to get into a lot of fights, it seemed to be that I was only arrested on many occasions for being drunk and disorderly. I felt safer down union street, than when I grew up in Estover.

General Ron was always around back then too, he spoke so fast it was hard to understand what he was saying, He was a nice skinhead, who loved his drink, but if it came to a fight, he loved it and would never back out of a fight. General Ron he went away games back then and still too this day with Argyle, a faithful TCE lad to this day.

I was in the cherry tree pub was my favourite pub. Kingy introduced me to Adrian Bailey who lived down the road from my Grandparents house, I often seen him with his long dark Swilly bobbed hair as a kid when I took my Grandparents dog for a walk, he was a gentleman and the good looking one out of the bunch. I was friends with Molly a mad skinhead with a heart of gold originally from London. Loves West Ham and he is a well-known TCE lad National front and proud comes to mind Molly great fun to be around always winding me up, but he made me laugh and was always good to me he is hard as nails a fat version of Vinnie jones. Mark Trenaman who was a laugh he lived in the cherry tree was his second home always up for a fight loves his party drugs I often had a smoke of weed with Mark back then. Duffy was in the pub this day I learnt a lot from Duffy. He bought a box of glucose from the chemist and would mix that with amphetamine. He was smart, he would make so much money by mixing it up, it tasted too sweet he put lots of glucose in the mix. Mark could always be easily identified with his orange Stone Island jacket on and Burberry hat and scarf on. He did not take amphetamine or any drugs, he loved his lager, it was just extra pocket money for him selling the speed and fake clothes, he referred to it as a load of shit. I enjoyed the sensation it provided, but I tried to limit how often I used it. We used to go drinking in the daytime in the Noah's Ark a pub in the city centre of Plymouth.

They told me lots of stories of fights they got into and Kingy was convinced he introduced me to the TCE, he did not but Kingy had ADHD. Duffy used to wind him, up he made me laugh, I looked up to Duffy as he was a decent lad with a heart of gold with a wicked sense of humour. I was in a lot of fights for someone so young, I saw Duffy at football games and saw him fighting but I never saw Kingy in a fight, at Argyle. In fact, I never saw him go to a football game he was always in a pub, but I had to listen to all his bullshit about fights he had, including the one he went on and on about, punching a policeman off a horse. That is the only thing Kingy had done, his stories were made up, he had ADHD.

Ian Gibbons told me Kingy was full of shit, he told me that Kingy ran from him as he made Ian angry one day.

Ian was hard and three years younger than Kingy but nuts to say the least, he chased Kingy for miles with a ball and chain. Kingy did make me laugh. He thought he could kiss my sister, but my sister's ex-boyfriend was in the night club. He went to smack Kingy, I punched her ex-boyfriend, it all kicked off with the bouncers. They grabbed me, I was on amphetamine while a, another bouncer was punching me in the face. While the other two bouncers held my arms, so it was free hits, he was punching hell out of my face. I laughed as if it did not hurt.

I was fighting all three bouncers outside; they did get the better of me, I left before I got arrested. When we went downtown, fighting with bouncers happened all the time for some reason, I never stayed home back then, I was always out clubbing back then, the amount of people I met was unbelievable. We would have laughs, meeting up in bars in our hundreds.

I went out drinking in many different areas, I hung around with Devonport and Keyham lads, they were a group part of the TCE. Mark Doyle was there too, he lived near my grandparents in Swilly, I used to drink with him all the time. Christian West Ham Del was there, Scooby, Rocky and lads from Keyham, there were loads. We ended up in a bar at St Levans gate, someone tried it on with this bird on the dance floor, then after that all hell breaks out with another mob from Devonport. I got punched in the head from behind, I got bundled this lad to the floor, rolling him around the floor. I managed to get the better of him, I looked around, Schofield was swinging kicks all around the club, I saw West Ham Del get booted in his ribs, even the DJ got knocked out, it was like a country and western film, we then ran them out of the pub. I loved going out and meeting all these different gangs in Plymouth, there were so many separate groups, but we all became one, at football.

Mark Doyle, He let me and Christian back to his flat that morning, I got stoned with Mark, he fell asleep, I could not believe what Christian did, Mark had no toilet roll in his bathroom, Christian used his bath towel, put it back on the rail facing the other way around, he came in laughing and showed me. Mark woke up due to all the laughing, he had a bad hangover, he went to the bathroom and splashed water on his face. All you heard was spewing from the poo on his face from the towel, Christian was in laughing fits, we got out of there and left Mark to it he was not too pleased. He shouted out the window you wankers, I rang him later and said "it was not me" he laughed it off. Christian brought Chris Ashton along to join the TCE, he was a year younger at school, he worked with Neil at the ice cream factory. In the film Id, Gumbo worked in a pickle onion factory, so that's where Neil got his nickname from, as he worked in an ice cream factory, we all called Neil Gumbo I am not sure if he liked the name or not.

Chris Ashton was like a born soldier, he had royal blood linked to Celtic Cornish Devon, through his dad, and he was like a philosopher. Chris was intelligent into his history, especially about the wars over the years, he was so knowledgeable, but he made a perfect hooligan. Back then I became good friends with Chris, he loved to fight, and we got on well. We went out one night, it was student night on a Thursday, he said to us all, let us go student bashing. We were outside the Candy Store, there were fifteen of us in a little mob looking for the students who started coming out of the club. Chris told us all to take our belts off, to attack the students. We were chasing a load of them up a street, whilst hitting them with our belts.

I stayed at his house where he lived with his parents, who were kind and lovely people, he had a tarantula. He scared me in the morning with it. My Gran, Mum and sister used to get their hair done by his Aunty who had a hairdressing shop nearby, my Grandparents house she was a friend of my family I discovered that night.

Nonetheless, the following week I went to an away Birmingham match with Gumbo, a friend Jason joined us on this away trip. There were no hooligans going on this day, we drank beers all the way up, Neil was driving. He loved his beers, but he could not drink that day. We decided to take a break at a service station near Bristol, when we returned to the car, he was unable to put it in reverse, the clutch was no longer functional. We had to wait for the RAC to arrive to solve the problem, he arrived one hour later.

The decision to watch the game was debatable, we only had an hour and a half to get there. We arrived ten minutes after the game had started, we talked to two teenagers about finding a parking spot for Neil's car, they directed us to a parking spot. We got to the ground and sat behind the bench where the Argyle manager at the time, Peter Shilton, was standing, we watched the game there.

When we went into halftime, there were Birmingham fans in our section of the stadium above us, they threw money at us, a Mars bars came dangerously close to hitting me on the head. I did not mind. I picked them up and ate them, but we did not win the game. We returned to Neil's vehicle, unbelievably they had removed two wheels from it. It was necessary for Neil to contact the RAC once more; we were taken to a garage, and they put two wheels back on, we were finally on our way again it was a nightmare I just wanted to get home. Jason repeatedly requested permission to pull over on his way home as the alcohol he had consumed earlier made him sick. He was sick all the way home, it was a fun day out, but I was relieved to get home.

Chapter 8. The Battle Scars on The Pitch

Neil played goalkeeper for the St. Anne's Chapel football team in Cornwall. Neil asked me to play, even though they were not the best team in the world, I decided it was worth it to play football again. Despite being out of shape and frequently out of breath due to smoking, I managed to play well. Nevertheless, I was able to assist them in winning their first game in a long time. Following that, we played a friendly match against the TCE, I took on the entire team against Lenox, Chris Ashton, Popeye Tristan, Rutherford Christian. There were more Plymouth hooligans, but my memory is not that great to remember all eleven players. It was such fun playing against them, I dribbled from one end of the field to the other, weaving in and out, doing nutmegs spinning on the ball with dazzling skills. I took on all eleven players scoring a goal. Going up against the TCE was one game to remember, it was hot, and everyone was out of breath, but I was unfit too, we won easily 7-0.

I played in another match, this time for a league game, I was playing like a pro at the time, I started to try to get fit again. I ran so fast for the ball, the other team passed the ball through to the centre forward, as I kicked the ball out of bounds, my knee gave out, I had to sit out the rest of the game. Just walking was excruciatingly painful for me, I needed help getting to the locker room. My leg was severely injured because of my knee being twisted so badly; I could not even put my foot on the floor because I was in so much pain. The football club summoned an ambulance, the paramedics arrived, they advised me to use laughing gas to relieve the pain, which worked perfectly and made me laugh. Regardless, they attempted to transport me to a hospital in Cornwall, I pleaded with them to take me to Derriford Hospital, they were gracious enough to do so. I twisted my knee and tore my anterior cruciate ligament (ACL). After nearly regaining my fitness, I discovered that I was unable to play again. I was in an unpleasant situation; I could not walk on my leg. My career on the football field had ended, I did not get any compensation money either. It improved over time, but the problem with my leg never completely went away.

After three or four months had passed, I could finally walk again. I was working at The Range for Chris D. Mum went out with him once when she was younger, but really, she fancied his friend so that did not last long, he was worth millions. I got the job through my friend Christian; I always went out drinking with the staff on a Friday.

Molly used to go out with a girl from The Range, my sister would sometimes come out as well, we all would meet at the Golden Hind pub. Then we would get a taxi to the Barbican, before hitting the nightclubs in Union Street, we had a good laugh dancing, sometimes getting into a fight, that was just the way it was back then. There was an Indian lad, who was being nasty to me, trying to get me to do his job as well as mine. I told him I did not have to do his work as well, he screamed "yes, I did." It made me so mad, so I opened the case of a music CD, and threw the CD at him. The CD smacked him in the head, and he went screaming to the office. Paul, a manager I knew from school, was in charge when Chris was not around, we got on well, but he had to give me the sack. I was only there for a week.

Christian asked me whether I wanted to go Butlins with him, Dan, and their girlfriends. They said they would sneak me in their car boot, the girls did not want me to go, but Christian and Dan insisted, even though I was banned from Butlins. We arrived at Butlins, I was in the boot of the car with suitcases on top of me, it was a doddle. When we arrived, there were Bristol Rovers fans in the room directly across from us, we could see them outside the window. We were watching and listening to them sing while they displayed their big flag outside their window. They were conversing and singing football songs, so we decided to sing Argyle songs in response after we had many beers. There were a large group of them, Christian suggested, that three of us would fight against twenty to thirty of them. We saw that the odds were stacked against us, but all three of us were up for the fight. We were singing our songs. They were singing back, we then decided to run at them, they scattered everywhere. They went running to the different venues, most locked themselves away in their rooms, so we started pounding on their doors. They were so perplexed that they called security, assuming there were more than three of us.

We eventually went back to where we were staying, I hid in one of the wardrobes when we noticed security approaching. I could see a gap through the wardrobe, and I saw Christian's girlfriend had taken her top off, I could see her huge nipples. Security insisted that the Bristol lads had seen more than just the two of you. They could not believe that the Bristol boys would try to avoid just two boys. However, after their investigation, they thought it was just Christian and Dan, they laughed about it but issued a warning to Christian and Dan. When we went out that evening, the guys had abandoned their women, so we all decided to go to a pub though we were already tipsy.

They were holding an auction to raise funds for a worthy cause. Dan and I put Christian's hands up to bid on expensive items, while he was unconscious due to his intoxication. He awoke quickly from his sleep when he realized what we were doing, as a result, we all fled.

A shopping trolley was outside the grocery store, after putting Christian into the trolley and pushing him down a hill, it was my turn, they pushed me down, dangerously, I was going so fast the trolley had speed wobbles, but I went crashing into a wall as a bouncer jumped out of the way. We had a great night, I felt awkward as they were not giving the girlfriends any attention, but they were giving me more. Even though I had entered illegally, I was granted complete freedom, I had no choice but to stay in the structure. We had to have our hands stamped, or a wrist band given to us when we went swimming, on the slides and tubes it was a great laugh. We went out every night to the entertainment and night clubs, they always left their girlfriends, it seemed like it was a lad's week away. The week flew by, it was a great holiday and such a laugh one to remember.

The following week I took acid tabs with Paul and some of the younger lads in my area. We had every intention of visiting the surrounding, subterranean, underground forts, in Efford. On foot, we made our way through the forest, it was about four miles away. I unexpectedly ran into Jason, the local psychopath. He would chase people with a samurai sword regularly, he was the last guy I wanted to see, while we were crossing a road, halfway to the fort. He came right up to my face rubbing his face on my face, he told me about my sexual encounter with his grandma. His grandma was completely unknown to me. He was completely insane, I told him he had gotten it wrong, "I do not know your grandma," I said, and he mumbled something back. His eyes were enormous, there was talk back then that he took angel dust a lot, which would explain why his eyes were ginormous.

He hit me with such force with a knuckle duster in my mouth, I flew back a few meters in the air before landing on my feet. I was hallucinating before I bumped into him, but as soon as he hit me the hallucinations went away. We were never able to make it to the fort, there seemed to be a lot of blood in my mouth, we walked the roadway home, I returned home, I looked in a mirror, my mouth was like a balloon.

I decided to try and get my life back into order and get myself a care job again. So, I applied for a position at this residential home for disabled people, I will not name the residential home. It was something I enjoyed doing. I had an interview, both ladies were flirting with me and said that I got the job because of my good looks. I could not believe my luck, the pay was excellent, and the shifts suited me twelve hours a day but lots of days off.

The two ladies ran the place, both in their sixties and one called Joyce who was the manager. The person who owned the residential home was a former member of Parliament, a rich ex MP, she had been caught having sex on a boat with someone half her age, she was in the Sun newspaper because of the affair, she left government. She got lots of money for the residents who stayed in her care home, it was not cheap to stay there. I had the opportunity to work with many people who I previously worked with at the Manadon Day Centre where I had worked before, so I knew a lot of the clients, I really enjoyed doing this kind of work.

In the morning, I oversaw bathing some men, assisting them in getting dressed, and getting everyone ready to travel to the day centre. We had to serve the patients with breakfast, it was my job to feed a blind lady called Christine. We then had to get them ready for all the different day centres they attended, we took some of them in our minibus and dropped them off at different day centres, some stayed at home, when I returned, I would have to clean their rooms. Then it was the dreading ironing, which was one of the few tasks which I hated. Another patient, Bob, would pitch in and help clear and help clean the dishes, in terms of abilities, Bob outperformed everyone else in the group. He seemed like he had nothing much wrong with him, but he felt safe being around other people, he was like staff always doing odd jobs, for extra pocket money.

Some patients were severely handicapped, and others were more mentally handicapped. I took Bob and Michael to Argyle, the minibus dropped us off there, they were enthralled when I took them to the game, Michael would sing and get so excited. Some of them, like Mary, were severely disabled, and it was my responsibility to help her when she needed to use the restroom. This was not one of my favourite jobs, but it had to be done, it was time for her diaper to be changed, I thought the job should be done by a woman, but it was occasionally done by me and another male.

Tom was a chargehand, stank of beer all the time, he lived in a cottage, which was built separately from the main house. He was such a slacker, I began by liking him because when I worked with him, he always told me to watch TV, there was not much work for me to do while he was on duty. He made a horrible homemade curry, which was one of my favourite dishes, but not his cooking.

Joyce' was the company's manager; she was quite authoritative and stringent with both the residents and me. I had done gardening as a side job in the past to supplement my income, only for families and some friends. She made me take care of the landscaping and clean all the windows inside and out. Joyce was like a slave driver, there was no sitting down when she was on duty, besides that, she liked a drink of wine too, she drank with Tom often, especially in the evening, she would then sneak out to his place. Jane, the proprietor, exuded superiority; she would ask, "OK, duck, how are you doing"? That was her favourite line, she was so posh, however she was not a difficult boss to work for, she let me leave an hour early most shifts. She used to wear miniskirts, which made her look hot, she used to dress the ladies in Laura Ashley clothing.

Then there was Martin, a care assistant, he was a control freak, nothing but an idiot. Everything had to be micromanaged by him, it was unclear why he felt such intense envy towards me. He imagined himself overseeing everything. He was a control freak, because he had been there the longest, this made him think he could tell me what to do. I hated him, he was lucky that he did not get a punch in his mouth. Fortunately, I did not have to spend much time working with him, it was mostly just twelve-hour shifts three days a week, with the rest of the time off we were always on different days on the odd occasion I had to work with Martin. Mandie was easy to get on with, we got on well, she used to tell me lots of news and this and that about people is why I knew about Jane, Mandie introduced me to her niece, a stunning looking girl called Tina. She was a model, so pretty she used to come to visit Mandie at work and after a while Mandie told me that Tina fancied me. I told her I would take her out, it was Wesley's birthday party, at Glenholt near the moors, a nice area of Plymouth.

Wesley is Chris Ashton's brother, the venue had a massive function room, I gave him some pink champagne. A form of amphetamine, it was pink in colour, it was so strong it was the first time he had ever taken it his eyes were popping out of his sockets. He had the biggest of grins on his face, his Mum was

Christine, such a nice down to earth person, her husband who was also nice., Neil and Christian, along with lots more people at his party. Next door to the pub was another group of lads, it was not long before a fight broke out. We heard a noise outside, Christian was fighting about ten lads, even Neil joined in this time, with a stunning right hook. Chris Ashton loved a fight, so he went straight in there I do not think he ever would have backed out of a fight back in the day. Then Tina wanted me to go to her place, it was a brilliant party, I said my goodbyes, Wesley said to me it's been the best birthday, but I'm fucked, with the biggest eyes and grin on his face he looked he was enjoying it, with pinging starring eyes. I was worried as it was his first time, and I was worried his parents would find out. So I went back to her place, she was so pretty you could not get prettier than her. I tried to be a gentleman and take it slow without jumping in too fast, she told Mandie I was too slow as she wanted sex that night. She did not want to go out after that, at the time I wished I were not such a gentleman about it, as I lost a stunner.

I went out another weekend, it was Ryan's birthday, there was twenty of us the more sensible people from my area, he was a born-again Christian, we went to a party before going to the nightclub, for a drink. I was telling all the boys that if I punch someone, they normally go down, the lads laughed at me as though I was making it all up. We were in the Ritzy club dancing. I saw the birthday boy get smacked in the head, Ryan the devoted Christian would never start a fight, unless he was preaching about God to someone.

I ran across the dance floor, I smacked the man in the chin, he flew from one end of the dance floor to the other. I was expecting the bouncer to kick me out, I continued to dance, I turned around to see Croke putting the finishing touches on him. Croke just turned up out of nowhere, he often did that, especially when I used to get into fights losing his friends downtown. I always seemed to have bumped into him, he was ejected from the club. Croke, he loved a fight, and he used to duck and dive a talented boxer and a ginger nut always laughing and smiling.

The following week I was surprised to see Wayne, a childhood friend of mine, he asked whether I wanted to go to a party. There were lots of people at the party when I arrived, several of them asked if I had ever used magic mushrooms before. Even though I had never done it before, I said yes, they presented me with sixty daddy mushrooms. They were quite substantial in size, I felt sick after eating them and had to use the toilet, I was sick all over the place. They could tell I was not feeling well and were concerned for my well-being, after admitting that I had never done these Magic mushrooms before, the look on their faces made me think I was in for a troubled time. Wayne and some of his friends took me for a walk around the block of the neighbourhoods, I noticed a road was moving up and down, the colours were all crazy, I was unable to complete the journey. We then returned to the apartment, they were playing on the mixing decks, which confused me even more because they were using two different mixing decks at the same time, so four records were spinning at once. There was about twenty people present, I yelled at the top of my voice, you must all leave the flat immediately, because my mother is due back from work, I am not allowed no one in so get the fuck out of my flat. They laughed at me which made me go crazy, I took one of the mixing decks and smashed it in half on the floor, the other mixing deck was still playing the dance music. I went to grab that one too, but

Wayne grabbed it off me, he calmed me down. I went to the toilet and was violently sick. I spent a good hour in the toilet, I then went to sleep after doing bongs, I was seeing the most wonderful colours even when I slept. Wayne had informed me of what I had done as soon as I awoke in the morning, I immediately gave the lad my hash for smashing his decks up. He said it was all right, but I insisted, he took it in the end, it was an ounce of squidgy black. He was nice about it, I felt like a total moron. The mixing decks were not cheap, they were Technics, the most expensive decks on the market, I said to myself I would never take magic mushrooms ever again. I used to make the most of the time I had off work, a few weeks later Jason and I went to Wembley to see Bon Jovi, we met Neil there with his mate Slug and a few others.

I chose to take amphetamine, I did it occasionally, I did not do it whilst working though. We took a coach from Plymouth all the way to London, we then took the train to Wembley. We smoked hash on the pitch with Niel and Slug and another lad from Plymouth, Andrew. Andrew was a posh lad, but such a gentleman, he was down to earth, always laughing at me in a good way, he was nice. Neil travelled in his car, he had Richard and his older brother there too.

He was a nice person who was a professional golfer. We watched Bon Jovi perform at Wembley it was an incredible show from start to finish. Bon Jovi was amazing; he was one of my favourites, after hanging around with Neil, who always used to play his songs in his room and car. White Snake was another band, the first time I ever heard of him, he was on after Bon Jovi, and he was nuts. We all held our breath, as he climbed to the top of the roof on scaffolding, with no safety rope. The roof at Wembley was so high and dangerous, he jumped from the scaffolding onto the roof, one wrong move and it would have been curtains for him, but he made it. The whole crowd was cheering, he was amazing, jumping like a mad man on the roof singing, and blasting out his guitar with a bold head, I loved the concert.

Jason was having an unpleasant experience with amphetamine; he was on a bad one. We saw Jane in London after the performance, "Hello duck," she said out of nowhere. "Do you want something to eat? "Jason said, "No" as we had to catch the coach. It was a bit of an odd encounter to bump into her in London. It is such a small world, bumping into my boss from work as London is miles away from Plymouth. It was almost impossible to eat on amphetamine, but I was up for going as she was a bit hot; I did fancy her as she always looked hot in her mini skirt. I did fancy older women when I was twenty years old, she was in her sixty's, but I would not have the bottle to try anything. She likes the younger man with her who was about thirty years old, he was a surfer man, with long blonde hair, who would use her for her money. That is what everybody said about him as she was a millionaire, she did, in fact, smoke flowers She referred to it as flowers which meant weed, she often got me to get her weed, when she could not get it.

Jason yearned for his girlfriend's company. He was constantly saying how much he missed her, we returned to the coach station and missed our coach home. They told us to keep hold of the ticket and put us down for a coach in the morning, we had no choice but to stay in London for one night. I really wanted to go to a nightclub, Jason was uninterested in doing anything, he was such a bore. As a result, we had to sit in the London underground in the gangways next to a shop. Luckily for me when you are on that amphetamine all you want to do is talk, a friendly tramp came and sat beside me. He said the only people to fear in London are the Chinese, he told us that they are the maddest and most dangerous people out of all the diverse cultures in London. He made a lot of money; he said on a good day he could make three hundred pounds and on a dreadful day fifty quid.

He used to be a wealthy man who had his own businesses, but his wife divorced him, and he lost his home, money so he started drinking, took drugs and ended up on the streets. He told me that he was clean from drugs, but he said he liked a brandy at night to keep himself warm. Jason fell asleep when taking amphetamine, even when there were four stunning birds sitting opposite. One kept winking at me. I tried waking Jason up, but he just kept snoring, as I really wanted to go over to the girls and sit with them, but I did not, how anyone could sleep on amphetamine was beyond me. The tramp collected a lot of food from people and fed us too. Jason would wake up when the food was being handed out, then he would go back to sleep when there was none left.

The tramp was a remarkably interesting character, with an old, checkered suit on with a cap. He spent hours talking to me, he told me he was going for a shower, where he paid a pound to feel refreshed, for the day, he loved being on the streets, and told me he would not have it any other way. Even though Jason was boring, it was a fantastic weekend in London, I had an exciting time.

I continued to use hash and sell it to my friends, which is how it all starts, once you start getting hash for friends. I would get it so cheap in Swilly, and once I saw a little bit of money coming in, I was hooked on such a straightforward way to make money, I was selling it cheaper than other dealers on my estate. I had lots of friends who wanted to buy hash. It did not make me a bad person as they would have the hash from someone else, I was just doing it cheaper.

We took the patients on a little holiday, not far away, to Pontins in Brixton, Devon. During our vacation, Martin must have assumed I was homosexual because I was the target of his advances, when he tried it on with me. I have never had a problem with other people's sexual orientation, but when I went to punch him, he quickly vanished, I was steaming, saying I am going to kill him. Joyce encouraged me to take time off work, to do something fun for myself.

I ended up in a club and talking to a stranger and spending the night with a woman in her chalet. It was a night of passion and no sleep, she lived up North, I was badly bruised downstairs, it killed. I was so paranoid that I had caught something or injured my manhood. I showed Mandie, she said hell that is really bruised bad she said, it will heal one day. I was not showing Joyce as she had a bad habit of drinking, she got so funny and jealous that I had slept with this woman. I was only twenty-one years old when this happened, she had a crush on me, Mandie had told me, it made me feel sick she was old and wrinkly and so ugly. Joyce acted funny for the rest of the holiday, Martin knew to stay away from me, the control freak, knew he could not mess with me no more. Joyce's husband called Ted, he was in his late sixties, he worked as a handy man around the residential home, he was a nice guy.

Mandie entered Tom's place, she discovered that they were drunk, kissing and a lot more than that. I returned to work with Joyce the next day, she was under the influence of vodka. She had a short skirt on with her legs spread open on the kitchen side unit, flirting with me, she asked me to come over to her, I said you are drunk, she said don't ever come back to work, you're a useless care assistant and you're sacked. I could not believe it, a few days before I was sacked. Mandie told me she saw Tom hit one of the patients with a hairbrush. I noticed Tom's more hostile demeanour because of the effects of alcohol. Joyce did the same; she also had hit a patient with a hairbrush.

What happened there was truly insane. I was a rogue, but I was good at my job and cared about the people I worked with. I was devastated, as were the patients I had grown to love and care for, I had enjoyed it so much. I did file a complaint about all the harassment, which was sexual in nature, and the way the patients were being treated I told the local council. As a result, they fired me but, just before leaving that job.

Chapter 9. The High and Lows

I finally passed my car driver's test after five attempts. It was such a relief, as I had completed crash course lessons in the past but had never been successful, however, I had succeeded this time. My Mum and I shared a Renault Le car, which turned out to be an excellent little vehicle, I could not wait to get out on the open road.

On my first night of driving, I drove Darren King and Mark Trenaman, to Torquay. I had no intention of drinking alcohol, but Darren talked me into drinking a couple of drinks in the bars, I did not want to because once you get a taste for it you just want more. I did not want to lose my license, Kingy was normally so tight, but he wanted to go to the Ministry of Sound. A rave in a church was unusual, and admission was often prohibitively expensive, but he was willing to spend twenty pounds to get in. When it was a football match, he would never pay, he would rather be in a pub with cans he had sneaked in. I would normally love a rave, but I was not in the best of moods, especially since Darren had given me such a headache all the way in the car. Kingy suggested that we should get an ecstasy pill, I initially refused because I had to drive. Even though the pill was blue they called it the white lady, I ended up taken one blue ecstasy tablets as Kingy came back with some I started dancing for about twenty minutes and noticed that there was a girl dancing in a cage, it was strange being in a club in a church, the room started to spin, I felt overheated and dizzy. I had to go outside and lay on the ground to get some fresh air when I became exhausted, I blacked out on the ground into a coma.

A biker in the Aquila named Stavros from Plymouth poured a can of coke down my throat, he was also in the TCE. Tristan introduced me to him at Tristans flat, I used to go there and get smoke if I got stuck, they were tripping on acid tabs when I first met him. He brought me another can of Coke, and after drinking it, I felt slightly better, he saved my life, as I was out for the count. It was my first ecstasy tablet; I was certain it would be my last. After three hours, I concluded it was time for us to go home.

I was still uneasy because the ecstasy effect made me feel dodgy, plus Kingy was constantly tampering with the heater controls in my car. I kept falling asleep at the wheel because it was too hot, he put crap music on when I had my Helter-Skelter tape on, he put eighties music on the radio, anything to annoy me. I slammed on the brakes and warned him that if he continued acting like a clown, he would have to walk home alone, I am not sure how I managed to get us home, but I did.

The following week It was Port Vale at home, we were all in the Lyndhurst End of Home Park, suddenly the Port Vale fans jumped the fence, and got inside our end. I got punched to the ground, I got up, a steward who was a kick boxing champion of the world, grabbed me to try to arrest me, so all I could think of was to spit in his face and managed to get away it's a dirty thing to spit in someone's face, but it had to be done.

I went to Exeter away, we hate each other especially when it comes to football, they are our local rivals, we all got up on the train this day. The usual lot went, we had hundreds marching through the town, we watched the game, I cannot remember the result. After the game the police were outside the ground and they tried to keep us all together in a group, the police got heavy handed, and it kicked off with the police Mark Trenaman got arrested, I escaped with about twenty lads, I didn't know these Plymouth lad's we ran through the police chain. We were in a street in the City Centre, when we came into battle with the Exeter sly crew, who is what they were called, as they used to jump people, when they were on their own. I looked behind, the twenty lads from Plymouth had run away. I had about forty sly crew big built men all with Stone Island on to me. I hit at least two lads, one I knocked to the ground, I had all forty, running after me through the town centre, I bumped into Christian and a load of police, I lived to see another day. Mark was free the gave him a warning and the mad head Trenaman was fighting again as it kicked off in the town centre, he was nicked again we had them all on the run then the police had us all in a big group and with no escape we was cornered all ordered to stand still whilst the police filmed us all then they took us all back to the train station.

The following Monday, I drove some different friends to the top of Jenny cliff where there are stunning views looking out onto the sea which surrounds Plymouth. I often done this during the week as I went out every weekend drinking with the football lads or going home or away watching football, but I never stayed in. My friend Mark was there too, he had a girlfriend shouted to him for a laugh, if I win, I win your girlfriend, he was driving a vehicle that was far more powerful and much faster. As a result, we engaged in a race from one shore to the other, about a ten-mile race, I used to be a reckless driver who performed the most daring stunts. My small vehicle drove up on two wheels around the bends where we were supposed to stop and look each way on a main road I drove straight through. Mark was on the give way section, if a car had come it would have been shocking news, that is where I overtook him. I weaved my way in and out of traffic and beat him all the way to Devil's Point, a breathtaking view overlooking Plymouth Sound and Drake's Island. However, I was able to seize his girlfriend until we arrived back at Scott's house.

Scott was a hardcore music fan with decks at his disposal, Mark was being disrespectful to his girlfriend, he hit her. I was quite a shy person, but on this day, I asked Mark 's girlfriend out, she said yes, however, the relationship did not last that long, Mark eventually forgave me for taking his girlfriend. Mark used amphetamine all the time, he thought that the cameras were watching our every move, in the room, he also assumed that the cameras were within the lampposts.

David came in carrying a hand grenade he had found near the army barracks, where the army were training. There were about ten of us in his front room, as well as his mother. Mark told David to hand over the grenade, Mark took the pin out and said, "Oh fuck." Mark took off into the air shortly after that, I went flying off the sofa with my ears ringing, the room covered in smoke. The windows in the front room were smashed, she was a down to earth Mother who had the whole of Mark's friends in her house, she told us all to get the fuck out of her house.

I phoned Andy from Swilly, to say I would give my friend a lift out, so that he could meet him so that he could get amphetamine, on a regular basis. Andy with his long ginger hair and a beard who I spent a lot of time with, especially back then, he said yes, no problem. Mark knocked on his door, Andy for a laugh was hanging out of his upstairs window, whilst pointing a real handgun at Mark, he sprinted back to my car and told me to drive off, I said he was joking, go back and get your stuff. He was shaking like a leaf and asked if I would go in and get it, so I went inside and got the drugs. Mark would never ever go there himself; he would always ask me to get it for him. Swilly was a dangerous neighbourhood back then, but I was able to have a good relationship with the locals, as over the years I got to know them all as it was so close to my Nans, I met a lot of people in Swilly. When I needed narcotics, I always went to the same location, it was less expensive.

I received a letter informing me that I was going to receive ten thousand pounds. It would be posted to me within a month, if I accepted the offer, I could have said no, for a possibility to get more but I accepted it. It was compensation money for the damage to my eye. I went to the bank with my letter, I asked how much the interest the bank would charge me on a ten-thousand-pounds loan, I got the following response, the man in the bank, said it would be six hundred pounds, for interest. He told me it would take a day, and it would be ready for me to spend, I was in possession of nine thousand and four hundred pounds, I could not believe they gave it to me, I knew I would not pay the money back.

After that, I was able to process the cheque, a month later I was able to open a new bank account. So, I had twenty thousand pounds minus the few thousand I had spent. I decided to go to Helter Skelter which was one of the biggest raves in the country, I brought Scott with me, as he was a major fan of his rave music. It was during a particularly cold season of the year, I went to Swilly and bought some hash, and some pink champagne, it was my favourite amphetamine. We drove to Milton Keynes, which was 231 miles away, as I drove up through the night, I stopped in a densely populated area, where we attempted to sleep.

Unbelievably it was cold, enormous amounts of ice had formed in my car, it was freezing, I could not fall asleep, I was on pink champagne which would not have helped at all. We were smoking bongs in my car, daylight came, we went to a nearby café, had a nice breakfast then we went to the river, we consumed amphetamine there and smoked a load of bongs before going to the rave. We had to line up in a big queue that went on for a mile, it was unbelievable how cold it was, with black ice everywhere it was freezing. My foot was numb, I could not feel it and it appeared to have doubled in size when I looked down at my feet.

I was tripping on the pink champagne, Scott was acting like a scab, as he did for most of his life back then, despite knowing that I had money, he failed to bring any. Scott persisted in his efforts to persuade me to buy some Ecstasy, as a result, I bought two each. I was having an enjoyable time until I took ecstasy tablets, it was far too hot for me, I was high on ecstasy. It made me feel so bad that I had to go to the bathroom, to pour water on myself. Then I was sick all over the place, I then crashed out on the floor. Scott found me in the toilet. We got some fresh air then after getting used to the spin, I thought I had to try to enjoy the rest of the night even though I felt so sick.

The music was incredible, but as I ascended to the Techno room upstairs, I made a concentrated effort to have fun, I was successful. When DJ Producer started playing his records, I had to sprint on the spot to keep up. I danced for an hour or two it seemed, but time just went so fast it must have been four to five hours. My eyes were rolling, and the ecstasy was making me spin with uneasy feeling, I could not wait to get out of there. 6 o'clock arrived, it was time for us to go. While sitting in the parking lot, we smoked bongs, as I was so messed up, the effects of my ecstasy hit me harder after each bong I smoked. After an hour of bonging, we decided to go to the main part of town, but the weather was so foggy with black ice on the road, it made driving extremely dangerous. I was driving on the wrong side of the road, a police car followed me, I could not believe it.

I was wrecked. I had an ounce of lovely hash in the steering wheel, they were watching me drive in the wrong lane. The police officer pulled me over and claimed to have detected the odour of cannabis, I will not arrest you if you turn over the item he said, as a result, I retrieved the hash and gave it to him. He ordered me to stand on it and break it. It was solid hash that was called a soap bar, it must have occurred to him that it would not break so, he told me to throw it, as far as I could. I figured that I would throw it towards a lamppost over the other side of the road, I would return for it later, I threw it across the road, just missing a lamppost. I was given permission to continue my journey by the police officer, we entered the town centre, our bodies still recovering from the ecstasy, we danced in the shops, people did not even look at us, as we danced insanely. We could not believe our eyes in this boring town, so we went in search of the hash that I chucked at the lamppost, we could not find the hash we searched for an hour, but we had no luck. We returned to Plymouth, as soon as we hit Plymouth there were lads dancing on a bridge, we knew we were back, the people were mad in Plymouth it seemed, especially compared to where we had just come from. I did manage to purchase mixing decks as well as a previously owned car.

Chapter 10. Riot of Shadows

 A week later we would be playing Millwall at home, Millwall were one of the country's hardiest hooligans, we all met in town in a pub. There were a couple hundred of us, we all walked up to a pub near Central Park, the pub the Pennycomequick next to the train station, it was not long before the Millwall firm walked into the pub for a drink. There were so many of us in there you could not move, this ginger lad gave a Millwall lad a headbutt. This was unexpected, the whole pub kicked off, we had Millwall on the run as they legged it towards the football ground. We won the game 3-1. After the game we were walking in the park, it was just starting to get a little dark, we walked back towards the train station. There were only about twenty of us, we could hear a group of lads over a hedge. We all thought stuff it and charged the Millwall mob, but it was Scooby and the Devonport lads who legged it, as we were making monkey chants, as we chased them. I soon realized it was our own supporters as Scooby was well known. We all laughed, as we were always going to matches with these lads. These lads from Devonport were older than us, so we thought it was hilarious as we had them on the run.

The following week I went to Wrexham away, we got up with a big mob. We stopped off at a pub, I was with Christian and the lads, we all went on the minibus, we played a game of pool in the pub. Christian decided it would be a great idea if we all had a pool ball, ready for the Welsh lads. We got to the ground and the police made us go straight into the ground, some of the lads forgot they had the pool balls in their pocket, nothing kicked off that day, sometimes the police were just always there.

 The next Friday night in the Ritzy nightclub, we all met up with the older and the original members of TCE, it was a good turnout, about fifty lads. Molly with his black leather jacket and leather gloves on while a lot had their leather gloves on in the club. Kingy embroiled in a fight, he never stopped bragging about being the hardest person in Plymouth. He was being severely beaten, he was not the toughest man he thought was, he was completely delusional, but it made him hilarious. Andy went to jail several times for stabbing people, he ran in and tried to help Kingy, by landing a few punches. The guy would not go down, he continued to brutally beat Kingy up. As a result, I ran in and landed a right punch square on the elder guy's jaw, he collapsed to the ground like a bag of potatoes and was cold out on the floor.

It felt good showing the mob what I could do, Kingy attempted to claim responsibility for his placement, to the floor. Everyone could see that it was the result of my one knock-out punch which had the man on the floor. Everyone in the TCE, including Andy, said "Well done," it felt good. Kingy did not even bother to thank me as he did not want to admit that he had lost, in such a manner. He was telling everyone, "Did you see me beat that bloke up?", but everyone knew what bull came out of his backside, they knew it was me who should have been taking the credit.

I phoned Molly at the Cherry Tree, a pub in Plymouth. I said, "Where are you Molly as we were going to watch Plymouth v Preston. he said Justin, you are a daft silly twat you just rang the pub, so you know where I am, laughing. I looked up to Molly. He was a hard skinhead, much older but he did have a caring side, proper old school, a good person to know. We were in the pub, there were about fifteen Preston lads in there, me and Molly were just finishing our drinks. We decided to run them out of the pub, Molly said let us chuck our pint glasses at them, so we did, we threw them at the same time then we were chasing them down the road, we then went and watched the game. I enjoyed drinking with Molly, who made me laugh.

We were playing Derby at home; we were in the Mayflower End of Home Park with The Central Element. We were just giving the away fans some noise and hand jesters, the police started waving their bats about, they tried to arrest Lenox. The police grabbed him, so we started fighting with the police, this went on for a while before the police left, Lenox got away, we got the better of the police on that day.

The following week Plymouth was playing Burnley at home, but I did not go to that game. I got a call from Christian asking, if I could meet down the Barbican for a fight in the evening, with the TCE. He could not make it, he told me Ashton was there and lots more he said, so I bought some amphetamine, in Swilly. Chris Ashton was the youngest, but I knew he would never back out of a fight, and was hard, especially for his age, he loved it. The top "boy" with a smart appearance, good dark looks, he was a financial advisor who was well known all over the country. Lenox was big built, with his own businesses in the building trade, these lads were the ones who asked us in the first place to join The Central Element.

Dave the spick half Italian, with dark looks, he was a smart dresser, he loved it, he stood out in a crowd. Tony," Popeye "that was his nickname, his eyes would pop out, he was mad always up for a fight. There was another Dave there, that made the seven of us, I did not really know him that well, but he was nuts too. We were drinking in the Gin Factory Pub on the Barbican; the top boy was waiting for a phone call from a Burnley lad. I was so nervous waiting for the phone call, we expected more of our boys to show up for the fight, but that was not the case. The Burnley guys called us, to let the top boy know, when they were in the Barbican. They had one hundred lads in the battle, we only had seven, we went outside the gin factory. Burnley had two huge guys who weighed about forty- fifty stone, I landed a single blow to one of them on his head, I knocked him out cold, he collapsed like a bag of potatoes, then the other giant huge fat man came at me. He punched me in the head, I ducked, I then punched him with a sweet uppercut, right in his chin, he went down in the same manner, one punch and he was out too. After that, there was a crowd of one hundred Burnley boys all in a big line. Chris Ashton and I raced towards them and dived straight into the crowd, we were fighting with loads of them and getting punched from all sides, right, left, and centre. I managed to punch one to the floor, I was fighting loads of them and was loving it, I got caught a few times, but knocking a few to the ground, I was fired up, this went on for about five minutes.

We should have gotten battered, but we were beating those who were in front of us, Chris was loving it, it was amazing as he was getting the better of them and so was I, there were so many bodies that we were fighting. The others kept running in and out, Dave and Mark went to the dumpsters to get bottles to throw at the group. The top boy shouted get back here you two, I needed to drag Chris away from the crowd, as he was still fighting with all one hundred men, by himself, he was holding his own, but it was time to get him out of there. I ran in and got him out, he told me to leave him alone. This lad was coming to the side of Ashton, he was to punch Ashton to the side of his head, I smacked the bloke to the floor. Ashton insisted on leaving him to fight, I dragged him back to our lads, then some of our lads threw bottles at them so we had them on the retreat. They went to regroup at the other end of the Barbican to the Navy pub. We were halfway down to the Barbican at this point, there was only one female police officer who was standing by herself in the gangway to a shop. She did not do anything to stop the fight; she called for backup. Suddenly they came running back at us down to the Barbican, bottles began flying back towards us, I had to duck because the bottle was hurtling towards my head, it only hit the top lad who was standing behind me smack in his eyebrow, blood splattered everywhere. I apologized to the top lad for ducking, he laughed and said, "its ok." We ran into pubs for any boys from Plymouth who could help us, but most of them were in the Navy, most of them did not come from Plymouth, one man said, "I am from Plymouth " Popeye said to the man "where in Plymouth are you from"? The man replied that he lived in Sheffield Road, Plymouth, there was no such a place in Plymouth. Tony delivered a hard headbutt to the man's nose that knocked the navy man to the ground, the other ten navy men just legged it, leaving their friend on the floor. We went back to the main bit of the Barbican, the police arrived in riot vans, they were running around everywhere. It was crazy the police ran after one of our lads, he was beaten with bats by the police and then arrested. I am unable to reveal his identity to you because he does not want his name to appear in my book, I called him Dave. We did exceptionally well, considering there were one hundred of them, we did more damage to them than what they did to us. And there were only seven of us. We caused mayhem and they knew they were in a good fight, the top boy from Burnley phoned a few hours later and said we were mad, but they held ample respect for us, we all went into town and had a fantastic night.

I managed to get a job as a theatre porter at Derriford Hospital, I went through an agency called pro-temps. Paul, the manager, requested that Mac would show me the ropes, Mac accompanied me on a tour, taking patients down for operations and then returning them back to the wards. It was enjoyable as we were having a laugh with the patients, Mac had a great personality, he was in his sixties, a good man but a bad boy too. He taught me how to steal the biggest bag of teabags and the biggest tin of coffee, we took them to the locker room and then he would hide the items in his locker. Then we went back to work, he sounded and looked exactly like Frank Butcher, from the TV series EastEnders he loved whisky. Mac told me the best place to hide whilst waiting for a job to do was in the smoking room, it was our favourite place. The walls were yellow stained with smoke, a little room with about twenty chairs going around. with people in there constantly, when there were no jobs that needed doing, some people were so lazy they would spend most of their shift in the smoking room. There were porters, surgeons, anaesthetists, and nurses all in the smoking room. I knew I could make an extra income because I could get tobacco and spirits cheap like vodka, whisky, rum, and brandy. It was not long before I was selling spirits to the surgeons and anaesthetists, I also sold loads of tobacco throughout the hospital. I was making some good money from tobacco and spirits, Mac loved it, a fiver for a bottle of whisky.

My Dad used to have a stool in the market, he made bonsai ornaments, Chinese men glued on bark, with fake bonsai trees. Dad would get oak out of the ground, clean it up and make things with it too. I helped him in the market, which is how I could get the alcohol and Tabaco cheap from an old lady on the fruit and veg stall, it was an unbelievably cheap price. I sold porn movies, it was amazing how many movies I sold, Animal Farm was one movie I sold, I never watched it as it was sick, people having sex with animals.

The staff would all play pranks on each other, Jim would frequently fall asleep, so quite often he would get a bucket of freezing water chucked over his head, to wake him up. Or if it were your birthday, you would get dragged to an empty theatre, stripped naked out of the green uniform, and buckets of water chucked over you the people in there were crazy. Kenny was also a major source of laughter, he was an ex-prisoner, however he lied on his application form, by not ticking the yes box for going to prison. He was from Swilly, just like a lot of the men who worked there, I caught up with him at a pub for a drink, he challenged every man in there for a fight he was nuts. Paul and Gary would always team up together, we normally worked in pairs, but they would try to avoid doing their jobs as much as possible by hiding. I had a good relationship with them both, but especially with Paul. He used to ask if I had been fighting at Argyle recently, I liked Paul, another man from Swilly.

Charge hand Steve was a laugh it was best to be on his good side though, he was a big, huge strong man who did not take any crap from anyone. We got along simply great, which was fortunate for me, we used to have such laughs, he loved to wind me up knowing I had a short fuse. The other chargehand was also quite large, he had it in for me. He pushed me to do a variety of tasks such as cleaning the theatres, while others did nothing, he made me clean so many things it was unreal. I used to work inside the operating room, where I would move patients around and turn them as the surgeon instructed. Furthermore, transporting them to the theatre's table, when their surgery was finished, and then taking them back to the recovery room.

We used to smoke in the smoking area while we were waiting for instructions to collect another person. Shaun was the name of this large man, he avoided every task imaginable, despite his belief, he was not amusing. He would frequently leave the hospital early to avoid cleaning the operating rooms properly, he would just run a mop through the operating room, which was so dangerous, especially with all the germs and bugs. Luckily, Paul swapped shifts with me so I could go to Wembley Stadium

Plymouth Argyle were in the play-off finals. It was the old division three, the year was 1996. If we were to win, we would go up to the old division two, which is now the Championship. Tristan Rutherford Ashton Christian was already up there the night before, I went up on the coach load full of The Central Element. We called it the fun coach, we could do whatever we wanted to do on the coach, smoke hash, drink beer, I took the fast drug speed, but others were on coke and all sorts, lads travelled up in cars. This young man, around the age of twenty years old was on his first ever away trip. He sat on the seat opposite me with his brother-in-law who went to many games. The older brother- in -law was well known from The Central Element, the young lad on his first away trip brought with him flat press hash, it was a nice smoke, he sold loads of it. We were able to meet many of my other friends at Marble Arch. Richard, Mark Chris, Christian, General Ron, Molly, Dan the man who loved to take photos he always brought his camera, a well-liked popular guy from Plymouth, many more I couldn't name them all, there was too many. I bought a beer, it was five pounds back then, so rather than pay that price, I walked to Tesco and bought eight cans of lager, then went back to the pub and poured my own, it made it a cheaper day out. We were breaking out into songs, which was great, "dance, dance whoever you maybe we are the boys from the TCE we need you all whoever you maybe because we are the boys from the TCE," this is one song we used to sing.

Argyle took up more than 30,000 people that day, so a sizable number of Plymouth greens were present, after that, we had to get a train in the underground train station. Some others and I jumped the gates and got on the train without paying, we filled up the train. It was jammed packed, I was stood up with no room whatsoever, a bottle of rush, a drug used for sexual stimulation, was being passed around. I sniffed some, everything went green, when I gave the bottle back, it kept coming back to me, by the time I got off the train I had a severe headache.

We marched out of the tube station singing lots of football songs, we were on the outskirts of the stadium, just down the road from the train station at the old Wembley stadium. There were easily three hundred lads, five hundred, it is hard to say when there were so many out on this day. We thought Darlington hooligans were running down from the underground train station, suddenly, it kicked off, they had a few hundred it was a massive brawl. No one had football shirts or scarves showing, it was just stone island, or design clothes that is what hooligans wear. Then unexpectedly, someone punched the lad beside me, he hit his head on the concrete so hard, he died it was shocking. Someone yelled it is Plymouth against each other, as someone had recognized a friend. It all went quietly; the police came in riot vans and most of the fans scattered. We were fighting each other because each different group thought it was Darlington, but it was not, it was Plymouth versus Plymouth. I was thrown into the police van, I had not done anything, they said before you go, we must look through the CCTV footage to make sure I had not been involved, with a knife. It was the first time I heard anything about a knife, I was shocked, but I knew I had not even had a fight on this day. The camera showed that I had not been involved in any way, I was so relieved and to be released from the police van. It was so incredibly sad on his first away trip that the unfortunate boy was killed by one of our own, it was such a terrible start to our day.

 I watched the game, but the fight before the game, killed us all, we were so sad losing a supporter in such a fashion. We won the division three playoff final with a goal, scored by Ronnie Mauge. I was not overjoyed like you should, after a big win, it was no fun on the coach on the way home, I sat next to Molly. When we returned to Plymouth, he told me that I had not stopped talking from London to Plymouth. That amphetamine had made me talk some garbage, a lad from Plymouth, was charged with man slaughter for killing the lad.

My Dad got sick and refused to eat, he felt useless, depressed, and suicidal. I mentioned to him that I would try to find him a job at the hospital like mine, most of the guys up there slammed Paul who was the manager, but I thought he was a good guy. I worked for a temporary staffing agency, but it was still full time just like the NHS, but they were more secure, being an NHS staff member, they had more rights, where I could just get sacked for nothing. With the NHS they had paid holidays, sick pay, and a pension, it was much more beneficial with more pay. I asked if Dad could do the same and work through the same agency I was with. The Manager Paul said he would do his best to find Dad a job if one became available, so I told Dad that he would be the first in line if a job became available. Dad expressed great concern that he would not be able to do the job, he did not have any confidence to be around people and just thought he would not be suited for such a job. It did not take that long for him to be taken on as a porter, he was fantastic at it. He worked meticulously, cleaning all the theatres, and jumping up for every job, not sitting around like all the rest of us, his confidence grew and grew, as time went on, he really enjoyed it and made lots of new friends.

There was a cleaner there who was flirting with me, she was all over me like a rash she was married to a naval man, he was away at sea. I went out clubbing again with her, we were kissing on the dance floor, then we decided to leave, it was late. We carried on kissing outside the club, I suddenly got a tap on my shoulder, one of the cleaner's husbands navy buddies, spotted us kissing one night, after we had come out of the club he punched me right in the nose, I was seeing star's it knocked me right back. I was with her for a week of passion. She told me she was getting rid of her boyfriend. Then the next day, she told me she did not want to see me anymore.

There were vacancies for the NHS, coming up, I figured I had a good chance after being there for a few years, I was not lazy, I worked harder than most and I had a good rapport with the patients. The NHS hired my father, I was unsuccessful, I could not believe it, but I was still working as a pro temporary worker. I was happy for Dad as he was much happier again, a substantial change from when he first started.

Wayne Robinson, a friend of mine, from football was regularly going in for treatments, he was in a tough situation following having various body parts removed. He kept asking if I could wheel his bed down for his operation, so I did. I ran on the pitch, at the end of the season when Keith Hill, the captain of Plymouth Argyle, gave me his shirt. I gave Wayne this shirt because I knew he adored Argyle and desperately needed a kidney donation. Wayne eventually received a kidney transplant and was fine for a year before he died, he went to most games, because he just adored Argyle, he was a great guy. I enjoyed my job at Derriford Hospital, but one charge hand named Keith, made me do loads of jobs while his favourites sat on their asses. On one day he made me clean all the theatres, which there was eighteen theatres to clean far too much for just one person, I thought ok I will then. He was finding faults saying I had not cleaned them properly, he was getting moody, I told him to get fucked, he then got mouthy, so I offered him out for a fight, as he had wound me up something rotten. He told me I was sacked and told me never to return, he was a gigantic obese bully. Over the speakers, the staff in the whole of Level 4 heard me stupidly, say one day I will kill you, you fat Teletubby. I was gutted as it was a brilliant job that I was good at and I enjoyed so much, just ruined by one bully of a man if I had just ignored him and kept my head down things would have been so different.

The last game of the season was against Burnley, Ian was driving the minibus despite his lack of enthusiasm, as the boy who was supposed to drive failed to appear. Ian, like the rest of us, wanted to drink, but he had to drive, we were getting drunk and smoking cannabis, he advised us to keep our cool because he could not concentrate whilst driving. We were misbehaving as we progressed up the motorway, Ian slammed on his brakes and cried that he was not going to drive anymore, so Chris Ashton took over the wheel after drinking buckets of lager. Chris was driving for a few miles when he nearly collided with a pile of cars, so Ian resumed driving. We stopped off at a service station, everyone ran in as it was full of Argyle supporters, plus loads of hooligans, we ram sacked the place, pinching food, but there was not much anyone could do about it. General Ron and I were playing football with a crushed-up tin of beer, he kicked me in the shin, I kicked him back in the shin. We kicked the hell out of each other for ages, my leg was badly bruised, but we were still friends afterwards, I always saw Ron, he was always game for a fight, we got to the match, eventually.

It was a crucial game in which we needed to win to avoid relegation, if Burnley won, they would move up a division. We went to the nearest bar we could find; the Police and horses quickly followed us. The Police forced us to go to the ground, and everyone marched down the street yelling, "We are The Centre Element!" There were loads of us that day. I took amphetamine, it kept me in control, as the beer caused me to do some crazy things, but not when I was on amphetamine with a drink, it was as if I was normal, but a lot faster. We lost this match, and we were relegated, Burnley fans all dashed across the field towards us. Thousands mocked us as they surged onto the pitch in front of the away end, some of our lads' flung chairs at them. Burnley then tossed pound coins of all shapes and sizes in our direction, I collected every coin that came my way.

Outside the stadium we were apprehended in a group by the police, some were on horseback. Then just as we were about to leave a lad who does not want his name to be mentioned was caught on video, flinging seats at Burnley fans in the stadium, he was on our minibus, the police arrested him. So, we had to wait and stay up there until the police officers released him, I just wanted to go home. We were all terribly upset about being relegated to a lower league and hating being stuck up there, we went to a pub while we waited for the lad to be released, the lad was let out at midnight, we did not get home till six the next morning.

Chapter 11. The Tree Demonstrates

I tried lots of different jobs, but one that I admired was that of a security guard. They were constructing a new highway, protests had become very prominent in the area, Swampy had dug a tunnel to hide in, he was like a mole in a hole, the remaining protestors were up in the trees, they were all new age hippies. I knew Jason, another lad who lived near my Grandparents, we really got along well, there were security personnel from all over Torquay, Exeter, Plymouth, and Bristol. There was a lad who was mouthy, and he moaned constantly, so we decided to bring some laxatives, that I had for being constipated, in the next day. We put them into his flask, we watched him all day, as he ran to the toilet all day long, not knowing that we had spiked him.

The job itself was quite easy as we just had to stand there working alongside the police. We would start at five o'clock in the morning, the coach would pick us up at three o'clock from Home Park, the home of Plymouth Argyle. I stayed with my Grandparents as it was only a ten-minute walk, I had to be up at two o'clock to work a twelve-hour shift. It was a long day, it was so knackering getting up so early, but the money was well worth getting up for.

Jason and I would have dinner with the Bristol boys every day, we got on with them better than we did the Plymouth lads.

Some of the security personnel were far more disorderly than the protesters, some of the security officers from Torquay took off their yellow jackets they were wearing and joined the protesters, the police officers arrested them. Some guys from Plymouth informed Jason and me that they wanted to fight the boys from Bristol on Friday, they were going to jump them. We warned the Bristol lads as we liked them, we went on our usual coach on the Friday. It was incredible, a man on our coach was carrying a gun, which he then dropped, and it slid down the coach just before we got to our destination, but whoever it was, was apprehended because the driver of the coach called the authorities just before we arrived. I had no idea who the user of the firearm was, all we knew was that he was sitting at the front of our coach.

The fight that was supposed to happen never took place as everyone was shocked with what had happened with the man with the gun. No matter how hard the Police tried, Swampy would not get out of the hole that he was in. This one hippie who could not get back to the trees, was stuck on the other side of the fence, he lunged at me with a knife through a fence. I grabbed the knife while shouting at the police to arrest this angry protester, the angry protester was taken away by the police. I had been there for a month or so, many of the demonstrators hid in the trees with tents high up, but every day the authorities were getting the protesters out of the trees, however, Swampy kept us in a job as he was down a forty-foot hole. Regardless, we stayed for a month and a half then Swampy came out of his hole and all the protesters were also removed. Jason and I were told that we would still be able to work for the company somewhere else, they lied though, we phoned up all the time and were told the company had gone bankrupt.

Chapter 12. Decent into Darkness'

Paul introduced me to a load of lads from Plympton, I sold them hash, I was better off on benefits and selling hash than I was working. Andy stood out from the crowd, we were driving across town in Paul's car when Andy, who came from Exeter, jumped out of the car in the centre of Plymouth. He smacked a lad in the head, then ripped a Stone Island jacket off the lad, in broad daylight, I thought he was nuts, but a nice enough lad to me, and we got on well.

Andy and I spent time with gypsies. Andy introduced me to them, and I got along well with them. We went to Bovisands, a nearby beach that looks out to Plymouth, while we were there, there were young men with fancy watches and apparel sauntered up the way. The Traveler's stole their costly watch and leather jacket, they pinched stereos, and other objects in the parking lot, and then they demanded that I sell everything, they had foolishly handed it to me, as I was so sneaky. I sold the goods and kept all the money for myself, they were always nice to me, even though I kept all the money for myself, the gypsies would frequently fix my car for free, whenever it broke down.

Andy and I found a good little earner, we knew at Bovisands, where there were enormous bottles of gas, which could be used for cooking and heating the gipsy's caravans. We could take one at a time, as they were the biggest gas bottles you could get, I could just get it into my car, the boot had to remain open with the chairs reclined. Andy held on to it so that it did not fall out of the car, we were mad as it could blow up at any time. We supplied the whole camp with gas bottles, we made a few quid, the gypsies loved it as well as saving them a lot of money.

I was also selling amphetamine and hash to the gypsies. Andy and I went to the Travelers site, the entire camp was deserted. Andy was so crazy, he was always looking to make easy money, he was like a gypsy boy himself, he said to me "they are always robbing people, shall we take their televisions"? as some of the gypsies had left their caravans open, so he filled my car up with TVs, I think we took five televisions all together. We sold them to a drug dealer, the gypsies phoned Andy saying, "have you been up to the camp today"? Andy said "no, why do you ask."? They replied we had been robbed. He said, "I've been at my Gran's house all morning, so it wasn't me," as we sat in McDonalds eating having used the money we had made on the TVs.

Chapter 13. The Phantom of Rave

I went into town with this lad called Scott who Andy had introduced me to, he loved the rave scene. He took me to the Dance Academy in Plymouth; it was the most enjoyable place to be on a Saturday night, people from Devon and Cornwall would travel all the way to Plymouth, to enjoy the best club on Saturday night. From nine

o'clock in the evening to six o'clock in the morning, it reminded me of the phantom of Oprah's theatre. It hosted some of the most well-known performances by house residents, DJs Tom Castillo, and Brandon Block. The sensation I got and still get from trance music is like being in paradise on earth. I do think that I have one of those odd faces, "could you please get any little ones"? that implied ecstasy. I had no idea who the people were because they were unknown to me, they could have been undercover police officers. Everywhere you looked, there were people selling ecstasy, right, left, and centre, it was like a pill factory, a plethora of gangs, all selling products for the bouncers. "What are you on, where are you from, are you having a good one,"? This was the most common manner people communicated. This old nightclub exuded a dark aura, a drug lord owned this nightclub. If this club had been in a major city like London, Bristol, or Manchester, this amazing sleeping behemoth would undoubtedly have been one of the best clubs in the whole of the country. It was fantastic, most people are often pleasant while high on ecstasy, therefore, this is a pleasant location to be. The building has three balconies going up high and a waist-high railing, making it an exceedingly dangerous place for those under the influence of narcotics. There were many stories of jumping from a high balcony down to the dance floor over the years, being in this club felt exactly like being in Ibiza. The music put the partygoers into a stupefying trance, you could listen to the music that the top DJs in various rooms played. I would be completely immersed in trance; everyone should have been present on the main stage, but in the VIP lounge, there was a little dance floor, in this space with stairs heading up, there was a lot of jungle music playing. We started looking for pills, when this little chancer in the toilet told us he would offer ten pills, for thirty pounds. He had a crushed face, indicating that he had been hit with a baseball bat several times, he was given the name "spud face." Following that, he began naming all of Plymouth's tough guys, "Do I know Joe Blogs and Peter Pan, do you know who they are"?

I have done this many times before myself, as many people have done this. After listing fifty well-known names of hard people which most people have heard of, in Plymouth, He took my money for the pills, I was waiting for him to hand me the pills then before I knew it, he dashed down the stairs as he exited the building and ran into Stonehouse, I chased him he was like a little fast rat. I never saw that Stonehouse scab, with the potato face again, I ran into Scott, I told him that someone had taken his and my money, I did not have much cash left over. Then Scott introduced me to someone I heard of who lived in the next estate to my Mums, I will call him Captain in my book. If we knew he was in the Dance Academy that night, we would not have gotten ripped off. The captain and his pill gang sat in the VIP lounge with the bouncers. They were the captains' friends, who the captain was paying off. The captain asked Scott whether he would be interested in sneaking pills into the club. "Are you having a laugh"? "I am not sneaking any ecstasy into the club," Scott said, "it was never worth a prison sentence," Captain. gave me a strange look, as he struggled to place my identity, before Scott had introduced me. He recognized my name and had heard a few stories about me, we got along simply great. He gave me a Mitsubishi ecstasy tablet with brown speckles, he did not charge me anything for the tablet. This ecstasy felt so nice as it was burning through my body, the emotion I felt was pure love, I relished every single moment of it, the excitement was out of this world, my eyes were twitching, and my jaw was trembling, uncontrollably. He had the most gorgeous sister in the world.

The captain's best friend at the time was called Peter, he went to my school, he was a year younger, and he was a sports fanatic, particularly about football. You might not expect him to be a cokehead, or even his best friend, I had no idea he was the type of person who would be into drugs. He used to live with his parents in an expensive house up on the higher estate, but then, what kind of person does drugs? I vowed to myself that I would never experiment with drugs, but I did. This ecstasy was turning me into a dancing king, the energy was extraordinary. It was nothing like the horrible experience I had had, in the past, it was nothing less than perfect. The lovely individuals surrounding me in a blaze of affection, the ecstasy raised the hairs on the back of my neck, I felt fantastic, my entire body was tingling. What was in those little magic pills, I was addicted. That saying "once you pop, you can't stop" was surely true.

We heard shouting at the entrance of Dance Academy, Scott pointed out that the overweight man and his friend had shoved the bouncer out of the way. Scott went on to say that there were tunnels visible on the CCTV, where the bouncers stand in front of the red curtains, the tunnels are located behind them, the tunnels go under the city for miles. We were in stitches as it showed the obese bouncers, chasing after them, shouting come back here, they just kept running, so did the bouncers into the darkness. It made up a chunk of the entertainment for us that night, why anyone would want to sprint through there, I will never know, but a lot of people did. This club was extraordinary, there were so many rooms in this club it was like a huge maze. It was the most incredible night of my life, in contrast to the other clubs on the strip, which were teeming with drunks, this institution maintained a calm and welcoming feeling. Fights would erupt everywhere, both inside and outside, the other clubs of Union Street would be like something out of the country and a western movie. It was amazing how many fights I had in the other clubs over the years, I even got into a fight with a sovereign gold print of a horse, with a knight stamped on my forehead when I went to a club called

Jesters one night. It was not like that in Dance Academy, it evolved into a place where the locals were so friendly that people flocked to Plymouth from Devon and Cornwall to discover this closely guarded secret from the local riffraff. I found myself in the restroom on my first night at the Dance Academy. I was a full-on amphetamine demon back then.

I was selling the nasty drug and taking it all the time, the drug that made me feel wide awake, I thought I looked normal. Nonetheless, I looked like a mess, I lied all the time, especially to my family members, it was not fair to subject them to what I was doing to them. When I took speed, it was like that old porridge advertisement from back in the day, where people ate it, while surrounded by a white glow. That luminous ring wrapped around me, I suppose that it was at that point, that I felt like He-man, I felt invincible. Gary was no longer a threat in any way, shape, or form, how the tables had turned, I had transformed my hands into a gun, so every time he crossed my path, I drew my hands into a pretend gun and pointed my pretend pistol at him. He knew not to fuck with me, as I would kick the shit out of him as I had so much fire in me and I hated his guts, in other words, he was now scared of me. We decided to go to Ernesettle because we needed to buy some hash, we normally got it at Swilly, but nobody had any. We tried everywhere, the only person who had it was Danny.

We went to see an old friend of mine who lived near to me as a kid growing up. We made our way back across windy, rainy terrain, Paul was in the lead, driving his newly purchased used car, he let me have his old Nissan by selling it to me. It was quite large and square in shape, to put it mildly, it was an old and sluggish drive, but it did the job. I could see Gary walking his dog, the dog dashed in front of my car as I drove past, the dog went onto the curb, the other side of the road. Gary walked out in front of my car after crossing the centreline of the road, I hit him hard he sailed over the top of my car, I did not come to a stop until I reached a higher point on the slope, where Paul was waiting for me. When I got out of my car, Paul informed me that I had just run over Gary, I asked if he thought I was to blame, Paul stated that he did not know. A local policeman that we knew drove past us, however, it was time to get out of there, we both jumped in our cars and drove to Paul's house where he was living.

The crazy two that we were, Paul and I went to the Dance Academy the following Saturday, I took a Mitsubishi pill. The Trance music was truly divine, the best rushes tingled my body hairs, better than when

England scored a goal. I had some dancing ability, but the ecstasy made me dance a million times better than anything I could normally do. People kept approaching me, wanting to know if I was a professional dancer, I am not sure where I learned those moves, but I felt like a superstar for the rest of the night.

I was dancing with an invisible football, and I felt like I had invented a new dance because I was spinning it in beautiful motions, transforming it into dance moves, the moves that I could pull off, while flying as light as a feather with a ghost ball, astounded some people. I was never able to find my way around the club, there were numerous chambers, each with a door leading to a different section of the structure upstairs or even into lots of different rooms where people could hide, while skinning up joints. Even though I was a speed freak, my street cred was growing all the time, and people began referring to me as, "You are such a great person" people thought I was so laid back, as a result, my phone book grew, with lots of people purchasing ecstasy hash or amphetamine. They thought I was a hero, the people who were doing drugs at the parties and raves, rather than the slime bag that I was to the rest of humanity.

I stayed at my Grandparents' house after Dance Academy after three days of no sleep. I could make out my brother's words, telling Rebecca my niece, who looked like an Indian squaw, she was a throwback, he told her to poke or kick me, she poked me in the side, I went ballistic, shouting and screaming, my head and my mood were not the best that day. They found it hilarious, especially my brother, he resembled a young child from the film Home Alone with his blonde hair. Mathew stood tall at the highest point of the road; he took immense pleasure in giving my friends the middle finger as they drove past.

We returned to the Dance Academy, Captain asked if I would be willing to sneak in some ecstasy for him. He offered me to do it for one hundred pounds, plus commission, if I brought him extra customers he would give me extra money on top. I told him no way, I am not up for it, he put the price up to one hundred and fifty and said you are safe, you will never get caught. I was an idiot high on drugs, I said, "ok I will give it a try." So, he suggested that we meet at the Windmill Pub, near his house on a particular Friday night, "I will show you the best place to hide them" he said. I went to the Windmill Pub and met the captain. He rolled the tablets into a roll-up-like substance, with a Rizla wrapped around my privates and a rubber band, making it appear as secure as a bullet. As well as that, there were approximately fifty more pills than he originally stated that would be there. Even though I was a mug, I would not participate unless he gave me two hundred pounds, he thought my price was reasonable. The insanely fast pace of amphetamine boosted my confidence, so I went ahead and did it, Paul would tremble uncontrollably while we waited in line to enter the club, even worse, he did not even have any on him. We were tapped in our pockets, by the bouncers I had to pay ten pounds to get in, I should have been the one shaking. I did nothing but sprint up the stairs and throw them at the Captain, I was eager to finish and move on, it turned out to be much easier than I had anticipated. Coachloads of people were arriving from all over the country, as it was the most enjoyable night I had ever spent in a club.

 I returned the following week for more, by then I had begun smuggling the ecstasy in on a weekly basis, it was hard to believe how many people I had met. Paul Walsh was a nice young man who I met in the club, he told me that if I went to see him on a Friday, he had loads of people wanting pills. Paul was like me, a speed freak, he was a Cornish lad from across the Tamar, he lived in Saltash. So, on a Friday evening I would go over most weeks to meet Paul who was helping me sell ecstasy, he did not expect anything for his effort, but I did sort him out with amphetamine for nothing.

I knew this greedy guy who sold me amphetamine, he was less expensive, he also lived close to the same estate. Even though I could not stick him, I bought soap bar hash from him and got amphetamine cheap from him and sometimes ecstasy from him, even Captain harboured ill will toward him. The man was despised by many people, particularly those who owed him money. His base, a type of amphetamine, was so strong that it could be purchased for as little as sixty pounds for an ounce which could make two hundred and eighty pounds. My friend Duffy demonstrated how to do mix it with glucose, add as much glucose as you want to the mixture and stir it with your credit card, it tripled my money easily.

Paul V would meet Lisa, his girlfriend, at two o'clock in the morning, he despised having to go home. He would always leave at this time; I would always go dancing. The dance moves I could do were amazing when I took those pills. The trance anthems were amazing too, it made my hair stand up all over my body, with a tingling sensation, with the feeling of overwhelming love, it was like being in Ibiza, most ravers would stay till six o'clock in the morning. I would routinely perform the same actions, six o'clock in the morning it was time to count my money. God knows what happened the money, my twenty-pound notes and ten-pound notes were stuck to chewing gum, in my pocket. I used to lose so much money every week.

I did not have any mot or insurance on my car, I was constantly getting stopped by the police for drug searches on a weekly basis. I used to get a ticket to produce my paperwork at the police station, but I never turned up, my tickets were mounting up. I could not understand why I was always allowed to drive on after receiving over seventy tickets with no insurance, unbelievable but true. I would drive around the coast to find a beauty spot looking out to sea smoking, normally smoking a bong and on amphetamine daily. Then as soon as Friday came, I would go over to Saltash, meet Paul Walsh and we would get out of our face taking lots of amphetamine, it was the messiest room in Great Britain with floorboards ripped up, walls all smashed in, it was in a state. We got on great, I would always meet him in dance academy,' sometimes he did his own thing, but he always brought people to get pills, the captain did not trust him, but I trusted him more than I trusted the captain. I bumped into a friend, Gary, in the Dance Academy, we used to work together at Derriford Hospital.

Gary was blonde, he had a tattoo on his neck, and he looked like Eminem. He invited me back to his friend

Will's house for a party at Dunnet Road, West Park, a rough neighbourhood about three miles distant from the Dance Academy. The captain gave me all the pills that were left over, that he could not sell inside the club, I had about twenty extra ecstasy pills. Me, Gary, Will and crazy Lee from upstairs would crush them up, sniff them and make joints to do bongs, the smell and taste were absolutely disgusting.

William was also blonde, a lovely lad, I became good friends with him at the time, we got on well, I would sometimes pick him up in my car and we would go for lots of smokes. Lee lived upstairs, he would always come down when we came back from the Dance Academy and always bought a pill or two. He was weird, his eyes would be pinging, his glasses staring at me with his bobbed haircut, and he spoke so fast, it was so difficult to understand him. He was so cold blooded, and he looked like a psychopath, he was in and out of the local mental hospital. It was a brilliant little party which we had every week after Dance Academy.

 I constantly had the worry that this drug lord who lived on my estate would always be after my money, daily. He was greedy for money, he used to give me more pills than I was able to sell, he worked as a bouncer, before he became a drug lord, and was in an international drug ring, he had a normal job as well. He had the most speed and ecstasy I had ever seen in one room, full of bin liners full of ecstasy, and amphetamines.

The ecstasy was so cheap, only one pound-two pounds depending on what ones he had, the amphetamines were dirt cheap and so strong it would have put a hole in my tongue. I could not stop thinking about how much I owed him; it consumed my mind. He was a hard-little man who was only interested in money, I was not that scared of him, it was the stress of owing money that was the headache. It would not surprise me in the least if he turned out to be a millionaire right in front of everyone's eyes, the number of narcotics he sold over the course of a weekend was unbelievable. He presented himself as a regular person living in a council house, I knew too many things about him. He was involved in several activities, including growing marijuana with a local farmer, even if he was not aware, I knew exactly what they were doing it in the middle of nowhere, in the countryside.

My friend went to a farm in Devon with them to set up some grow lights and a special kit so the plants would be watered through this special set up. The cannabis factory, which he bullied the farmer into letting them grow weed on his farm, in a big barn is still going to this day, from all those years ago. Adam this lad who loved his speed phoned me up for some hash, he was at this lady's house on the next estate, with a friend called John. They were both obsessed with speed back then, we were all badly on it.

Adam just bought loads of hash from me and offered me to play a card game, called blackjack. The bet was not money, we were playing each game for an ounce of hash. I cheated on every game, I would frequently hide my cards, making victory much simpler. The biggest, ugliest, nastiest bitch looks after the obese, greedy man's drugs. The crafty woman then calls him into her home, I owed him a couple hundred pounds, plus an additional hundred pounds in interest, for being late with his money which I refused to pay. Then, out of nowhere, he punched John in the mouth, causing blood to flow and knocked him to the ground, John inquired as to why he had punched him, as he did not owe him a penny. He said to me "that is what you will get if you do not pay me back," but there was no need to hit John, because I owed the money.

 I had money all the time and loads of Hash in my pocket after beating Adam. However, I needed to use that money to make more money, I was not ever going to pay the interest he put on top of the amount. The obese man even knocked on Croke's door, Croke's mother answered the door, he was only thirteen years old and still at school, the greedy man informed Croke's Mum, he owed him money for drugs. What type of man would go about knocking on the doors of school children's Mums, who goes about demanding money like that? It was like he was in with the police, and non-touchable as it was so obvious what he was up to, he was obvious. He was in his late forties and tried to bully me, but he knew he could not touch me, I knew some hard nuts and he knew that I mentioned their names to scare him, and it worked. I told him I sold drugs for one of the hardest men in Plymouth, a massive drug lord back then. I lied I never ever once got it of him, I cannot mention his name as I do not have his permission. When it came to selling hash, I never missed a beat, I simply would undercut everyone so the stoners would come to me, I smoked hash every day without fail, I became dependent on amphetamine, I could not go a day without it, seemed like I was on it for a month, but it had been much longer at least two years.

When it comes to people, it seems like I met so many everyone opens about their personal lives, when they are on that evil amphetamine. They tell you all their business, too much information, anyone on it would talk non-stop and most could not shut up. It made me look skinny and ill looking, I would lie through my teeth to get money from my family. It was not fair on them as they were not stupid but, on that stuff, it seemed I would even believe my own lies, it truly made me a nasty person.

I knew Mathew a lad from our area, he was like a gypsy boy from Ireland, originally. He came over to England at the age of about eight years old, his family had to move to Plymouth as Mat's Dad was being pursued by the IRA, he had a death threat for being in the URL and was in fear for his life, so he had to move to Plymouth. His Dad was a brilliant man very down to earth; he would sing songs in pubs by himself, he loved Argyle and would travel the country, a real character. Mat was streetwise and young; he was about sixteen but looked about twelve back then when I was hanging around with him.

While I was in Mathews' place, I ran into Kenny, who had dreadlocks, Matt lived next door to a Nigerian, he made the declaration that he was a Prince from his country, he resembled a young Eddie Grant. I advised him to have a look at the weed as it was so lovely, he was utterly bankrupt, he phoned a few of his friends and asked them if they wanted any nice weed, it was red in colour and was called Durban poison. His two friends on the other hand wanted to buy an ounce each, I had gotten it cheap, but I was going to double my money, so I told him to get in my car, but he refused.

Kenny had a mountain bike I had never seen anything like it before, Kenny started riding his mountain bike, Kenny roared for me to follow him and gesticulated with his arms the entire time, it was like he did not think I knew where I was going. We were driving so slowly behind him, I wished he had just said, "Meet you at Mutely Plain." Kenny's friend was so impressed he asked if I could get more, we exchanged numbers. I have one more place to show you, it is my friend Ginger's place, he rode his bike again, I followed. Kenny informed me that Ginger sold an enormous lot of different drugs, I sold him the weed, he looked like someone easy to steal drugs from, which was something, that what was on my mind, after watching films like lock stock and smoking barrels. I requested a thousand ecstasy pills to buy from Ginger, knowing extremely well that I would steal them. Ginger informed me that his friend would be arriving from Bristol on Thursday, he told me to go around at a certain time. He also told me the ecstasies would cost five pounds each because they were imported from Amsterdam. Ginger with his scruffy long hair told me that they were the best ecstasy tablets, he informed me that they were ten out of ten and you could not get any better and that I would love them. He told me "That he had them a week ago but was waiting for more to be brought down." I would have needed five thousand pounds, which I certainly did not have, but I always had a plan, I was a deep thinker, and it needed my physical presence. I called Captain and told him my devious plan, he was all up for it, he was of strong physique. I told the captain that I was going to be the one who takes the pills, all I needed was him to be my back up and bring loads of cash so that it would be easier to pinch if he saw the cash. I told the captain that I would give him two hundred pills for his efforts, and he agreed to help me tax Ginger. I was not the nicest of guys either when I was on drugs, it was not the first tax, I had taxed many little dealers before Ginger, but this one was worth talking about, I knew it was an excellent opportunity. I was simply an opportunist; I knew it was me against Ginger as he could not exactly phone the police, I thought long and hard about how I would nick the thousand ecstasies with no comebacks.

I also took a burglar named Luke, he was a little mad, but I got on well with him, he only wanted one hundred pills, Luke was there to make up the numbers. So, it was me, Captain, and Luke, we entered, I was armed with a knife in my pocket, however, I had no intention of using it, we proceeded to the top-floor of the house to his shared room which was massive. Card games were being played by several young males on a big table. The ecstasy bag was positioned directly in the centre of the table, Colin, an old friend was unbelievably seated at the table, which was the cause of an issue. It was difficult for me to believe that he was in the room, Colin was liked by me, I had played football for his stepdad in a charity match with ex-Argyle players, he used to be a neighbour of ours growing up as a child. He got beaten up as a child and made to do some cruel things by his stepdad. If Colin had been naughty, he was made to wear nappies when he was ten years old and made to go out and run around the block. Colin was not as bad as most kids, he just got dealt some bad cards with having such a strict stepfather. Colin got his own back one day, his Mum and Dad went on holiday, leaving all their bank information. Colin went on a massive spending spree spending over thirty thousand pounds, Colin went to prison for a little while so I knew or hoped he would not declare my name. Ginger was being friendly, he offered several types of marijuana, the ecstasies, on the other hand, was what I was after. I let him keep his marijuana, if it had been within my grasp, I would have taken it too. I was desperate to get my hands on that bag with the ecstasies in.

The most intimidating-looking one was a black man in his forties from Bristol with dreadlocks, but he did nothing but sit there and kept silent, he was puffing away on a large joint. Even though Ginger must have lost confidence in me as he moved the bag of ecstasy nearer to him whilst playing cards. I am opposed to the use of weapons, but I did it in a courteous manner while maintaining total mastery of the knife. Nobody was going to get stabbed; however, this was only a fraction of my act, I was reaching for the thousand ecstasy pills on the table while holding a ten-inch-long blade. I grabbed the bag right in front of Ginger and said, "You've been taxed, try to do anything and I will go mad" whilst Ginger went red in the face. He realized he could do nothing with dread in his eyes and followed us the entire time. Colin gave me a smile with a sly wink, I responded with a wink back. We ran down the stairs with a handsome profit, we were out of there before Ginger realized it, I rushed into my car, Luke followed me and jumped into the car, Captain legged it up to Mutely Plain to meet his girlfriend. He was a crafty little jerk who had snatched my phone from under my feet, I knew it was him because he was the only person in my car at the time, it didn't hit me till I dropped him off at Scousers' house, Luke was never seen again after that, he was convicted and sentenced to prison for burglary just afterwards. I looked for it when I got home, I could not find it, I looked everywhere imaginable, but the car was the last place that I had looked. I liked Luke, till he pinched my phone. The concept was that I should give him ecstasies in exchange for doing nothing, so that is what I did, he might not have pinched my phone as I was always losing stuff back then, only he knows if he did, or did not, even though I was a filthy scumbag too, you did not do the sly on your own. I owed Captain two hundred pills as he was a bit more expensive, he told me to sneak his two hundred pills into the club on Saturday night, we were back in the club with the best ecstasy tablets on the market for all the party goers, this evening.

This one bouncer would constantly look at me strangely, he was always looking out for the captain as if they were close friends and partners with these pills that I was sneaking in, or I was just being paranoid. The bouncer approached me and said "that they were looking for the captain" who had gone off dancing, knowing that I had his pills.

This woman appeared, she looked to be about fifty years old, dressed elegantly, accompanied by Chopper, he looked just like the killer Chopper famous for his murders in Australia, which is why he had the nickname. He was in the biker gang Aquila, the TCE do not really get on with them, we are rival gangs, but some did get on with each other. Chopper knew me from drinking in the Wellington pub, Chopper normally paid the bouncers as he had a gang of boys selling ecstasy in the club. They both made me feel anxious while I was spinning on the ecstasy I took; I was seeing double of everything.

The scenario became unpleasant when I had three drinks in front of me, still, there was just one authentic one, I did not pick it up at the time, but when I did, I knocked it over and smashed it in front of the bouncer and Chopper. Chopper said "For God's sake how much are the fucking things" with an angry face. I replied, "that they were from Amsterdam, and they were worth ten pounds each, that is it, we cannot do them any cheaper." He looked like he wanted to kill me, the captain climbed back up the steps, his eyes filled with fear, with the presence of Chopper. He smacked me across the back, and said, "four for twenty Chopper," then yelled, "Come on, fifteen!" I said, "no it is twenty." Chopper handed out the money without even a cordial thank you.

Everyone was able to take a deep breath again and relieved as he went walking back down the stairs. The captain told strangers who come up to us looking for pills, that I was the man. He was trying to make out in case they were undercover police, that I was the person selling pills, not him. I realized then how much of a user he was, to throw me under the bus like that, but I always knew in the back of mind he was a user. He used to imply that all the time, I could see why he took advantage of others, for financial benefit. It was my fault as I was fuzzed on amphetamine, the stupid amphetamine was horrible, there was no way in hell I would have done those risky things, if I hadn't been using the nasty speed, it was a dirty nasty horrible drug, which kills the soul and makes you act so Devilish. It changed me as a person and gave me a great lack of morals, if any at all, things that I would never dare, especially trying to get ecstasy in, for this idiot.

Someone told me that Gary was the person who was sneaking the ecstasy in for Captain before I started doing the dirty deed. On his introduction day at Primary School, I had to show him and a few others around the school, then we ate dinner together, they were having one day at school before they joined for good, it was my last week at junior school. He was a nice little cheeky boy, but in all his deeds he was completely innocent, Gary was sentenced to six years in jail, he was sneaking pills for the captain before me, it was never worth putting six years of your life at risk, for a tiny sum of money. If I had known this, I would never have sneaked ecstasy in, in the first place, with each passing week, the sum sank lower and lower, he would stuff most of his earnings up his big nostrils with cocaine.

Some of the others such as Scott, and the Plympton gang, regarded him as a hero, many fell for his false charm and licked his ass. He decided to purchase me some cocaine after we had helped him make a lot of money, I luckily did not like cocaine, I was sick after he gave me some, I did not like it, it was like having the flu for twenty minutes.

Captain had a smooth manner and a mysterious appearance due to his Greek ancestry; he had the appearance of someone who would be very at home in a mafia film, but he was addicted to coke. He merely needed ten pounds for each tablet so he could sustain his cocaine habit, I was quite aware that he was using me big time for his own gain. Yet others spoke critically about him in my neighbourhood, though the stories about him were terrible, I carried on with my business each week but with extraordinary caution.

The following Saturday came around far too quickly, the bouncers would act as if they were arresting Captain, as it was too obvious to the average person what exactly we were doing. Every week, we were selling ecstasies in the VIP room, no VIPs just ecstasies for ten pounds each. The fact that the bouncers brought him into a room, searched him to make it appear to look like he had been caught, selling pills. Even though the captain had no contraband on him, as he had passed them to me to sell, made it appear an excellent bit of acting, it had been pre planned a week before. He left with me while I was spinning out on ecstasy, I hated having them and went on a weird one constantly thinking I was going to get caught for real, it was about two o'clock in the morning, I had hidden fifty of my own ecstasy. I did not normally bring my own, but I did on this night, I was too scared to sell any.

My friends were not present on this evening, which made it impossible with the bouncers constantly watching me. So many people who fell for the act were coming up to me to tell me that Captain had been in trouble, I thought only if they knew the truth. The bouncers kept bringing strangers up to buy ecstasy, which made me feel so much on edge, as I really was thought that an undercover police officer was going to buy pills, and that I would be in trouble. I was so relieved when six o'clock came, I gave him the money owed to him, the weekends come and go before you know it. Captain bought one hundred yellow submarines from me which helped me to have a little extra cash. I still had to sneak them in though it was like an addiction, sneaking them in was easy but the sentence if I were caught would not be so.

Paul and I took two yellow subs an hour before entering the club, we climbed the stairs together, we walked past the Police with their uniform on. It was very scary with one hundred ecstasies to my manhood; my eyes were flying around like a swarm of butterflies, despite this, Paul was trembling like a leaf. Following that, the officers pursued us up the stairs, I put the tablets on the captain's sofa before sinking further and deeper into my double sofa's luxurious cushions. The couch was a pickpocket because I would always lose my money, it was red and so attractive to sit on, as it was so comfortable. The officers looked at us all before walking back down the stairs, it was difficult for me to see anything in front of me, my eyeballs were jerking and swirling in circles. The yellow ecstasies were the most powerful pleasure we had ever put in our bodies, the officers' bright yellow police jackets sparkled as they returned up the stairs. I was tripping on the radiance of the coats, which were glowing like glow sticks, now that I was whirling, the police officers were just staring at me with my jaw vibrating a million miles an hour. Paul said, "oh fuck, we are all going to die." I murmured, "Be silent," gripping the sofa for dear life, he looked at me in fear. The police officers were just there for a second before leaving, it was a huge relief for everyone in the VIP room. I could not concentrate either, or I had an uneasy feeling on the come up, oh crap, I was thinking the same thing, the scary sensation of dying was dreadful. I know what Paul was talking about now when he was fearing that he would die. When I turned around, Paul was trembling like a crazy person, his face had a grey appearance to him, he looked at me with fear clearly visible in his eyes and as if he were on the verge of crying, I had never seen anyone look so scared. Apart from me, he was certain that he was going to die, while Paul was having a panic attack and spinning out, the policewomen and the annoying policeman came back up the stairs and just stood there, it seemed like an hour, but it was only five minutes, they finally walked back down the stairs. Paul was sitting on his seat with his grips as tight as they could get, murmuring repeatedly that we were going to perish, then he just got louder, we were going to die. I said, "you will be ok," our eyes were all like grey aliens.

After the intense felling of death, then it was the feeling of pure euphoria When I went to go to the dance floor to have a dance, I bumped into a lad called Trigger he was a younger version of myself, he was in every week, we got along famously. He would sell ecstasy for me but not expect anything in return for his efforts, I would routinely reward him with freebies, whenever he helped me out. Trigger told me that somebody offered him four pills for the price of ten pounds, he told me that he looked like a Muppet. I said, "show him to me." We looked for him, no way I could not believe it, it was ginger, with his grubby hair and scruffy appearance. I took a break for it and told the captain to get him taxed once more, after the bouncers confiscated all his ecstasy, they kicked him out of the building. They handed over one hundred and thirty-five tablets, which is a lot of ten-pound notes, to us in exchange for a share of the profits, once we sold the ecstasy Trigger got a nice bonus from Captain too. I had been going there every Saturday for an entire year, I had become completely addicted to the atmosphere, since the very first time that I went there, I had not missed a single night.

I had tried many different pills, but I had never ever come across any like the ones that we had stolen from ginger. They were yellow, typically oblong in shape, quite large and referred to as yellow submarines. I was buzzing, absolutely flying, I went to the dance floor underneath the VIP room, there was jungle music in this room. I could see an attractive woman dancing, she was in her thirties, pretty with dark looks, dark hair, and a short skirt on. I asked her if she was searching for ecstasy, she was a friend of Captain, I told her that "I could sort her out with certain stuff like hash speed and ecstasy cheap out of the club," I was basically chatting her up. I gave her a pill for free, she could not thank me enough, I told her not to say anything about giving her a free pill, she promised that she would not. I was showing off with some brilliant dance moves, we danced for an hour or so, she was all over me, kissing and cuddling, we went for a joint in the VIP lounge on the sofa. She told me she was from Chudleigh Knighton, a place in Devon, thirty-six miles from Plymouth. I am normally shy, but I had the courage to ask her out for a date, she said "yes," I could not believe my luck. It wasn't long before Walshy came up to me, he had the pills I had hidden from the captain on him, his friend wanted to buy them over at Saltash, I explained to Debbie, that I would not be long, we got a taxi over the Tamar Bridge into Cornwall to Saltash. We sold them, jumped back into the taxi, and headed back to Dance Academy. It was an hour or so before we were back in the club, Captain said that Debbie was smooching Shane, I was gutted, he told me she had gone with Shane. Shane was someone that we knew who bought ecstasy pills all the time from Captain, we referred to him as "Superman from Exeter" as he always wore a superman shirt.

At that point, I could not wait to find out whether Debbie would be there the following week. I was in the club all night, I was tensely seeing if she would turn up, she did not, I like knew that would happen. After that, Debbie gave me a call unexpectedly, I could not believe my luck, her husky voice was so sexy. She got my telephone number from Captain, she asked me if I could bring an ounce of hash on Tuesday, along with some base, which is also another name for amphetamine, my car, unfortunately, broke down.

Chapter 14. The Green Gold Discovery

I asked Paul for a lift, I offered him some money for his trouble, I was not going to make a penny after paying for a lift. I was only doing it because I fancied Debbie, it was a dark, spooky night, Paul said "I got work in the morning," so he was not in a great mood and

was in a hurry. It was his first time driving out of Plymouth, it was not long after about twenty minutes that he started moaning. He said that we must be close so when he said that we believed that we had found the place, but strangely enough, there was a location known as just Chudleigh. We turned off and went down a dark lane, I told him to turn around, I said we got to go to Chudleigh Knighton, which was the right destination. He said come on, let us just go home, I knew it was near Exeter, we were miles away, but I had lied and told him that we could not be that far away. I really did not want to let Debbie down as I fancied her so much. I tried to phone Debbie but typically my battery on my phone had died. However, I had her number written down in front of me, we were looking for a public telephone box at the time. But at that moment, we were sitting on the motorway, awaiting the exit that would take us to a telephone box we needed to find as we did not have a clue which way we had to go, it was a bit further than we had anticipated. Since we had left Plymouth, we had been driving for an hour on the motorway, as Paul was driving so slowly, it was misty and raining, Paul however, had wanted to turn around throughout the entire journey. Therefore, we chose to take the next exit to the left, Heathfield is the name of this area, an industrial estate. From driving on the highway, you could just make out in the distance thick clouds of smoke, coming from the factories.

As we exited the freeway straight away, we were in a small housing estate, next to an industrial estate, we first spotted a red phone box. Two young boys were standing in front of the red telephone box at the beginning of the street, they were about sixteen years old. I asked where Chudleigh Knighton was, they told me that it was just around the corner, that the next exit to the left up the road on the motorway was about a mile or two, they seemed like good lads. Since I was running late, I called Debbie to let her know that I was unable to stop, as my friend was complaining, but I will be there in just five minutes. These two young boys gave off the impression that they smoked weed, as they just looked the type, so I said, "All right, boys; do you want to buy some hash cheaper than chips?" One of the boys asked, "how much"? I replied that I would give him a quarter of a clean soap bar for ten pounds, he said that he would fetch his dad as he might buy some. After leaving the red phone box, he proceeded up the opposite side of the road, up to about the seventh house up, I never missed a trick. After that, a more senior gentleman emerged, he was old with a smart appearance with black trousers, a black leather jacket, white shirt and the strangest of white hair which would make him stand out in a crowd. The gold that he was wearing was like BA, Baracs from the A team, he was plastered in the thickest of gold chains that could be found wrapped around his neck, his hands were covered in the thickest of gold rings. My first thought was, "Who the heck does he think he is, robbing Sir Fancies Drake?" I was at a loss for words because I had never seen someone wearing so much gold. At first, he introduced himself as Fred, he appeared to be a millionaire on a council estate, he got pen and paper for us because we could did not have any on us, he inquired as to where I was from, as well as the reason for my presence in that region. He was asking me lots of questions, I told him I was delivering some hash to a woman in Chudleigh Knighton, we decided to swap phone numbers. He bought cannabis that was two ounces in size, he said it smelt nice, he reached into his pocket and took out the largest wedge of fifty-pound notes I had ever seen. He asked if I sold anything else, I said that I sold amphetamine, I had some in the car, so he asked for a sample. He said, "fucking hell that is strong" he said, "it burnt a hole in his mouth." He went on to say that his staff would love that, he told me he had nightclubs, he had bouncers who worked for him, who would love that amphetamine. I told him about working for bouncers in Dance Academy, he liked me more after I said that he asked if he could have it on a regular basis, and we exchanged numbers. I told him I would be back on Thursday, he walked back up to his house. I could not believe the smell of weed in the air, I said "Paul can you smell that in the air"? Paul's response was" fucking hell that fucking stinks." I could tell that Fred was up to no good, the amount of gold he was wearing was truly unbelievable.

We made our way to Debbie's house; it was still stinking of weed when we got to her house. I said, "why do you want hash when the whole area was stinking of weed"? I said, "I just met a man called Fred" she said, "no way my ex used to work for him." I asked her what he was doing with so much gold, she said that she was not allowed to tell a soul, but she soon told me everything. Her ex worked looking after his plantations of weed, which was sent to London on a regular basis. I asked if Fred was a millionaire, she said" he was worth much more than a million." She said, "there were three different weed farms that she knew about," she also said, "he does not sell any of the weed locally, he had always tried to keep it a massive secret, from the locals." She said, "he is probably the biggest grower in the country," I could not believe what she was saying, but I believed her as the smell was so strong. He and a few locals were in on it, even a judge was involved in this massive operation. She said, "he grows the best marijuana she has ever had." She said, "since her ex-boyfriend had cheated on her and returned to London, she missed the weed so much, but could always smell it in the air." He was not allowed to tell a soul, but she knew everything that was needed to know about the whole thing. She told me she did not like him, I asked her that "if I did the weed farms over, would she say anything if I gave her a cut out of it"? She replied that she would not tell anyone and was well up for it, I thought, this is my sort of girl. I was buzzing when she was telling me the story of this magical place, it was like a dream, all I ever wanted to be back then, was a gangster. As soon as she told me the story I knew, I was doing him over, but I had to keep my cool, I got easily excited, a million pounds up for stake that was the goal, from that day forward, I was all out for this and going to chase it, no matter what the cost. I asked her if she could draw me up some maps of where the plantations were located. She found a pen and she drew me the three separate locations of weed farms.

I asked her out for a drink on the following Saturday, she said "yes of course." Paul was beeping his car horn to go; she gave me a nice big kiss. I loved the film Lock Stock and Smoking Barrels, these farms were much bigger than the one in the film, I watched that film, knowing that one day I would try the same thing. The smell of it was out of this world, I said to Paul, "you would never guess, you got to look at this, I have maps of where Fred is growing his weed. He said, "fucking hell," I said, "I knew he was not wearing that gold for nothing." Paul agreed, but Paul said that he was not getting involved with taking the weed, I told him that I was going to rob the farms all in suitable time.

Paul knew exactly what I was like, he was not a bit surprised, I was going to try to do him over and rob his plants, Paul thought I was insane, but knew it was just my cup of tea. I was a deep thinker, so I thought of lots of diverse ways of getting the weed were going through my head. I could not sleep with all the excitement, if I pulled the job off, I would be a millionaire. I really thought I could pull it off, if I got the right people to help, I knew loads of football hooligans and if they had my back, it would be easy. Since I had been raving, I had not seen them for a while, I like just went my own way, when I was on drugs, lost my morals and my good friends, I ended up hanging around with wrong ones and the users. I also knew the gypsies, if they helped it would be a walk in the park, I had a few options to think about. I had to go head hunting to see who would be up for the biggest robbery of a weed farm in England, the easiest way to get a million pounds and nothing in the world would stop me from trying, Fred and his farmers could not possibly phone the police, I was on amphetamine every day and every night I just could not sleep.

Paul drove me back to Fred on Thursday, he invited me into his house, he told me that he was the silent owner of nightclubs in Torquay. He said he oversaw most of the bouncers, which confused me, as if he was the owner, how was he in charge of the bouncers too, it was both. He also said that "if I ever I wanted to sell any ecstasy in his clubs, I was welcome to, and I could do it for free. He asked if I had the same amphetamine as before, as he thought it was so strong, he said all the bouncers loved it too. I said "yes, it is the same stuff" He pumped his fist in the air, with delight he bought some hash as well, he added that his son loved the hash. He asked if I could bring it up most Thursday's, but sometimes, he worked away as a lorry driver, he told me that he worked in Holland, sometimes not home for weeks. I could smell weed, but I decided not to ask if he sold it, as I had the maps to one day rob him, and he had told me loads of information. He seemed like a nice old man, in his late fifties, older, I told him I would return the next week. Paul said, "fucking hell you have been in there for heck of a long time," I needed to get back on the road and get myself a car, I could not stand Paul's moaning, he was like an old man. So, I went and bought a nice Orion car, with no mot, tax nor insurance, but it was a lovely fast car to go spying on the farms, we were in for the adventure of a lifetime. Shaun learnt to drive but he always failed his test, he was willing to go above and beyond, like no other person I knew, he was nuts and he could fight, I had my first person on board.

Debbie drives down to Mutely Plain, she parks her car outside Paul's flat, even though Paul's girlfriend Lisa had just given birth, he invited us in for a smoke. Lisa kept pulling faces to Paul for us to leave, he said "stay" when I said, "we had better go." We went to the pub, followed by the Dance Academy, we had a brilliant night, I was enjoying my night with Debbie instead of running around for the Captain, I was dancing all night and getting close to Debbie, I was getting on well with her.

Afterwards we went to Will's house, we had a little party in the front room as everyone fell asleep. I was all over Debbie, she was all over me, Will told us to get a bed, so I took her into Will's bedroom, we had a morning of passion, I really liked her and wanted her to be my girlfriend. I am not so sure she felt the same way. After that, we returned to a taxi to retrieve her vehicle, and drove me to Mum's house. The dark eye shadow was dripping down her face, I asked her if I could see her again. She said, "it was a bit awkward because of her daughter," she told me that she would see me again, she would ring me. I picked Shaun up in my car to take him up to plantations, to check out with the maps, he was the best sniffer dog in the area, he always assured me that he had my back, he claimed that we were a mafia organization. When we were younger, even though Shaun was insane, he made me his blood brother, after injuring ourselves, we shared our blood. He claimed that I was the Head of our organized little

Mafia, he said I was the Godfather, he was three years younger.

Shaun claimed to be a don and was number two in the organization, I thought he was mad and speaking his normal mad stuff. Shaun was loyal he had a massive heart and a profound sense of humour; he smoked a lot of hash. He was always telling crazy stories or doing crazy things especially after he had smoked the hash, he declared that he would never be in a relationship with a woman, as he had gotten married, with cannabis. He was not afraid of much, except for the insane asylum, where he had spent so much time, where his freedom was frequently taken away, from the age of fourteen years old, he had been frequently admitted to and discharged from the hospital. He put a Fly agaric mushroom in his mouth when he was so young from that day on, he was tripping for the rest of his life. The very first time I took Shaun, he was astonished by the smell of weed, it was so strong, we were in the middle of a forest. I was checking out one farm on our map, we could not see anything, but towering trees surrounded by million-pound cottages and big houses. The smell was getting stronger and stronger as we walked down a spooky lane, Shaun said you are on to something here. It was a mile down a lane with no houses around, we walked it, but it felt like we were being followed, we reached a farm with this huge barn and caravans, in a massive field, in the middle of nowhere. We noticed cameras on the outside of the barn, as I beamed the torch on the barn, we were buzzing as we knew that we had found it. We heard dogs barking from the caravan, it was time to get back to the car, it took us an easy half an hour to get back to the car, it was three o'clock in the morning. That was one seriously huge, massive metal barn to tick off the list, Debbie was certainly right with her drawings of the maps so far.

We decided that we would return at the same time tomorrow, to check out the second location on the map. Shaun wanted to drive, he would not take no for an answer, he kept saying that he was a good driver. I promised him a driving lesson the next day on the moors, as that was an ideal place to learn to drive, with no other cars around, on the off roads in the beauty spots that we knew. If he passed, he would get his wish, I would let him drive my car. He previously did a crash course in driving but failed four tests, he passed with me with flying colours. It seemed Shaun could drive, I was waiting to get taken to court by the police, I had been stopped by the police more than seventy times in the past for no insurance. Shaun was driving at 120 mph in the fast lane, I told him to slow down, we had missed the turning, we had to carry on till we could turn around, which was miles up the road near Exeter, we had to make a U-turn close to a garage. On the other side of the garage was a farm with cows, the smell of weed was unbelievable, we had found this one accidentally. Shaun climbed over the fence to get to the farm. The barn was located some distance from the road, I watched as a massive spotlight went all the way around the field, following Shaun, as he ran back, while the sounds of dogs could be heard. We came across this one in a debaucherously manner, but it was obvious that the odour was emanating from his barns. We drove back to check out the second place on the map, we stopped on the opposite side of the highway from Heathfield. We parked in a layby on the opposite side of the road, then ran across the motorway into Heathfield. As we walked, we went by the industrial estate, and a mile down a road that was lined with nice cottages in the woods.

The scent became more potent as time passed, we thought we saw a ghost when we saw a couple of shadows crossing the road, not too far in front of us, but it was just some people that were going into the woods, they probably were people what guarded the weed farm, it was completely dark. We walked in a lane and were behind a little school. The lane went up for a mile, then we came to a huge mansion with a built-in barn, in a field, which was in front of another field with huge metal sheds, the smell was out of this world, it stunk.

The school nearby must have been able to smell it, it was stupid how much it stunk, in fact the whole area for miles, just stunk. I had no fear of being caught stealing from him or his gang, or even from the people he knew at this point, because I was completely unafraid of everything or anything at the time. I was going to rob the weed farms, no matter what it took, my life was a gamble that I was willing to take, it was just like we were in a movie. This once-in-a-lifetime opportunity had been on my mind, heavily from the very beginning that I had smelt the weed in the air. I never once felt threatened by the work, I only had one chance to do it, so I decided to put it off until I had enough boys to do it, in the meantime, I needed to know when the crop was ready, so Shaun and I would get in the car and drive there at least three times a week. We did petrol runs from so many different petrol stations, I lost track of how many times we had stolen petrol from stations, every time we would take turns saying that we had lost our wallets.

When we had pulled the job off from the weed farms, we would then pay for all the petrol stations we had robbed, Shaun and I agreed to that. Shaun was driving for the second time, I had put my trust in him, many would not dare but he wanted to drive so badly, so I let him. He started off at Sainsburys, I made him do a petrol fraud first, he filled the car right up, petrol was spilling all over the place. He then went through his pockets saying he had lost his wallet, freaking out in front of the cashier, she made him sign some paperwork saying that he would pay it in a week.

Shaun drove on the A38 which was not the main motorway, which is past Exeter, it looks like a motorway, though with three lanes late at night. He was a natural in the fast lane, he was driving 120 miles per hour, I was scared, I would not lie, Shaun stayed in the outer lane brilliantly, all the way to the weed farms on which we were spying. We checked out the farm behind the school, there was a massive field in front of the mansion, it must have been worth a few million pounds. But in the dark, it was hard to see, but just like the other place it had a caravan in the field, with lots of cameras on the barns.

It looked like a Texas ranch with no animals around apart from a dog barking from the mansion in front of the farm. With that a spotlight lighting up the whole area, was coming from the mansion, it was time to get out of there. We found the second weed farm which stunk, but if Debbie had not given me the maps, I would have never found that one, as it was well hidden in a lane, which led to the farm. It was on top of a hill, looking down to an old-looking school, I could cross the second weed farm off our list as you could clearly smell it. They were up to no good here too, as there was someone in the caravan, just what Debbie had told me, her ex-boyfriend had done, the same thing, living in the caravan with dogs.

The next day I let Shaun drive again, as he had insisted that he was a good driver, I picked him up, he was living with his parents at a place called Plymstock on the outskirts of Plymouth. It was a nice bungalow, his dad was a union rep and had a brilliant job, he did not like Shaun smoking weed, which was fair enough, as it often made him so ill, that he landed up in a mental hospital. We drove down the hill to a bus stop, he jumped straight into the driving seat, stating that he was the best driver, with a grin on his face.

 I had a craving for one of Ivor Downey's pasties, the shop was in the town Centre, near the town's market car park. I saw a car coming from the other direction, I told Shaun to put the gear stick into reverse which he did. We heard a thud and shouting, Shaun had knocked over an older man with a walking stick, I got out of the car to make sure he was ok, his daughter and a little group of onlookers did not look too pleased. He was on his feet a bit shaken, but he was fine, I got back in the car, I told Shaun, "You have to apologize," which he did. After saying "I'm very sorry," he jumped back into the car and unbelievably drove off, I told him, I was going to drive the car. He said it was my fault for telling him to reverse, he begged to continue driving, he did have a point. It was my fault, but with amphetamine, with no sleep, it was exceedingly difficult to concentrate. We were on camera, especially in the town, I was worried that we would have a knock on our doors, from the police. That evening we ended up meeting some strangers, in Stonehouse, Plymouth, I ended up with these lads in their flat, I was off my head on speed, it was getting late it was 3 o'clock in the morning, Shaun said to me "I have left something in your car" he asked, "could I have the keys". I thought where Norman had gone, we call people by their second names in Plymouth, I could not believe it, he had only gone and left me, it was not even his car, I had to get a taxi home. On the way home he had only gone speeding through a speed camera and got me a fine. When I asked him why he had taken my car, he told me that he did not like the boys who I had met, I told him off. He feared me, as he knew me extremely well, he had seen me knock out men when I was just a kid, we used to play fight, I always got the better of him. He did, however, save my life, I was driving through Jenny cliff, the opposite side of the coast from Plymouth Sound. I was driving, I looked down to change my music on my cassette player, suddenly Shaun shouted "stop," which I did straight away. The car was right on the edge of the cliff, I was looking down on to a car park, overlooking a gymnasium, it would have been curtains if Shaun had not shouted "stop" so I did have a lot to thank him for.

Plymouth Argyle despises Exeter City in football to no end. I believed that taking the TCE would be a brilliant plan, as the weed farms were close to Exeter and as a result, it was necessary for me to see them. It had been a while since I had seen any TCE friends as I had been going to Dance Academy, I had cut down on the amount of time hanging out with them all. Time just flew by, especially as I was raving every Saturday, it was the events that had taken place at Wembley. Instead of remaining a hooligan I had developed an addiction to going to raves.

I had Mat in my car quite frequently, he was the Irish lad that I had taken to the secret location of Fred's house. When I showed it to him, he was completely in awe, due to the aroma that had piqued his interest, throughout the entirety of the enchanted region.

When I went with Mat there was a greater intensity than ever before, in the air, it had a putrid Odor, it must have been ready to be harvested to go to London. What would the loss be to someone who was so wealthy that they could not even call the police, however a fantastic opportunity for me to become a millionaire overnight. I had to take the appropriate people with me, that was the key, Mat recommended that I would need a gun, his dad had a twelve-bore shotgun buried on the moors. Mat said, "you need to stuff a tissue up your nose prior to firing the gun, if do not do this, the gunpowder will get up your nose and leave evidence," he always went on about this. He never stopped going on and on about that subject, he did not appear to be the type of person who would fight or shoot anyone, to be honest. He was skinny with black hair, very streetwise, he was the second person who I was taking, as he was up for it from the start. He was like a gypsy, he told us some amazing stories that he had learned about his father, who was a fascinating and lovable man. His Dad was insane, he was known to throw a hand grenade, made from dynamite, into the river at Plymbridge, it was the end for the salmon. I had no fear when it came to amphetamine, I went to a notorious criminal who shall remain anonymous, he could get away with murder and was untouchable. He told me that I was messing with some serious gangsters, but if I pull the job off, to see him would buy the weed and plants.

He lived in a mansion on the moors, he wished me good luck and to be careful, he told me I needed to be incredibly careful in whom I told. The speed had made me into a roaring mad lion that could not shut up, I was telling everyone. If they wanted to be rich easily, I told them to come with me and rob some weed farms. Most people thought I was crazy and that I had lost the plot, they did not want to know me, nor believe me, as I looked like a speed freak, so they thought I was chatting utter nonsense. The best plan I could think of was trying to get as many people as possible, to charge at the plantations, tooled up. I had the notion that the hooligan approach seemed like a clever idea, just take a huge group of boys, a couple hundred should be sufficient, charging the farms, whilst chanting the Zulu song, which would have those sneaky Londoners running.

The individuals were transporting enormous quantities of the weed, from the vicinity of near Exeter to London, without even bothering to share it with Plymouth. On a Saturday, Fred phoned me unexpectedly, it was his son's birthday, he wanted one ecstasy tablet and hash plus amphetamine. The trouble was that I could not drive, I was in a pub, I had four pints of lager, I told him I would have to ring Paul for a lift. Paul would only ever do it if I gave him a decent bit of petrol money, so Paul took me up there. Fred said, "I am only getting it from you because I trust he will be safe on the ecstasy that you have." I told him that "he should only take half as these yellow submarines were so strong and I did not want his son dying." He told his son to "take half tonight" Fred cut it in half, he said "the other half of the ecstasy he would give to one of his son's mates." I got out of my pocket some awful weed, as it was full of seeds and sticks. Plymouth always got rubbish weed back then, I asked Fred what he thought of the weed, he said "that he thought it was like shit" he went off somewhere saying" that he would be back, shortly." His wife made me a cup of tea and gave me a massive slice of cake, she was a nice, kind lady, she made me feel so welcome, she spoke with a London accent.

Fred returned, he had been to his massive shed, which was built onto the side of the house. He brought me a black bin liner, full to the brim with bud mixed with leaves. He said I could have it for free, I thought it was my birthday, there was so much in there, I could not believe my luck. I thought he was such a nice man. I said, "thanks so much." He said, "you have helped me out, for my friends, who really liked the amphetamine, my son, and his friends who love the hash, you are a nice person, and I trust, you." I said, "in the future can I buy this bud that you gave me"? He said, "I will ask my friend to grow extra for you, so that he still has enough for his customers", he explained "he got full price in London, as he supplied the whole of the capital, he sold it to one person who then supplied the whole of London".

Fred was a rich gangster, worth millions, he told me he had one friend in Plymouth, who Fred sorted him with weed, he had known him for years. He asked me if I knew him, but I did not know the name. He also said years ago, a group came up from Plymouth, they tried to rob him, he does not trust anyone else from my city. He told me that he filled the giant lorry up full of weed and that he was the one who drove it to London, he delivered it there every three months. He could have been doing it more than that, he was not going to tell me everything, although he was excessively big headed, I thought, I really thought that I was the last person he should be telling. He was so kind, giving me that weed, so was his wife and his son was always nice with a great big smile. I felt guilty that I was spying on his mates' farms, even though he was the one really in charge of the whole operation, just like Debbie had said, you could tell by just looking at him, he was one rich man. I was thinking I cannot do it over now, as he had given me a bin liner full of weed, and he said, "nine ounces would only cost me six hundred quid for the best weed in the world."

I could make loads if I did not do him over, he told me that he sneaks the seeds over from Holland and that is why it is the best weed. He had been waiting for the date of the harvest, ever since me and Shaun had been spying on his friends' fields. He informed me that he would be gone for the next few weeks, when he returned home, I would be able to buy some weed, if his friend agreed. I was like a big kid at Christmas time, I asked him "do you think he will say yes"? Fred said, "yes probably." Fred told me that I was not allowed to phone him whilst he was away, driving his artic lorry. He told me that he would phone me, otherwise he was not going to sort me out, he made me promise not to say anything to anybody about what he was up to. I could not believe he told me all of that, but he was on amphetamine, it makes you tell your life story and always makes you talk far too much; the drug is designed to make you speak a million words an hour. I wished his son a good birthday, I thanked his wife for the cake and cup of tea and thanked him so much for the weed.

I returned to Paul's car, which was around the corner, he said "fuck me you have been in there for hours." I showed him the bin liner with the weed, he freaked out and said, "put it in the boot." He was buzzing, when I said, "I will give you a load of it, "fucking stinking," was his words with a big grin on his face. We stashed it in his flat, well not his flat, his girlfriend's flat. We agreed that he would be looking after it, I would sell it, and he would get half of the profits. I was always a little sly, and pinched some out of it, so I had more of the profits. It was simply the best weed we would ever smoke in our lives, it was unbelievable, the best grown in the country. The weed was so tasty, I had never had anything like it, it was so pleasant words could not describe how nice it really was. People who bought it wanted it all the time, those who tried it would never get a better smoke than that weed, in their lifetime. I managed to pay off my debt with the fat greedy man, I owed him a lot of money. The bud that Fred gave me did not take long to sell, even mixed with a lot of leaves.

I had no money left, but I did have lots of ecstasy, which was hard to sell out of Dance Academy, I drank in the Hyde Park pub all week, feeding the stupid fruit machines with my profits. Fred called me, as soon as he got back to his house, to catch up, I asked him "was the weed ready"? he replied, "I have only a little left."

Fred yearned for amphetamine, I just took Mat he had his Mum's nine bar of hash on him, we were near the motorway, I said, "Do you mind if we go and see Fred first?" Mathew agreed that she could wait. Fred reminded me not to bring anyone, Mat was sitting in my car, outside his house. He asked whether I had any hash, which he adored, I responded that you should have asked me earlier to bring some, I have your amphetamine, he said "that is good." I said, "my friend has got his Mum's hash in the car, I think he will sell it," I said. Fred said, "I will swap nine ounces of weed, for nine ounces of hash from your friend." I wish I had had a bar to swap, but I did not have any on this day, which was most unusual for me. The bar of hash would cost no more than two hundred and fifty pounds, Fred's weed would cost one thousand six hundred pounds in Plymouth or even more as it was a million times better than their weed.

His Mum could make one thousand six hundred pounds, but most importantly it would keep me in Fred's good books, the transaction would be beneficial for his Mum. I went to the car to tell Mat the great news. I said, "Fred wants to swap a nine bar of his weed, for your Mum's shit hash." Straight away he said, "no, it is my Mum's if it were mine, of course I would do it." I tried to persuade him that he was making a significant error of judgement, as it just did not make any sense. I told him to phone his Mum, she did not answer her phone, I kept telling him that his Mum would want it, as she would be over a thousand pounds better off. "My Mum would go mad," Mat said. I could not believe that Mat would not swap, Fred appeared to be a little aggravated with me, at that very moment. I told him that "Mat could not do it because he did not have his Mum's permission." I said to Fred "give me a few hours, I will swap it," he said "no" abruptly. He told me he was going away, when he got back, he would ring me. I said "Sorry about what happened, but it was not my fault. He said, "look I will ring you," I asked, "how long are you going away for"? He said, "for a couple of weeks."

I was nervous and felt that he was annoyed with me, and not going to sort out the weed that he had promised me. He was in a mood, telling me I was not allowed to bring anyone near his house again, apart from Paul, I gave Mat a lift home, to his Mum's house. The car I was driving broke down, I was out of transport, it just would not start. Debbie phoned up for hash, I did not think she was really into me, I was not too bothered at the time, I was thinking she only phoned when she wanted drugs. I said, "I cannot get up there, my car had broken down." Debbie told me that she was selling her car, as the fan did not work, and because it was in such poor condition, she was only asking fifty pounds for it. I had no choice but to ask Paul for a lift, it took some bargaining, some smoke, and money which he could not refuse.

I sorted her hash and bought the car; she seemed a little more interested in hugging and kissing me, while Paul was beeping his horn. I wanted him to follow me home as the fan was dodgy and it did not go around, she told me to keep putting water in or else it might blow up. I said my goodbyes. She said that her kid was not around tonight, I was welcome to pop up, I told her I would pop back later. I was driving home, the reading on the temperature gauge was so high, in the red, I had to keep stopping to pour water into it.

Captain called, to ask if I could give him a lift to Exeter, where he was dropping off a load of ecstasy to someone, he offered me a good amount of petrol money. I was going to see Debbie anyway, I warned him about the fan, we agreed that we would visit Debbie after, he dropped the pills off in Exeter, Debbie fancied Captain you could tell, but the captain had a girlfriend. I phoned Debbie to make sure it was ok to bring Captain and his friend to her house, after we did a drop off. I went to pick them up. Captain had a massive bag full of ecstasy pills, it looked like an easy thousand.

We were driving, it was incredibly quiet, with not much on the road, it was pouring down with rain. We were driving for approximately thirty minutes, on the A38 carriage way, I checked my rear-view mirror, I noticed a truck off in the distance, I was driving in the fast lane. Suddenly, the engine went through my car, and onto the floor, which caused the car to flip over three times, before narrowly avoiding and colliding with the truck which was in the slow lane. We collided into the barrier, a fire broke out in the vehicle, we legged it over the barriers on the left side of the motorway and down a big slope, we heard the biggest bang, and saw thick black smoke in the air.

Captain freaked out, he stashed his pills in a bush, it was pouring with rain, there was a red telephone box right next to us. We phoned Debbie, she got us a taxi, Captain went to get his pills, the bag was open, he dropped loads, the pills in the bag were soaking wet. She knew the taxi driver, so it was cheaper since we were near to her house, we dropped the pills off in Exeter, then we returned to Debbie's house for a couple of drinks, the same taxi driver gave Captain and his friend a ride home. Debbie asked me to stay for the night, I had a great night with her, we made love all night, long. In the morning, she took me to the local train station at Newton Abbot, I caught the train back to

Plymouth, I wanted to be Debbie's boyfriend, but she made it quite clear, I could only see her when her kid was not around. I did not register the car in my name, Debbie had to pay a fine as her car had been left on the carriage way, she was not happy about it. After that, Debbie asked over the phone for a kilo of hash for a friend, I was only selling a small amount, but I pretended to her that I was selling a lot to impress her, I was able to convince Paul to give me a ride. I informed her that I would need the money right away and that I would return with the kilo of hash. She provided me with one thousand two hundred pounds, and I took the money without ever intending to go back.

I made Paul promise to pretend that the police had caught me, and to let Debbie know that I had been arrested for possession of the kilo of Hash. I would then give him four hundred, as I was the one who was taking the risk, I kept eight hundred pounds. He complied with my request and called her, I could not listen to the call, I asked "had she fallen for it"? He replied that he thought she had. I purchased a used car from one of Darren King's friends, I spent all the money right away, as I always needed a car to travel up and down the motorway. I did go to the bookies and wasted four hundred pounds, I lost every race, I was being greedy and thought that I might have won more.

Fred gave me a call, and informed me, that he could sell me whatever I needed, in a couple of days, how typically I had spent all the money that I robbed from Debbie's friend.

It happened all too quickly, I had no money, Fred told me the least I could buy was ounces of weed, it would cost me six hundred pounds. A couple of the dealers I dealt with said they would buy a couple of ounces each, as they knew it was the best weed. I asked them to give me the money up front, which was the only way I could pay for weed from Fred, they told me to collect the money on Saturday morning, before I went to see Fred. I was in the company of Paul Walsh, my car broke down on a Friday night over in Saltash, I only had had this pile of rubbish for a week. Just my luck, or was it Karma, getting me back for robbing Debbie's friend. I stayed at Paul's house in Saltash, we were on amphetamine, we did not sleep, the morning came quickly.

I phoned another Paul for a lift, he said that "he was with his girlfriend so, could not do it today." I had three hundred pounds, but I needed to collect the money from my two dealers who were friends, who would not answer their phones, I had to be with Fred at two o'clock. It was eleven o'clock, I was nervous and panicky, I felt like everything was going to go wrong. I had loads of ecstasy stashed away, but no one wanted any that weekend. I phoned the two dealers who said they would give me the money up front, but both let me down. I then tried to borrow the money from many people but no joy, not even my dad, my Mum, Nan nor Grandad, nobody would lend me the money.

I phoned Shaun's friend, Cathy, and asked her if she wanted any of the best weed cheap, but could I have the money up front, I knew she had money. She asked how much an ounce, but she would only do it if she went to Fred's with me. Cathy told me that she would buy two ounces for a hundred and twenty-five pounds each, she said that is all she had enough for as I asked if she would buy more that gave me two hundred and fifty pounds. She said, "I will only buy it, if I come to Fred's house with you," I told her, that she would have to wait in the car, because Fred will go mad I had enough for a taxi and I was only one hundred pound short I thought he would not mind me owing him the rest.

Cathy was a friend I met through Shaun; she loved Shaun, she knew him years before. Just like Shaun, she was in and out of the mental hospital, she loved her weed and most party drugs. She was glamorous, she was like the Marilyn Munroe of Plymouth, she was a kind soul always talking about God, telling stories about how we are all god's children, and we are all angels. Paul said he knew a taxi driver who would take us there and back for fifty pounds. The taxi driver was a nice bloke he turned his meter off and knew what we were up to he then drove me, Paul Walsh, and Cathy up to Heathfield, as the taxi turned off the motorway, I warned him not to go anywhere near Fred's, but he accidentally went into the same street.

The group of friends that Fred was with had already observed the taxi, I quickly approached and expressed my regret that I did not have all the money. Fred told me that he had warned me not to bring any strangers to his house, I told him I was so sorry, I said they were all sound, the taxi driver was someone that we knew. He went mad, very red in the face and said you have blown it now. I just stood there in front of Fred's friends, who were standing in front of a large quantity of weed in bin liners, like a mountain of weed, in an open-top land rover. I never saw so many bin liners full of weed, it stunk. I informed Fred that I was only one hundred pounds short, that as soon as I got home, I would get a lift and return, once I had sold the weed, I begged him. He told me to get the fucking hell out of his presence, and to never return. I walked down the road back to the taxi thinking, I am going to come back one day, I will have the last laugh, when I rob you of your weed, you are a fucking idiot. He made me mad; I was truly gutted as I could have been very prosperous with him. The taxi took me back home, I went to Dance Academy in the evening in a bad mood.

The day after, on a Sunday, Frank down the road asked me if I could get thirty ecstasies,' I had stashed ginger pills down Paul's flat. My mum had some vitamin tablets. They were brown, Frank fell for it, He asked for thirty more a week later, I could not believe it, he said that they were amazing, can I buy another thirty? I went to the chemist as there was none in Mums cupboard and got some for a couple quid. I had a lot of money from him, enough to purchase a rubbish car, with no Mot or no insurance but I could keep an eye on his plantations. Shaun served as my nose on the ground, but it would be me who would have to find the right people to take. I was constantly using amphetamine, I was unable to get to sleep as I had severe headaches, and a feeling that death was approaching quickly, a comedown that made my head hurt. Sleep was the only option, but I found it impossible to take advantage of it, as I was preoccupied with the thought of the plantation.

My undoing was the fact that I only got a few hours of shut eye every few days, I made some extremely poor choices and due to the pace, I was living at, people thought I was completely insane. When I think back to that time, I was completely obsessed with weed farms, before I even took possession of it, the million pounds belonged to me, that was insane. I imagined it to be the same as taking candy away from a child, even though it was never legally mine to possess, to begin with at the time, I was under the impression that it was. Before I had even gotten the weed. There was no mention of firearms, so that thought never really occurred to me. I was relieved that the situation was not as difficult as it could have been otherwise, I would have needed the A-Team with their Armor. I was on a major come down with no sleep for a couple of weeks, I felt awful. I took Paul Rowe and Mat to see TCE to ask them for their help with taxing the weed from the farms.

Before a game there were an easy one hundred lads, some I knew, most of which were new guys. After speaking to Mark Trenaman, I could tell he thought that I had lost the plot, he must have thought I was talking crap, off my head and had made it all up, this made me frustrated. I said to all a hundred of them, "do you want to fight"? They thought I meant to fight Brighton, who we were playing that day, there was a big roar "yes" they said, I said "come on then, I'll take all of you on," I had my fists up. None of them wanted to fight me, so I went up to the hardest one, a well-known hard nut. "I said "come on, then me and you he backed down." Mark pulled me to one side and said, "I think you had better go home, which I did. I was not going to the game, as drugs was my thing, it had taken over my life, I dropped off Mat and Rowey, I went home to bed, I was feeling well rough that day.

A week later I was driving on a Saturday night with Mat in the car, there was a tub full of weed, it was the first time I had not gone to Dance Academy for a year or longer. The police had their flashing blue lights on, it was like they had been following me all the time. We pulled over, I had forgotten that there was a knife in the door pocket, it was to cut hash up. We were both arrested and were in some holding cells, Mat was going crazy, fighting the police, and spitting in the policeman's face. It was torture, Mat was let out early in the morning, I was let out about 10 o'clock that evening. I returned to my car at Mutley Plain, I could not believe that they had not taken it away. I jumped back into my car I was driving for one minute, and they pulled me over and arrested me again for no Mot or insurance. It was a hell of two days in those cells, it felt like a week, I promised myself I would never visit that place again. I had to get another car as nothing would stop me from trying to rob those farms. Shaun and Mat then put me in touch with these London boys, and Shaun told them about the farms who had recently moved to Plymouth, they were eager to take advantage of Fred. I spent the day with them came across as right hard nuts, they were the sort of people I was looking for. They informed me that we were on our way to Liskeard, in Cornwall, to purchase a twelve-bore shotgun. I said "No, we do not need a gun." I was under the impression that Fred and his crew were a bunch of fools, farmer boys, and the only animals that they had were dogs. So, I suggested, that we acquire crowbars and other weapons, rather than firearms and that we focus on accumulating numbers instead of fire power. However, they told me not to worry about the numbers, we would be able to make it work, they told me that I was the leader of the gang, in charge of the operation. It was up to me to decide, "we will respect your wishes," Ronnie said with his glasses, on wearing a cap. Then Reg turned his gaze towards me, he claimed that he would murder anyone for me in exchange for just one ecstasy pill, he meant that. He was a dangerous man, white as a ghost, simply by looking at them, murderous sickness cold blooded I could tell they were infected with that disease.

Ronnie was insane, he had too much energy to burn, whereas Reg had no emotion at all, he seemed very sure of himself, but there was a significant screw missing in his arguments. Both had spent more than half of their lives in jail, however there was one thing I did not want anyone to get killed on my call, not at all, they exhibited the utmost level of extremism, they were both young men from London who were not afraid to kill.

Ronnie and Reg would not stop talking about a stupid gun, the situation was becoming extremely stressful, they made me feel paranoid, and that I was taking the wrong people with me who might have pulled a gun on me in the end. Gary, a good friend of mine, knew them from jail, he told me they were ok, he told me they respected me, and they would not rob me at the end of the job. That was my worst fear, we all agreed the weed would be going to his house, if we pulled it off, I had complete confidence in Gary, I went ahead and let them into our gang.

They came highly recommended to me by both Mat and Shaun, Ronnie was now talking about the Mafia, he said that he was a Don, and I was the Godfather, I had heard this from Shaun all my life. I suppose we had made our own little Mafia, as I needed to put my faith in them, hearing that they would look after me was comforting. but it never did, I did not have a choice. I enquired with the gypsies, but they were aware of Fred and his gang, they also cautioned me, that I did not know who I was fucking with. They wished me luck and would not say anything about what they had heard, they were the ones that I wanted to take with me, as they would have been willing to do anything for me. Reggie and Ronnie were natural born killers, but the fact was that I did not want anyone to get killed, it was a major concern for me, that the London boys kept going on about guns.

My primary objective was to finish this job without any comebacks, or serving any prison time, related to it. I did not tell anyone about the plan to kidnap Fred, as I did not want anyone to get hurt. That would have been the easiest thing to do, to kidnap him, he was worth many millions. I frazzled my brain of every thought in my head to pull it off, my first couple of plans were not on, so I had to think of every option which could lead me to the gold.

 Mat was up for pinching the weed, which was all that mattered at the time, he had always been up for it, and he was the one who introduced me to the Londoners, he was the most courageous person in the world. However, despite his inherited Irish eccentricity, he was so young sixteen, I had complete respect for him because he was game for it, when other tough nuts were not. Since we had first caught the aroma of heaven, we had witnessed far too much.

He was one person who knew that I was telling the truth, after he had seen Fred's gold, his eyes lit up, he was buzzing just like me. Me and Shaun saw those barns hidden in the forest that went into an underground maze, we saw the maps, we smelt the smell that had been ridiculously potent. We saw the caravans that were parked in the fields in such large numbers that the area resembled a labyrinth, we saw one plantation at the back of Heathfield, behind the school. They were growing loads in a mansion that had a barn built onto the side of the house with cameras. Nevertheless, we were in a field in front of a mansion on the map, a judge was growing weed, part of the gang, that I was targeting.

I bumped into Andy W he said your right about Fred he is growing shit loads, Andy comes from Exeter and found out that Fred was a silent partner and owned lots of Pubs and night clubs in Torquay so all our friends from Plympton, was up for it I didn't tell the Londoners or Shaun we just went there in the moment there were twenty to thirty of us, I took them to one location, it was secured with massive, barbed wire fencing, we had to cut the gate open with bolt cutters,

Gavin cut through the fence eventually, there was a caravan in the field, we checked that out first, it was easy to get into. The lights for growing were in there, it was stacked to the ceiling with equipment, we walked up to a mad sort of farm, built with aluminium, everywhere. It was like a Texas ranch, it was a huge place, you could tell by the structure it went underground to tunnels. There was a fortune hidden behind those doors, but it was impossible to open, Gavin had his crowbar, and making lots of noise a dog barked at us from the direction of the man's mansion.

We could smell the weed; it was in the air and so strong. They were all terrified of the dog, all of them ran away, I was not at all bothered about the dog, but it was getting closer, we all went back to our cars and vans. The Plympton boys were disappointed.

When I went to visit the mansion, during the day a week later with Shaun, we drove up the lane to spy on the place, there was a huge barn next to the house, it had cameras, the place stunk of weed.

A man came out with a dog, he looked like a hard gangster, he gave us an evil glare, we drove off. I could clearly see that the field belonged to him, there was a judge involved in their growing gang and this was his mansion. I reckoned it was his son walking the dog, as

Debbie had told me that he lived there, when she gave me the three different maps she had mentioned the judge to me. I had a good feeling about the five of us working together at the time, as Reg and Ronnie, in addition to Shaun, were among the meanest people in Plymouth.

All four of us could fight, Mat was mad too, but he was so young, I did not expect too much from him, but to fill those bags up with weed would have been enough from him, we were all the maddest around back then. However, we were going to need a van and some weapons, we also needed Gary B to get rid of the bud, he had a brother in Cornwall who had a massive place in the middle of nowhere. He also told us he had a twelve-bore shotgun if we needed to borrow it, I straight away said "no need for that." Ronnie on the other hand was saying we need the gun, I said it is my job, and there is absolutely no need for guns.

I wished at the time Gary did not mention the gun as Ronnie and Reg would not stop going on about it, yet again. Everything was ready to go, down to the plants and Mummy trees that we were going to try to take, millions of plants, I was constantly thinking about it.

The boys from London were able to tell that I was heading in the right direction, they agreed with me, which most people were unable to comprehend. I walked them through the storyline, they were absolutely astounded when I took them in the dark, late to each location on the map. They could not believe the smell that was so intense, and the area that looked so magical in the massive forest. Ronnie said, "You have found the largest plantations in the whole nation, they wanted to get guns on the same day that they saw it, but I told them in a few days, it would be bonfire night. We would hit the field with the one massive barn, about a mile past Fred's, I really did not want to take the place behind the school as it went so wrong before. This barn was in the middle of nowhere, apart from maybe some people in a caravan, and dogs, Shaun and I always heard barking, when we got close to the barn, it was the easiest one to do, we thought. It would be bonfire night, I suggested to Ronnie and Reggie, we all agreed that it was the perfect time to do it.

Reg loved me, Ronnie. I did not trust him. Ronnie was like a fuse. Ronnie was the oldest out of us, ten years older than me with the loudest cockney accent; he just could not shut up. They were very cold-blooded, they had beaten up the greedy man, the one who I always owed money to and his brother, who was the hardest on our estate. Someone owed them money, but I am not saying who. Reg and Ronnie had a screwdriver and applied it to the fat man's head, Reg put a knife to his brother's throat, I was glad to have them on board. Mat beefed them up, telling them that all I needed was Ronnie, Reg to come with us, and Shaun. I was looking for people who use weapons without wielding them, I erroneously believed that the fact that I had some dangerous boys on my side, was all that I required. Shaun made sure we had done our homework, we had three stinking plantations to hit, they were a mile apart from one another, Still, we discovered what was the largest plantation in England. Shaun and I went there religiously every other day, owing thousands of pounds to petrol stations, but completely overcome by the aromas that we could detect.

The barns lockups were enormous, the largest metal barn had several smaller barns lockups located alongside the larger one, all that was required was to strike the plants when they were fully grown ready for picking. They were much more straightforward than the mansion.

Chapter 15. The Devil's Harvest

Bonfire night arrived and I went through the storyline all again with Reg, Ronnie, Mat, and Shaun. Reg drove to my sister's house first, as I wanted to see her before I went, in case things went wrong. I told her what we were about to do as she knew everything from the start. However, they did not tell me, but they told my sister that they had sneaked a gun and had hidden it in the van. My sister was worried after the gun was mentioned. I took them to the large barn surrounded by caravans on this field, when we finally got through the gate with the barbed wire, and cut the fence open, all the lights came on, people were hiding inside the caravan, they did not seem to care that the dogs were going crazy, with their barking. Ronnie opened the barn door, with a crowbar inside were millions of plants, it was just unbelievable, it was massive, my mind blown away, enough for the whole country, not just London, genuinely unbelievable.

However, one of the people inside the barn shot at us, with a twelve-bore shotgun, Shaun ducked otherwise it would have hit him in the head, Shaun, and the rest of us just ran back to the van. Reg turned to me and said, "I told you we needed a gun." I nodded. In the van, Fred's gang were proper gangsters, not dumb farmers as I originally had thought. Reggie was right, we would need five guns, not just one. On the way home, Reg stopped on the edge of the moors, Lee Moor, they got out the van, knowing that I didn't know about the gun at that time I think they had hidden the gun in a hedge but, I did not see it myself so I will never no. I had a tub full of yellow ecstasy on me, I stupidly took two it was about 2 o'clock in the morning, we all took some yellow ecstasy pills. Ronnie said I would get the most significant reward if I went to the police, he said, all the newspapers would pay loads for my story too.

We knew he was the biggest grower in the country, the amount of the plants was out of this world, it was just like something out of the film Lock, Stock and Two Smoking Barrels, apart from there was a lot more there, than on that film, I was super pissed off that we had got shot at. I was not thinking straight, I hated people who grassed, but the gangsters were telling me that the law was bent, it was not the way it should work. I knew the law was bent, often hearing stories about these bent coppers, were a common thing back then. I worked so hard trying to pinch that weed and it seemed such a promising idea. Fred had really made me angry, when I had turned up in the taxi and he told me to piss off, never to return, after seeing millions of plants worth millions of pounds, the size of the place was truly unbelievable. I said to Ronnie, you are the best at speaking, you tell the police as I am tired, I said "I'm smashed on this ecstasy." He told me that I would not get the reward if he did the talking. How gullible was I? so, I said, "ok I will do the talking." We all went to Charles Cross police station, it was only a week after I was last there, with Mat.

Chapter 16. Hells Cross

I hated the place, the police receptionist got some undercover police officer, who was dressed very smartly. He could not believe what we were saying, I even told him we got shot at, I told him the whole story from the beginning to the end, I said I have the maps of the locations. He took the maps straight away, and another undercover police officer said that they would get a negotiator from Exeter. It will take about an hour before he arrives, he said, that we should return in an hour. It was three o'clock in the morning, freezing cold, buzzing on ecstasy, and the usual amphetamine in my system, which made me extra paranoid. I had to trust these experienced ex-prisoners on what they were saying as I was so out of my mind, having had no sleep for a month, I felt deathly and insecure. We all walked in, a police officer said, they only want to speak to "Me." he told the rest of the lads that they had to leave, while they were speaking to me. They took me to a room quizzing me about the farms for an hour. I was so out of my face on the ecstasy pills. The undercover police officer had told me that, at the beginning of the interview, if I answered all their questions, I would be let out.

I was dying for a roll up, I could not wait to get out. Suddenly unexpectedly about ten police officers bundled me to the floor, ripping my clothes off and putting me in a white all in one paper suit. It was sick for simply trying to get a reward. I was in a cell handing three maps in, I was thinking how this is even possible. What had I done wrong? I thought it was so strange the way that they were treating me. I should not have given any credence to Ronnie's plan, as look where it had landed me, in utter hell.

The police had just abandoned me to rot, I was constantly pressing the red button to get some attention, for a roll up. I was shouting for an explanation as to why I was being held in the cells for three maps. It was so stressful, the whole situation, one-minute thinking that we were in for a reward. The only reward I got was staying in a Hell's cross cell, it was a huge nightmare, especially on an ecstasy tablet, I was begging for water, it felt like I was truly going to die. They would not let me call my family, to let them know that I was ok, or a lawyer, which was surely against the law. It was so corrupt back then for sure, it has not even changed that much, now.

I was starting to lose my mind as it seemed like hours had passed since they had just abandoned me. I yelled at them that they were breaking the law by not letting me make a phone call, after hearing keys, I started singing songs. "Why am I waiting"? "I am suffocating, let me out, let me out, let me out." After that, I sang, 'Old McDonald had a farm, and on that farm, the grew some plants Ei, Ei o and on that farm, they had some weed with Police here, Police there and nicking it every fucking were. Old McDonald is a thief Ei, Ei, o.' I repeated this song many times, other people in the cells were telling me to shut up. I told them to "get fucked" and started singing football songs. 'Dance, dance, wherever you maybe, we are the boys from the TCE, we need you all wherever you maybe, because we are the boys from the TCE' is how it went. I told the lads who were mouthing off to me, they were getting it as well, when I could get hold of them. I sang loads of football songs, it was my way of releasing my anger, I was getting angrier as time went on. The police came and suddenly there were no others in the cells around me, either they had been moved, or let out. I was hoping it would not be too long till it was my turn to be let out, or at least I could have a roll up. It seemed to go on forever, and it was a long night, with no water, or explanation, why I had been locked up. I felt trapped, and so anxious, I knew that I was not getting anywhere, so I started banging and kicking on the doors. After a significant amount of time had passed, and I could not get any water, I started getting afraid that I was going to pass out and die. It had been hours since the event, I could hear gunshots coming from outside my cell window. Worzel had a gun, the noise from the gun was so loud that it was causing discomfort in my ears, he warned me to stay clear.

I jumped up onto the wooden bench, the window was so thick it sounded like a twelve-bore shotgun. With each shot that he was firing, the window cracked increasingly with each shot, glass flew all over place. I had splinters of glass all over me, Worzel shouted, "I'm going to get you out of here soon." I could not get out because the small windowpanes were far too small to fit through. I was just losing the plot and was having the worst hallucinations; this was the worst living nightmare.

Gary had told me stories about his friend Worzel, I did not even know him, but he shouted that Gary had sent him, to fetch me out of there. He assured me that he would return, and there was no need to panic, that is what he shouted as he left. I attempted to flush myself through the toilet by pulling the flush down, thinking that if I put my head down the toilet, the power of the water might help me to escape through the pipes, I felt like I had shrunk in size to make it happen. I had tripped out so badly, it was like I was in the Matrix, but there was no escape, it was the worst intense illusions that I could have ever experienced.

I experienced a real death situation, like I had died and come out of my body. I was out of the cell at Devils Point in a caravan with friends who had previously died, I spent an hour with Wayne Robinson. He told me all about heaven and hell, I was in heaven for an hour talking about football. He told me that when you die, you come out of your body. He had been walking the earth ever since he said that he passed over to the other side. He told me to believe, to be good. I then jumped back into my body, and back to the cell, in other words, I was back in hell, I had tripped out, that I was at Devil's Point.

I had never experienced anything like it, it was truly strange but at the same time it was so real. When I had entered the police station, I was not experiencing hallucinations, of this nature, I had a horrible Police Officer who had been bulling me, he was like the devil himself. The bully said that you are locked up for the rest of your life in the cell, he told me the key for my cell door had been chucked away, he said organized crime does not pay. He claimed it was a serious offence to organize a robbery, it totally baffled me, he was taunting me for real, just pure evil, I really believed that the key had been chucked away. I was raging red in the face, shouting that I was going to kill him and his family, as soon as I was out of the cell. One entire day had passed, with no phone calls, or smoke.

I had taken the London boys and Shaun and Mat to my sister's house, before we had intended to tax one of the plantations. I wanted her to know that we were going to rob the farms on that night. So, if anything went wrong then at least she knew. I did not have any food, nor water, I shouted I need water then this voice, shouted shut up little Boy I said who is it. He introduced himself as Chopper, your worst nightmare, he shouted screeching my ears I could not see him he would not leave me alone, for some unknown reason, he began to torment me, he told me that I was responsible for his funeral. He was a menace, the voice grew louder, and suddenly, I saw Chopper as a ghostly figure in front of me, a terrifying black shadow. I looked down at my arms, I could see loads of little spiders and ants, crawling out of my skin, all over my body with millions of flies emerging from my mouth, just like John Coffey in the film The Green Mile. When John was in the cell, I experienced worse than that. It was terrifying, all these bugs and spiders continued to fill my cell, I was drowning.

I begged for assistance, but the officers just laughed at me when I begged, there were insects all the way up to my neck. I wished for their departure through prayer, I was naked as they had eaten through the white paper suit, and thought I was going to die. Eventually, I saw the spiders, bugs and flies leave the cell and then went down the corridor. After that, my fear subsided, I regained my ability to breathe, Chopper had left the cell, but I could not get rid of the sound of his voice in my head. I yelled for assistance, but the police officers only laughed at me. Someone brought me food, I threw it directly back at him, all over him, but I kept the plate, and I threw it all around my cell like a frisbee. After being there for two days, I had not received a single phone call, or a visit from a solicitor, Chopper appeared and warned of the trouble, I was, in his terrifying voice, what sent shivers done my spine. He called the prison the devil's playground is the place where you are going and labelled me a scum bag. I shouted why he kept repeating you are going to the prison and the devil sent me to haunt you it was so scary and so real I believed the voice. Chopper's voice revibrated through the cell turning it into a living nightmare. I feared I would be locked away forever as he blamed me for his demise. The ruthless sound of his voice grated on my nerves me accused of his fate. was so loud, threatening to the point he would not leave me alone, I was terrified. I still thought that they had thrown away the key, which was my forever thought, I felt trapped, no escape with the sound of his voice grating saying, I was in hell. I screamed to the authorities who had just abandoned me there, left me to rot.

There was a camera in the cell, I thought, does anyone care? If they were watching I was thinking of suing the police for not allowing me to make a phone call, or to see any solicitor for committing no crime whatsoever. I was going to do this act and try to get them into trouble later, by getting someone to play the camera back. I was thinking of a way to get out, as it felt like I was in hell. I thought if I pulled it off, they might take me to the hospital, where I would not get bullied by the police, nor haunted by the terrifying voice of Chopper, I was raging mad at this point. It was the first time that I had gone without a roll up, since the last time I was in the cells, for something else I had done. I was crazier about not having a smoke than anything else, so I went into an acting role. I ran headfirst towards the wall and gave it a massive headbutt, I had dived back in the air to make it look good, I laid there for a few hours as I had nothing better to do. Absolutely nobody came to help me, the care in this place was appalling, I was raging, shouting for a roll up, a phone call, a solicitor, which was the law. A peculiar man with a devilish demeanour, was cleaning the cells as I looked through the spy hole. I begged him to help I shouted they are mentally trying to make me lose my mind, they will not let me have a phone call please help. The evilest police man acted like the devil himself making me rage as he should have never treated someone in his manner, he made me lose my mind as I believe every word he said. me told me, that I was going to be there for the rest of eternity beside him cleaning cells, which would be the only time I would ever get out of the cell; to clean, I would never see the light of day, he taunted me my heart raced. The next thing that I knew, after days of being there, was officers break into my cell, wielding wooden baseball bats, with helmets with shields. They beat me so badly, battered, bruised, and covered in blood, they gave me an injection, it seemed as if a psychiatrist was watching my every move from the camera in my cell.

I was still hearing the voice of Chopper, taunting me, "they call you, Braveheart, you're not so brave now, you will pay for my death." I kept thinking, why is Chopper's voice in my head when he is alive? me and Chopper hated each other. It was so puzzling why his voice was haunting me for days, the voice and hallucinations were terrifying, coming and going wherever they pleased. I am never going to get out of here that is all I thought, forever needing a roll up was pure torture. Days later, still no phone call, a female officer appeared through the flap of the cell door. I was shaking, I begged please, "I'm going crazy, please can I go outside for a smoke." The female officer who was more friendly announced that I was leaving and going somewhere else, I said would I be able to smoke there. I begged her to tell me where exactly I was going, she told me I would be ok and walked off.

Chopper started shouting "the only place a scumbag like you is going is prison, and I am coming with you," he said in an angry voice. He kept telling me that I had killed him, "I did not kill you," I pleaded my innocence back. Then I thought, what if I had killed him, but my mind was a blank. I started to believe what the voice was telling me, it had taken total control of me, I was so worried that I had killed him, the prison I was going to, especially in a white outfit, had me worried like never before. I had so wished that I had never gone to that stupid farm, which had now totally landed me in this hell of a state. I did not know what was going to happen to me, whilst hallucinating a crowd of police had all jumped on me and wrestled me to the ground. They were so heavy handed, nearly breaking my arms whilst putting cuffs on my wrist, they even tied my legs together. They bound straps around my body to the bed trolley, the police officer who had been very heavily handed with me, pushed my face against the bed, I could not breathe. I managed to free my head for one second, enough time for a gob full of my spit, right into his face. He pushed even harder, with my nose already broken from the beating they gave me. Then a mask went over my head, I felt like Hannibal Lecter. Chopper was shouting, "who is going to have the last laugh"? and burst into laughter.

Chapter 17. The Web of conspiracies

After a short trip that lasted somewhere between ten and fifteen minutes, they took me to a mental hospital called the Glenburnie Unit which is a mental hospital. The mask came off, I was welcomed by a little elderly nurse called Jackie, she made me feel at ease. I put my hands together as though I was praying and begged to make myself a roll-up. She said that I had to see the doctor first, I said "I have not had a fag for four days, please" I begged, I was so irate, like my life depended on it. She said, "you promise to behave I am not supposed to do this." She said, "it was the rules of the hospital for me to see the doctor first, promise to be good and don't run off" she said.

We went to a balcony just outside the ward, a green cage in the open air with a red brick floor, looking down to a big garden next to an open forest. Finally, after waiting for what seemed a life sentence, since I last had a roll-up.

All I could think about the whole time in the cell was a roll-up, after waiting all that time my roll-up tasted vile. She was down to earth, and straight to the point she was a Swilly bird, she knew all my dad's side of his family. She said, "I have been speaking with your Mum and Dad on the phone." They were so worried, but you are safe now she was such a caring person, I felt at ease to be there, she made me feel safe.

The psychiatrist, who was smartly dressed, said that he had been watching over me through the camera, in my cell, at the police station all day. We talked for ten minutes about several reasons why I was detained under the mental health act, under a six-month section. I was a danger to others and myself, I argued my case about being stitched up by the law, but it got me nowhere. He told me that I was suffering from drug psychosis, and that too many drugs had caused me to hallucinate. I could not see the reasoning, but I also could not see the state that I was in. He told me that he was just doing his job, to make me better, and told me to trust the process. All that I wanted to do was to go home, go to sleep, sleep for a week and I would be fine. I said, "if I hadn't gone to the police station with the three maps I would not be here right now." He was nice about things and gave me a Valium, he also believed me about the plantations, he told me that was not the reason that I had been taken there, the reason for me being there were the voices and hallucinations, I was convinced back then it was all a massive conspiracy. Then the doctor told me that I needed to have a ruthless injection in my bum cheeks, oh my god the horror stories Shaun had told me about the dreaded injection.

My worst fear was staring me in the eyes, the biggest needle I had ever seen, I begged, that there was no need for all of this. I refused and said, "you are not doing that to me", Jackie told me that I had to have it, she said "you been through so much, you need sleep, you are going to kill yourself, so listen to me and dam well take it, then you can go for another fag". I listened to her; the doctor gave me the injection; I was shown around the building. The bedrooms were boys' and girls' rooms with about four beds in one room, there were two single rooms, I was going to stay in one of the single rooms.

There was a music room, where people could play music, a quiet room for reading books and chilling. There was a garden, but I was not allowed there until I was trusted, I was told I had to behave, keep my head down and my nose clean. She said "you cannot go fighting in here, there is a place downstairs, the secure unit, which has three rooms, it has the highest security, for the most violent dangerous offenders. On the other side of the building, downstairs was a ward, next to the garden with people mostly from outside of Plymouth, with the odd few from Plymouth, the ward which I was staying in, they were all from Plymouth. The showers and baths we all had to share, which was not the most ideal. Jackie left me in the smoking room, it was a large room with uncomfortable seats going all the way around the room, with a TV in the corner of the room, I was set loose, still buzzing on a high.

I still felt chatty, but relieved not to be in that police station, I went to the smoking room. A scruffy man was sitting there, his appearance was diminished by the growth of a ginger beard, he was sweating and looked overheated and uncomfortable, itching with rashes on his dirty face, it looked like he was on heroin that was my first impression. I quizzed him and wanted to know the reason for his stay in the hospital, he cautioned me to stay out of his personal affairs, I was just trying to be friendly. He glared at me trying to scare me with his evil ugly face, I glared back to show I was not scared of him. He walked out of the room but made it quite clear that he hated me. Over in the corner of the room, a scruffy lady with black curly hair, and with black teeth was seated in a wheelchair. She shouted, "Thomas is that really you"? in a Scottish accent. I said, "no you must have mistaken me for someone else." "Give us a roll up please Thomas," she yelled. She said, "I have no money, no one will give me a roll-up," she went on to say that she only was paid ten pounds a week, she begged, holding her hands together. I felt so sorry for her and gave her a handful of tobacco and some Rizla papers. She said, "bless you Thomas, you are so kind we used to get on so well she said." "Let me give you a big kiss, Thomas it has been so long." I said, "no you cannot kiss me, and I am not Thomas, I am Justin." "You might not remember me; it was a long time ago in our past life. you died on the cross next to Jesus, you were so funny telling jokes, whilst being crucified next to Jesus, you had such a wonderful sense of humour." She claimed in a previous life, we both had lived in Nazareth, even though she kept going on and on about Nazareth, which had been the first I first heard of Nazareth. Before that, I had no idea that it was Jesus' hometown, she obviously was not well.

I had to tell her that I was not Thomas as she would not stop going on and on about me being Thomas, it started to do my head in. Mel was a big built lady who had a hunched back with a skinhead, was smoking in a chair, she came across like she was a hard nut. She introduced herself by saying do not give your stuff away, they will fleece you in this place. I said, "I do not mind, I get Tobacco cheap, I told her my Mum will bring more up for me later." Mel said" it is up to you, but I thought I should tell you." I told her that I would get her tobacco or cigarettes cheap from my Mum or Dad, she said that that would help her a great deal. She said, "do not tell all the patients," she warned me that some would grass to the staff, most of them are nice, but she said there were a few that were horrible.

Mel told me to be smart about it, she said that there was a cigarette and tobacco machine in the cafe. Mel said it is so expensive from the machine, and told me to charge the right money, so that it would benefit me. She told me the characters that were staying in the unit, in her Cornish accent. She said there is lots of people messed up on drugs, murderers, paedophile's, self-harmers, heroin addicts, mental patients and people who just wanted to kill themselves. She then asked me if I smoked cannabis, I was dying for some, I said "yes," hoping she had some. She warned me that hash would be detrimental to my health, Mel said, "it is bad and does not agree with everyone, and that it causes psychosis," she warned me, she was dead against cannabis. I tried to tell her that I was dependent on amphetamine, I said that "no sleep has made me ill and being locked up for four days has sent me wild." I explained all about the farms and what happened in the cell, she agreed that the law was bent, she told me to keep my head down, and not get into any trouble, was the key to getting out of this place.

My Mum walked in for a visit, she brought me a bag of goodies, crisps, a bottle of coke, sweets, chocolate, and tobacco. Mum sat with me and Mel, Mel straight away got out of her seat, she said, "I must leave you to enjoy your visit, you only get one Mum, make sure you look after her." Mum said, "do not go, sit with us," Mel with a big grin sat back down, we sat together around a table. I chatted about the farms, Mum knew all about them, as I even told her about what I found ages ago, so she knew everything about it, I could not understand why I was there just handing three maps in. I did not consider that I was hearing voices nor hallucinating. Mum said, "that was the least of my worries, just to get better." The voice was constant, I was still having psychosis to the max, which in other words was that I was hallucinating which would come and go. Mum asked the reason, Mel was in the hospital, Mel openly said that she there due to depression, she had tried to kill herself lots of times, but always failed, but she could not cope with life like some people. She was mentally abused as a child, raped, locked in a cupboard for years, the only time that she came out of the cupboard was to be sexually abused by her father, her mother had died at the tender age of when Mel was five, she had self-harmed herself, covered by a bandage on her arm.

We sat chatting for half an hour, she told Mum that she would look after me, and make sure I did not get up to any mischief. Mum said, "goodbye and thank you to Mel." I made Mum promise to come back tomorrow, she said she would if she could, the unsecure feeling was unreal, with the psychosis. Mel said I was so lucky to have a good mother like that, she told me that she would keep an eye on me as she had promised, and Mel walked off to the garden. A lady whilst in the smoking room, asked for a cigarette from a lady called Joyce, who had blue piercing starry eyes. Joyce shouted, "fuck off no you are not having a fucking fag fuck off." I asked Joyce if she wanted a cup of tea. She was an elderly lady about seventy years old, Joyce said "thank you, no one has made me a cup of tea before." She then asked why I was in the hospital, I told her I tried robbing a weed farm and that was the reason for my stay there. I allowed a few of the patients to have some of my tobacco, everyone wanted to know what happened, I told them all the story trying to rob the farm they thought I was making the whole story up.

This man named Paul, who had previously been to Broadmoor, had a tear tattoo under his eye, he fancied himself as a tough guy and believed that he had the ability to frighten me. I was now afraid of no one, apart from the voice, which was the scariest thing, I could beat anyone in there in a fight. I was a dangerous person and had no fear, I did not like Paul, as he thought he was the main man, the alpha dominant monkey. He was annoying a girl named Sarah, who told me he would not leave her alone. She told me that she was hearing voices and seeing things, she told me it was all a bit too much, she was seeing him, but she told me she was so ill and just wanted him to leave her alone and get better.

 I did fancy her a little bit, but I could tell she did not need anyone at the time, as she was extremely ill, I talked to her about her problems, and she had many. She had even sold her body on the streets to fund her drug habit, I told her if he annoys you, let me know, I will sort him out. I was ten times my strength at the time, I would not let him bully her. I got the impression that the man with the ginger beard was a scum bag, he would not stop staring at me. There was tension in the air when we were in the same room, he was guilty of something, he always looked so nervous. He was a heroin addict, as he was perspiring heavily, when wearing a blue sweater. I explained to Jackie that I constantly heard Choppers' voice talking to me, in my head, we discussed who Chopper was, she revealed to me that he had been killed. It was so unbelievable to me. How had I known that he had died? I did not even know he had been murdered. She said, "how odd you must not worry, the voice will go with the help of the right treatment." She said, "when the voice comes, do not be afraid to tell a member of staff." Jackie said you might get a chill pill to help the bad thoughts which were normally Valium, she was a little hard lady but a very fair lady, the easiest to get on with, and the nicest staff member, patients called her smack head Jackie. She was well thought of and after everyone liked her, she always had a smile, she was very caring and had an enthusiastic sense of humour. At ten o'clock, it was time to line up for medication, I had to take sleeping pills, Valium, and an antipsychotic drug. I was always thinking that I had blown my dreams, and it was over. There was a buzzing noise in my ear, just like on the radio, when searching for a radio station the noise was constant, I was up and down like a yoyo, in and out of bed, that night. The staff were outside my room telling me that I should sleep, to get better, but it was my freewill to go for a Roll-up. Cathy and Michelle where the only two people still awake, it was something like 3 o'clock in the morning.

Cathy in her late fifties looked like a real witch with pointed nose, her black perusing eyes, and jet-black curly hair, with the brightest of red lipstick plastered on her lips. She screamed just for the sake of screaming, she asked me to dance with her, while she had the radio on, I said "no thanks." She grabbed my hand, when I asked the reason for her being here in the hospital, she sat beside me and told me she had a mental breakdown, then told me stories about her Italian husband, who was in prison for murder. He will come after me next, she said, I said "why would he be after you"? Cathy then told me, the horror story of her husband who had killed someone, and then chopped the body up into pieces. She told me that she often got beaten up, she was the one who grassed him up to the police, as she had witnessed him commit the murder. He killed the man in front of her in a jealous rage, he then took his body onto the moors, into the depths of Dartmoor, I told her "He will not get you; you will be ok." I said "goodnight" to her, and added if you ever wanted to chat, I am always here to help. She said "give us a kiss" as she tried to kiss me on the lips. I went to try to go to sleep, but I was tossing and turning the bed was so uncomfortable, I did not sleep a wink. Morning came, 8 o'clock was medication time, a little queue would form, with the nurse, with a trolley. Valium to wake up with, and the psychotic drugs was what they made me take, just what you needed, to start the day to get sedated, I then had breakfast, porridge and toast, no fry-up here. I could not wait to be allowed into the cage, or the garden, the staff kept a close eye on me, they just wore normal clothes, no fancy uniforms or anything like that, the doctors wore suits, there were easily thirty to forty people on my ward.

More tablets at 12 o'clock followed by dinner, there was a lad, who introduced himself as Jason, who was deaf he asked, me to keep an eye out to make sure that staff were not coming. He started putting skins together to make a joint, he said listen out for staff coming. I sat by the door looking down the corridor if someone had come along, I could not exactly have told him, which made me laugh, I said "do not suppose I can buy any Hash please." He said that he could not hear after a couple of attempts, he can lip read only, he pulled out a couple of ounces of hash, and bit me a massive bit off. He said, "give me a fiver," so I gave him a tenner, as it was worth it, he gave me easily a quarter, I went to the toilet and skinned up. I then just went to the front room, a man called Derek was there, he had a beard, he did not talk to anyone. I opened the window which had a restricting vent, it opened a tiny bit, I had a sneaky sly joint, it was lovely I felt relaxed, nice, and chilled, it seemed a good place to be. I made friends with Tony, a rocker who had long blonde hair, he wore a leather jacket, he was a smoker. He sat on the round table with a woman called Anne, she was good to talk to, her boyfriend always sat at the table, with us at night. Lots of people in the hospital had a sneaky spliff, the heroin users stayed in their own little group, they were always grassing each other up, for smoking hash, it was just like being at school. They simply got jealous when another had a spliff, I was allowed to go into the garden and the cage after a week, a tiny bit of freedom, after being stuck in. I hung around with all sorts of people, I always had someone to talk to, I was quite popular there. If somebody had a problem, they would come to me to talk to me, as they trusted me. I looked after the older ones, making them cups of teas or coffees, if they needed tobacco or fags, I got them for them. I only sold it to those who deserved it, as there was the odd idiot here and there who did not deserve any discount at all, I was well respected and most of the patients looked on me, as if I was a hero.

Ian Gibbons, a football hooligan, not to be messed with, he was one of the nuttiest boys I had ever met, had a blanket around him to keep himself warm. He was someone well known in Plymouth, I knew Ian well from the football firm. Ian went to visit a priest, he asked for his blessings in prayer, as he was going to kill himself. The priest blessed him, Ian went to the Tamar Bridge he dived off it, he hit the sea as if he were hitting it with a brick, he was truly short of breath, he was in a bad way, but survived it.

Most people would have died, because of the enormous 80 ft fall and the mud beneath the sea. I went and chatted with him, the last time that I had seen him was, before I went to Heathfield, I had needed to get money for weed, it was the time Fred had told me to fuck off and never to return. I asked him why he wanted to die, Ian told me that he had been sexually abused, and the nightmares were constantly there, the pictures of being abused were in his head constantly. He had been abused by the worst paedophile ring in Britain, William Goad the rotten human, who had raped, loads of children.

William used to pretend he was Ian's Uncle, Ian was in a boarding school full time, Ian was in care for most of his childhood. The sick man would pretend he was taking him out for an hour or two but really, he was taking him to the woods to be raped, Ian was only eight years old, this went on for years. Ian had escaped, that is why I had not seen him on the streets for such a long time. Ian used to hang around with me and Shaun. When we were kids, I had no idea that he had escaped boarding school, as he was smart, he had not told us that he was on the run. He lived in a cupboard at the tender age of ten years old, it was somewhere he felt safe, underneath a little shop in Estover. Above that there was a flat Ian stayed in the outside cupboard, his sister used to bring him food and warm clothes. Ian cried when it was zero degrees, but he always thought it was better than being raped by that evil thing. The police caught Ian, but it did not stop him from escaping again, he would always return to the same cupboard, as he was close to his sister.

Ian eventually was out of care at sixteen years old and free from care, he joined Plymouth's Youth Firm (PYF), before later joining the TCE, from the younger generation, from all the different estates in Plymouth. Ian was one of the hard guys, I never could understand why he had the childhood, that had, and that he went through. He only survived life, at that time, because he was loved by the hooligans, so-called thugs, some of the most caring people, who would fight for their clubs and country, who were the most caring people in the world.

Meeting his friends in the football element gave him the opportunity and the chance to build trust and some sort of life for himself. He was a warrior, not afraid of going into battle with other football firms, one of Plymouths top boys, he was simply ruthless never backing down from a fight, once he and three others took on thirty Cardiff lads, called the soul crew, at The George in Plympton, Cardiff held the greatest respect for the four central element boys, as they more than held their own, it was written in the soul 2 crew book. Ian was in and out of hospital, I had often seen him in there in my younger years. I asked him why he was in there, he was very clever and told me he used to come in voluntary, as it kept his benefits going. He explained that he would be ill for years, so that he would never lose his benefits. Ian tried to kill himself ten years previously, by taking two hundred and forty olanzapine, he was in a coma, on a life support machine, for a few months. how he survived that is beyond me. He is doing well these days, he has children, grandchildren, and has a good family unit around him, which is good. Ian is a nice person, especially to let me share his story.

Anne Robinson and The Weakest Link came on the TV, I would start hallucinating whenever the music came on, just after taking the medication. This happened every day at the same time, it lasted for a few hours, it made me feel lightheaded with blurred vision it was like using an ecstasy tablet, it felt quite good but weird, and then it would wear off, after a few hours. I loved the garden; it was my favourite place to go, where I met other patients from the ward downstairs. They were all country bumpkins, from Tavistock, Devon and Cornwall, there were about forty people in the ward too. I used to go out for a sneaky smoke, I would walk around the corner where the garden was so big, where no one could see me and light my spliff, I used to go in feeling nice and chilled. They had cameras everywhere, and knew everything you did in that building, it was just like Big Brother.

A receptionist who worked in Glenbourne, in the ward where I was often listened to my stories. She also dealt with all my paperwork; she was a successful author, she was going into retirement and was about to leave her job, she told me to write a book on what happened on the farms, and my life story, she said I will know when the right time it is to do it. She said, promise me you will do it, it is the only reason I ever drafted this book, as I was the worst at school at English, I was in special needs at school with dyslexia, so this has been a major challenge for me to complete. Because of all of this, I decided to draft a book about my experiences. If she had not mentioned authoring a book to me, I never would have thought of doing it myself. To begin, I enjoyed being there, I was safe, but I did not enjoy it when anyone tried to restrict my freedom. Reg, Ronnie, Mat, and Shaun paid me a visit and sneaked hash in, Mat passed it under the table.

They told me they returned to Chudleigh Knighton, at five o'clock in the morning, the same night I was being held in the cell. They went to returned to the same location when fifteen men warned them off by shooting guns in the air, they knew it was impossible to steal their weed. They informed me a day after they got up that they believed the police had found it, and said it was the biggest cover up, and it was corruption, but there was no evidence, just as I heard the same from staff as well.

My friend Andy saw Fred in Exeter, a long time after, so his weed was still being produced. As many years later, I heard that a Judge from that area had been caught with loads of plants he was in the paper, he had been questioned, regarding lots of plants, I could not believe what I was reading, it was the Judge, he said if only you knew the whole story. I knew they were still growing, after reading this in the paper. I do not know what happened after I was locked up, I heard stories that the police had found loads in one location, they had kept millions, it could have just been just a rumour, but the law was so bent and corrupt back then.

I had no sleep and was not thinking properly and taking Ronnie was the reason I grassed he was giving me false information and I should never have listened to the scum bag. I hate grasses I only done that because I was delusional with no sleep. My sister knew a hairdresser from that area who had seen loads of armed police around that region with guns a few days after I went up there. Or they just continued, and the police did not even believe me and thought I was mad, but I will never ever know the truth of what had happened.

Ronnie disappeared after that, I never saw him again, I had heard that he had killed someone on the Hoe in Plymouth, he had run over someone in a car, while in reverse, and that Reg had gone to prison for stabbing someone, who was having an affair with his girlfriend. I used to enjoy going to the cafe it served delicious food, and the two women who worked there were friendly, I got on well with both, they even bought tobacco from me, I used to make them laugh, they told me that all the time. One smoked Hash, I told them all my stories, I became particularly good friends with them and the cleaners.

Jackie was without a doubt the nicest person and nurse. Jackie informed me that I was extremely fortunate to be placed in Glenbourne because the other units that the police had attempted to place me in, were already at full capacity. Blonde Cathy, who I took to Chudleigh, was admitted, it was like her second home, she had taken an axe to attack the owner of the local shop, she had also used the axe to break the window. She brought loads of hash that she had sneaked in, her ex-boyfriend had accused her of being a paedophile, towards her own child, this was the main reason for her madness, as she really had wanted a child, the lies about her made her into a nervous wreck. However, she had had her child taken away, by a biker from a gang, one of the leaders of the Aquila, was her ex-boyfriend, it is highly likely that he lied to take the baby to Spain. It seemed to me that the reason, why she was going crazy, was because someone had taken away her baby, she had explained to me in detail. Cathy was generous, she shared her hash, and she let me buy cannabis, it was night-time, and we were in the TV room.

We would hide behind the curtain, sitting on the window ledge, with the curtain shut, you could not see us hidden behind the curtains. The room would stink of hash, we would sit by the door and look down the corridor looking out for staff if they was going to walk up the person looking out would cough when staff were approaching down the corridor, we had such a great time, especially when we got together in the evening, someone ratted us out and told staff we was smoking cannabis. It was Mel.

Cathy attempted to escape with the joint, just as a nurse arrived, Cathy was giggling, running around the room, smoking a spliff, dodging the nurse, while the nurse ran after her. The nurse caught her and took her spliff away, Cathy knew how the system worked, she had been there many times over the years, she was about three years older than me.

A woman in there was trying to get off heroin while pregnant, it was so sad to see, as she seemed such a nice person, but being addicted to something was not easy, even being pregnant to try get off that. Every time she needed hash, I helped her out by getting it for her, she was one of the nice people in there on the heroin program, most of them were just horrible, but not her, she was really trying as she was carrying a baby. She had been in and out of prison, she told me, for shoplifting.

After speaking to Kelly years later, she had given it all up, for her kids, she was married, clean and did not even smoke hash anymore, she was one of the lucky ones to survive, she had done amazingly well. Cathy went on and on saying all the time that her baby had been stolen, I could tell that she was telling the truth.

They would not tell you anything about their personal lives, if it were bad, they would keep that to themselves.

Cathy would yell and cry, while telling you her story, she impersonated Marilyn Monroe, completely even with her signature blonde hair, "pretty but mad" demeanour, and love of party drugs, like ecstasy. Sarah F, although she had a poor reputation, she was a speed addict just like me, she was well known in the city for stabbing people, with a voice inside her head which told her to do some crazy things. I had heard of her name in the past in connection with being a bad girl.

However, I found her to be acceptable, she was itching and scratching as if she was hallucinating, and she was attempting to get the bugs and insects off her. I spent so much time with her, she always had a staff member beside her, she used to hold their hands. She explained to me that she stabbed people, as the voice in her head told her to do it, she was like me in many ways, as she was such a dangerous character. One of my doctors was an Indian, he was a horrible person, I complained that the medications were too potent, as I had lockjaw and had trouble keeping my mouth close, my mouth would not close properly, I could hear the muscles in my face ripping as they attempted to do so. Hilary the nurse claimed that I was lying, but that was not the case, they called an ambulance and told the dispatcher that I had an allergic reaction to the tablets. They provided a pill that was supposed to aid in the management of lockjaw, but it did not work.

The doctor was sent from the main hospital, he gave me an injection, it still did not work, hours later, I thought I was going to die. The doctor said I was allergic to the medication, he prescribed something to help me with the lock jaw, it felt amazing the buzz of the pill, I still suffered with the problem but with lesser severity compared to before, I still had the issue, even after receiving some relief from it, time went on, I struggled mightily with terrifying panic attacks.

Shaun arrived at the hospital, he would make people laugh, by singing Elvis Presley songs on his guitar. The police arrived in Glenbourne and informed me that I had received seventy-six stops, in which I was required to produce my driving license tax and insurance. Shaun had been responsible for knocking over an elderly man in the town, in addition to the fact that we had had, thirty-six fuel runs, during which we had not paid for the fuel at a variety of different petrol stations. The officer told us to hold our hands out, he gave us a friendly slap on the hands, and then informed us that Shaun and I had been exonerated of all charges. Shaun and I had hash, we even smoked it in the toilet, we would run out of the toilet as it could have been anyone who was smoking in there.

Shaun was getting increasingly ill in hospital; one night when I went to bed, Cathy was having a joint with him, staff had caught them, he had transformed himself into Bruce Lee, he had used his karate kicks to beat up the entire staff. Cathy informed me that the riot police arrived and transported Shaun to a secure facility in London, whilst I had been asleep. There was a user of heroin, her boyfriend continued to supply her with heroin even after they broke up, she was carrying an unborn child, I believed that if she took the heroin, it could kill her unborn child, I informed the staff about what was going on. I was able to help others there, especially the kind people, as some of them did not have families like I had, I engaged in conversation with them about the challenges that they faced.

Dad would come to visit, he brought me a bag full of sweets and Tobacco, played cards with me, my Gran, my niece Becky, my sister, and my brother visited. Mum and Rachel would sometimes bring lots of treats, and Tobacco, I was one of the lucky ones I had family, while many of the fellow patients did not.

I was there for about three months, during that time I was watching TV, I unbelievably saw the ginger man on the news, he was walking into court and was on trial for murder. He had left heroin on a table, and his baby had eaten it, I could not believe what I had seen on the television. After about an hour, I ran into him again in the television room. He said, "what are you looking at?' I immediately leapt from my seat, and booted him in the head, I properly laid into him with right and left punches, and more boots to the head, as he curled up into a ball. When there was a confrontation, the alarms would go off, I quickly got back into my seat and pretended that nothing had happened. He

was a large man, bigger than me, but one thing I learned through my life is it does not matter how big anyone is, it is who is the angriest or maddest on the day. He was battered and bruised, he had broken his ribs and his arm, he had been admitted to the hospital, which was next door to the mental hospital. They tossed me into the secure unit, which was called Stalford Ward in the basement, where there were only three of us, they gave me a lethal injection, when I awoke three days later, my eyes were stuck together, like glue for a few hours, I could not wake up.

There was a large built man who claimed to be God, I am God, he said in a deep husky voice. I am pleased to meet you, he said. He would not take the medication that was offered to him, he claimed that all the nurses were going to burn in hell. The nurse said, just take it and you will be out of hospital quicker, just take the medication. He said, "I'm never going to take it, I will live for eternity, I will never take it if I'm in here for the rest of my life, it doesn't matter I'm mortal, I will live forever," he claimed.

He promised me that if I played the drums and told the Queen where he was, I would receive one million pounds. He looked so serious, he was someone special, he was fit all day every day and would do sit-ups and press-ups, all day long I have never seen anyone as fit, he had such a strong physique and a bulky frame. He was in his forties assured me numerous times, that he was the all- powerful God, and that he resided beneath Buckingham Palace, where he had a television that was larger than our living space room. I could not stop questioning: "What do you mean by beating the drums for a million pounds"? He told me that I would have to investigate that matter on my own, he was forced to take the medication after initially refusing it for days, he was held down by about twenty staff who piled on top of him, he was so strong, but he gave up and was given the injection.

The doors were locked in the single rooms, so that the other patients could not get into the other bedrooms. They did not allow lighters, so we had to ask a member of staff for a lighter if we wanted to smoke.

The other man in the secure unit was a man called Charlie, he was old, about eighty with pointed ears he looked like Lucifer. I was locked up with God and the Devil it seemed, I gave Charlie a tap on the shoulder I was offering him a fag. He gave me a right hook and broke my nose but that made me breathe better, I had broken my nose before, and I had sinus problems I could breathe so much better after that. He told me that it was it was rude to tap someone on the shoulder and you should never do that to a man, when their back was turned. I was quite hurt but not from the punch, I liked him, because he was interesting to talk to, and I thought we were friends.

Charlie's two sons visited him most days in their suits, they were very smartly dressed, Charlie only smoked woodbine cigarettes, which the sons brought in for him. He had certain ways just like an old coke head, the reason he was in there was because he would make his own cocaine as he told me, Charlie was about eighty years old, was a rich man, he owned his own pharmacy in Tavistock. I spent some time in the secure unit, I was in there for three months, I never thought the door would open again. It seemed like I had been down there for a year; I could not wait to be free of this whole place. I knew though that everything was a test, just like a game, I would have to behave on the open ward before I was allowed to go home for good, and that is what I really wanted.

We had a ward round every month, which would include my nurse called big Joe, she was a little on the large side, she always told me that I would never get better. That was so true if I kept taking their zombie drugs that they were giving me, which made me so drained, I hated those feelings and side effects, but I could get better, I argued.

The psychiatrist, the Indian man was so thin, he had the biggest black eyes, said orange juice is better than amphetamine, and it gives you good energy, it is good for you. The doctor would always ask me questions like would I ever want to use amphetamine again? The answer I gave back was a big no, to tell the truth back then that is all I thought about, I could not wait to get back on it, and feel awake again. After about three months, I got back to the open ward, which seemed such a long time since I had beaten the ginger scum bag up. I was told he had moved out the day before I returned, he had been found guilty and sent to prison, I found out on a much later date.

The open ward was a completely different place as obviously there were a lot of new people, and others had moved on. I met this pretty lady about ten years older than me, she was an attractive ex heroin user, we got on well, having sneaky joints together in the garden. We listened to music together, I was told by someone that she really liked me, I could tell, as she held my hands. I was told I had to go and see the doctor, I went to see him, he informed me that he wanted to give me even more medication, I said to him, "I am not ill, I just need to stop taking drugs, if you want to know me, let me tell you my life story from a baby to this present day, then you might get to know where I went wrong, rather than feeding me up, with these evil drugs". He told me he did not think I was very well, I told him, that I was not a guinea pig, taking these evil soul killing drugs, each day, they were killing me, to the point it was stopping me from even be able to talk.

My confidence was slowly being taken away by the evil drug which has you depressed in a deep hole, so that you cannot be a danger to anyone, you can barely move, and it is a fight to stay awake, and that is where they want you. It had taken away my life and it had killed my soul. After hearing him say, "No, you are very ill, I must put you on another six-month section as your other section is nearly up, how do you feel about that"? I was drained from it all, as I thought I would be getting out. I told him he should be sectioned, and that he did not have a clue what he was doing, so I decided to sing a vicious and offensive song to him, to wind him up. I made this song up when I was younger, just to make my friends laugh, not mean offence against to anyone. I had to write something, as it would be racist if I did not, so you will have to guess what the rest was in my song. The song went ding ding everybody sing sing, listen to the something rap, there int no something in the union jack, so send that something back, he pressed the alarm on his key. When the alarm went off, the staff would come from every ward in the whole building, I was bundled to the floor. I got an injection for my troubles, which instantly sent me to sleep. Before I knew it, I woke up three days' later in that darn secure unit,

now I am stuck with God, and a woman whose name was Lynn, who was being released from a room which was like a padded cell. After having been locked in there for days while she constantly screamed. She ran through the ward with no clothes on whatsoever, it was not a nice sight. She had worked as a nurse, she had been responsible for the death of one of the patients that she had cared for, an old lady who wanted to end her life, she had asked Lyn to help her assist her to die. She claimed the elderly woman had expressed a desire to die, so she had administered an injection to kill her, I did not like her. She kept questioning why I am in the hospital was, so I finally answered her questions, by explaining why. Her brother came to visit her, he always looked down on me, like I was the devil. I was friends with one of his sons growing up, and in the same year as one of his daughters. How ironic that he, who had always considered himself to be so superior to everyone else, now the tables were turned! He gave me such a dirty look, like he always had done he used to beat his children up for nothing, a so-called Christian, a catholic wife beater, he never let his kids be kids. He was so depressed and hated me with passion, he thought that he was perfect. Now his sister had committed murder, which is what he hated, me knowing the truth, that his family were not so perfect.

Tom never stopped trying to convince me that he was God, I got on well with him as the staff always reminded him, who he really was, but the trouble was Tom really thought that he was God. There was a TV room where we watched videos, the tablets and injection made it impossible to concentrate while watching TV, you had fight to keep your eyes open, whilst the legs would shake, my arms would just flap in the air, to say I was twitchy would be an understatement, I looked such a mess. It took me about another three months before I was able to go back to the open ward, being locked up in the secure unit, was a very unpleasant experience.

On the open ward, things were much better, you could not smoke hash in the secure unit, while on the open ward it was quite easy to smoke hash, I was always thinking about amphetamine, I was an addict. I went back to the open ward, the woman that I had been getting on with, had left, I knew that she had moved on. I played football in the garden every day, I was showing off my football skills, I really had the thought of trying another go at getting back with Plymouth Argyle, I had had a bad injury to my cruciate ligament, but it was holding up. Some staff members who watched me play said, the same thing, that I should try to play football again, once I am out of hospital. I thought that if I train myself every day, anything is possible.

I was still smoking hash, and on the strongest medication, so I had no chance, but my mind saw past that and thought it was a possibility, as I was still good at football. We used to have little games, a few of us would play, and each day more patients would join in. The medication did make me feel ill, I was fighting life or giving up, what the tablets and injections were designed to do. I decided to fight on and try to get fit by going to the gym too, I joined a gym group which got me out for a few hours a week. There was a gym in the back of Union Street in Plymouth, bouncers trained in that gym, I recognized some of the bouncers who worked in the Dance Academy, I just ignored them. I was on Valium, the owner told me that I could not train at his gym on Valium as whilst taking it, it was dangerous to work out.

I asked my doctor to stop giving me the Valium tablets, as it would stop me from going to the gym, so they gave me something else to take as well as my antipsychotic drugs. I enjoyed going there, there was a little group of around fifteen of us, we used to go to the cafe next door afterwards, to have a fried breakfast, which was not ideal after doing our workout. Scouser, my friend, got chucked in, he was someone whose girlfriend had had an affair with a policeman, so he phoned the police while he was at home, poured gasoline all over his house and himself, then lit the gasoline with a Zippo lighter, he tried to burn himself as the police came through his house. Scouser was full of burns, when he arrived at the hospital, he was one of those people who always smiled even if he was feeling bad, he hid it behind his smile. He resumed his relationship with his girlfriend, and after some time, he forgave her.

I was granted a couple of hours of leave; it was eleven months after I had been first admitted. A friend called Vinnie, which was the name of the friend who I had a smoke with after Dad had dropped me off. He was missing one of his eyes, as he had suffered an eye injury. He bumped into his ex-girlfriend and her new boyfriend, out of nowhere the new boyfriend was hitting him with a baseball bat. The girl grabbed the baseball bat and smashed the bat in his eye she was the one who had hit him, in his eye Vinnie was awarded a substantial amount of compensation, however, he was living with a DJ, who I cannot mention and had stolen thirty thousand pounds from him. Vinnie lived with his Mum, she was so lovely and friendly towards me, she made me feel very welcome, and his brother Paul was sound, originally from Birmingham, Vinnie liked to drink and take Valium. They spent time together smoking hash and seemed to get along well; they were so poor that their only source of food was egg sandwiches. Dad was so kind to drop me off there but had told me to say to the staff I had been with him, I used to go back to the ward so stoned.

I have mentioned a patient at the hospital who went by the name of Tony the rocker with blonde hair. He was in his forties, he decided to hang himself by a belt on the door of his room, he did not tell anyone that he was planning to take his own life. I was shocked because Tony seemed happy the night before he died. Every four weeks, my doctor would come and do ward rounds with us, they would extend my leave or lessen it. They always told me that speed was not good for me, but I could not wait to get back on to the dangerous drug, which got me into trouble all the time, most of the people that I met in the hospital were remarkably interesting.

Cathy, with black hair, was the one starting most of the fights, she would start fights with others, whom she thought had nicked her purse or cigarettes. She would scream from the top of her voice, then attack patients who she thought had stolen from her, she would punch them and pull their hair out at the same time. She was always kind to me; she would ask for a kiss. I told her "No," but she would never take no for an answer. I started to feel rough again, with deep depression, it is not the way anyone should want to feel, but it is the doctor's job to make you feel like this for society's sake.

I was so against the injections, as it made me shake, dribble. I did not even want to speak to anyone. I just wanted to sleep my life away, there was nothing to get up for, I was in and out of bed. Then a man called John, who looked like Jesus Christ was admitted because he had jumped off the Tamar Bridge. He was shivering with lots of blankets covering him, I made him a cup of tea. He nodded his head to say thanks, as he did not talk at all. He had decided that he did not wish to continue living, but he managed to survive the eighty-foot fall into the water, where many other people had perished at this well-known bridge. He was such a meek and delicate human being, he was a fragile, scared man, he was on hunger strike and refused to eat. He wanted to die in any way possible, he could not take the pain of living. Joyce would never put her faith in anyone, but she liked me though, and often talked to only me, as I made her cups of tea, and I got her cigarettes cheaply. She was an elderly lady who would always tell everyone to fuck off and say what the fuck are you looking at.

Tony, another man, enjoyed playing role-playing games, he was a member of the Looney Party. He would dress up in bright clothes and mad big hats, he looked like the mad hatter, but he was a jovial, always laughing and a smiling individual, who was generous with both money and tobacco. Tony would often smoke a cigar, he was a man of enormous stature with a full-grown beard, very charitable.

I had panic attacks and felt like my heart was racing, unregularly fast then slow sweating and a fear of dying, I had spent my last four weeks in bed, my time had ended, after a long two years. I was free but the medication was a prison sentence, in fact worse, as the tablets took a massive control, I was free, but with no life, nor spirit, free, but a dead soul. It was the strongest, meanest, drug in the whole wide world.

The nightmares were terrible, just like being in hell, with no escape, permanently trapped, just the same as I was living. Almost immediately I was provided with a support worker after my stay in the hospital, it was her intention to help me in finding suitable housing for me. She was able to secure me a short-term apartment at Mutely Plain, there was a man who lived downstairs in the first room he said to me "I know you, but you probably don't remember me, you are now a don" he declared. He told me that he was the Godfather, and I was entitled to twenty-one wives, he was completely insane. I lived there for a while feeling so hopeless that I wanted to throw myself out of the window, I was taking Prozac and I felt so depressed they made me feel suicidal. I would just stay in bed for weeks, just lying in bed, I was totally a zombie that could not even crawl.

The medication for psychosis was too powerful for my brain to cope with, for my mental health, as well as an antidepressant, which caused me to feel ill. Dad was concerned, because no one had heard from me in two weeks, so he came pounding on my door, I did not answer the door.

All my family thought I was dead, I managed to ring him, I told him that I needed to go back to hospital, as I was obviously mentally institutionalized. All the medication had made me feel lazy, and in a permanent panic attack, the feeling paralyzed to the bed, my legs arms were shaking and my mouth constantly dribbling. I could not wait to get out the whole time I was in that hospital, now, I could not wait to go back. That was unreal as most would be going out partying or celebrating, I had lost all my friends that I previously hung around with, my confidence had been knocked right out of me, the unsecure feeling was intense. I went back to the hospital voluntarily.

My friend's brother from School a few years younger had just got a job and was staff nurse there, he was a decent lad. He was the new manager on my ward, he told me the doctor thought I was not well, I was ok apart from feeling so low, but I did not want the injection as I knew it made me feel so ill. So, when I went back to the ward, I did not say a word, I thought, if I did not say anything, they would not have any reason to give me the injection, as that was always my worst fear. The injection used to wipe my mind right out, asleep for three days, it killed my soul, I had so many nightmares about this it was so unreal, it sent me into a massive bottomless pit, where it was impossible, to get out of the deep hole of depression. So, the lad I knew from school said, you must go into a room for an injection. I told him, "Look I have come here voluntarily, I can go if I want to, you have no right in giving me that lethal injection." Him and loads of staff came from all directions, I said right, you lot stay back, I did mad karate moves with three sixty spinning kicks just missing the lad from my old school. I did not intend to hit or kick anyone, it was more a case of showing them, if anyone came any closer, this is what they would get, they all took a back step, there was a standoff for about five minutes.

The boy from school talked me into taking the dreaded injection another three days of being in darkness, I woke up feeling like I was totally drained of all my energy. The feeling was as if I had taken a thousand sleeping tablets. I spent about two boring months of being in bed, I did get up sometimes, but bed was the best place for me. I still had a sneaky joint sometimes, but the medication always made the paranoia so much worse.

Cathy with the blonde hair came into my room late, she told me to make a joint, she was buzzing; after coming back from leave she met a new Moroccan boyfriend at the bus stop. She was so excited, as she left my room she had left the three ounces of hash on my side table. I was waiting for her to come back; I was also hoping that she had not realized that she had left it in my room. I was sneaky and sly back then, I had had enough at this point, and wanted to discharge myself, with Cathy's three ounces of hash. It seemed the right time to go, if she had not left it, I think I might have stayed. The staff threatened to put me on a section as soon as I left the building.

I went to my Mums where Gran was staying, as Grandad had died, Mum let her live with her, as Gran had Alzheimer's, she was forgetting things, but she was always very upbeat. Gran was an amazing woman even though she had this dreadful illness.

After about half an hour Cathy turned up, I had only gone to the toilet and walked back down the stairs. I was totally gob smacked, Cathy was just glaring at me, saying that my Gran was so nice, she just let me in. I kept a poker face and said, "Hello Cathy, you left your smoke on my table, staff found it and chucked me out," she said, "you are surely joking." "Nope I am gutted," I said, "plus I have nowhere to stay it has totally done my nut in" I said, that hash has landed me in big trouble. She looked at me like she did not believe me, but. She could not prove I was lying either, so I managed to get away with that.

I had help from a social worker who found me temporary accommodation, until I eventually had my own council property in the same area of Plymouth where my mum lived. The location was lovely, offering stunning views of the woods. After settling into my new flat, I felt a sense of freedom. Although the accommodation was pleasant, I started taking amphetamine again, to pull myself out of the depression, so I decided to stop taking the medication.

Shaun had been discharged from the hospital, I had been on amphetamine for about a month and started to feel alive again, it was the only way out I thought.

Ashley had a nice tan as his dad was Spanish, he brought a girl to my flat. She was already on a mad one before she came to my flat according to Ashely, she had taken far too many drugs and was on amphetamine and had tripped out. She shouted from the top of her voice, "get the fuck out of my flat." She went to get a knife out my kitchen drawer, Ashley stopped her, we phoned for an ambulance, where I believe that she herself was eventually taken to Glenbourne. I warned Ashley that the drug was extremely dangerous as he was under the influence of amphetamine as well, he had just started taking the evil drug we liked him, I tried to dissuade him, we told him how evil the drug was, and we tried our best to put him off. I told him that he did not want to be like me, to have no future and end up in mental hospitals. Even though Shaun and I both took some of it with him that day, we still called his Mum to let her know that her son was on it.

Ashley went to the hospital to check on the girl and make sure she that she was ok, Ashley was one of the only people to ever listen to us, and his mother knew so least he had a chance of a life rather than being a nobody, whilst being on the crap that I was taking. Ashley eventually became a care assistant for the elderly, and after that was a porter and then a nurse at the hospital.

After that, Mat and Mark came to my flat, I had no sleep for a few weeks, I had started to hallucinate again, I looked around and saw what looked like green luminous spiders, they were massive, they would light up, crawling around the walls and on the carpets. I asked Shaun if he had seen the spiders and Shaun said that he had seen them too. He was covered in the spiders crawling up his legs, I booted Shaun so hard in the leg. Shaun screamed "why boot me"? I said, "I'm only trying to get the spiders off you," he could not really see the spiders, he was just going along with me, he later said. Eventually the spiders went away after that freaky hour, I then attempted to make a roll-up, but the tobacco transformed into wriggling worms.

I tried and tried but it was so hard to make a roll up, after many attempts, I made it, but the worms were making a popping sound as I smoked it tasted vile. Shaun stayed around for the night on the sofa, he attempted to go to sleep, I was talking to him and did not let him sleep. He told me "You have not shut up for twenty-four hours, he was right, I could not stop talking, I always buzzed too much on amphetamine, but my trouble was I always had no sleep.

Chapter 18. The Conspiracy of Shadows

Then two days passed, it was a spooky night, the wind was blowing, the tree was shaking and there was thunder and lightning. I ran out of electricity, I was alone, a spirit jumped out from the trees and into my body, I felt strange. I looked out the window and saw lots of black shadows walking down the street, it resembled me to be lost souls. The following night after a day with no electricity I decided to walk to my mom's house, a five- minute stroll away, I saw spirits everywhere. I thought she could be at my Auntie and Uncle's house which was a ten to fifteen minutes' walk. I walked there; a cat walked with me for five minutes, there was another cat, it was a long walk up the steep hill, which in turn took me to a third cat, I was escorted by the cat gang, my Aunties and Uncles' cat was the last cat to join me and the rest of the cats. I knocked on their door, hoping they knew where Mum was, but it was quite late in the evening. My Uncle leaned out the bedroom window, he told me he had not heard from Mum and that they both had to get up early, for work.

The plan was for me to walk back to Mum's house, I kept to the road, I saw a spirit crossing the road in front of me. It was pure black, the same shape as a human, but it seemed so real, it was as if I was seeing lost souls, many different spirits. I eventually got to my Mum's house no one was there, I didn't have a clue where she was, nor my Gran I made a roll up, I looked up to the top of my Mum's drive, this beast of a spirit was looking at me, waving a gun, pointing it at me. This spirit was so scary looking, it was bigger built than all the rest that I had ever seen, I really thought it was the end of my life. I honestly thought I was going to die. I jumped over Mum's fence, there is a lane of fields and woods which were quite near to Glenbourne, and Derriford Hospital, so I made a dash up there, as that was the only place that I could think of, to go for help. The spirits were on the banks, in the trees, looking down on the road, on me, with guns, pointing at me, as they were terminating me, suddenly the dark shadows started chasing me through the dark lane. I got to the main road, I ran to the mental hospital, and pounded on the doors, and demanded entry.

After that, a malevolent spirit crept up at me and I could feel the sawed-off shotgun in the stomach, I looked down, I watched as the bullet tore a hole in my stomach and entered my body, I flew in the air and was in complete darkness just as if I was dead. The next morning, I woke up in the hospital with Jackie and Mel, they were cuddling me, and said that they thought that I must have been having nightmares, as apparently, I had been going simply crazy in my sleep. Mel would have been a good nurse, she kept her promise to Mum, the very first time that she saw her that she would look after me, she told me not to worry. I had no idea how I got there, nevertheless, after a while I remembered everything, the last thing I was able to recall was being shot at. Jackie watched the CCTV and said it looked dramatic, she said, I took off in the air before laying there like I was dead, she added it looked like something out of a film.

Mel was so kind to me and always kept to her promise to Mum and watched out for me. When she noticed that I was associating with undesirables, she reprimanded me, around new people, there were more distinct characters to be found. One of them, named Phil, appeared to be a wizard, some sort of sorcerer, we got on well, he had a thing for crystals. Phil informed me that a lot of people were carrying crystals with them, these people believed the crystals radiated a unique energy, he had the best crystal which were thousands of years old, he said that one day he would let me hold it. He kept going on about his Mum who had died, and that his dad who was in the Navy had remarried and had a new family, but his dad had abandoned him. He was terribly upset just losing his Mum, he had found life exceedingly difficult back then, but he was so clever.

Old Cathy acted exactly like a witch, she presented me with a present a red crystal that, according to her, would provide me with a great amount of energy, I did not believe her until I tried it for myself and realized that it worked. The crystal helped me feel much more energized till unfortunately I lost it a few days later. Taking the pills, especially in combination with the injection, made me feel extremely sick, however, it was a necessity for them to carry it out, to make me better. I looked around and saw souls and dark spirits everywhere, all of them walking past me just as we do.

Voices were constantly surrounding me, one of them being Chopper. The phone started to ring, there was no need for me to answer it, as I was resting in bed, Dad received a call from Chopper. The telephone was located down the hall, it was for the purpose of Dad. Chopper took Dad to be crucified in a cell, from my bed I listened to it, and it was pure terror as I bizarrely saw everything. Dad was yelling and screaming as each nail hit his hands and went into the wall. The disturbing sound of the phone rang again, it was Mum's turn to be crucified. I ran and told a member of staff what was going on with the spirits mocking me, while they haunted me. Jackie was always there for me, she reassured me that it was just my mind playing tricks, and that I should call my family to see if they were all okay. They were all fine, it was a huge relief to hear and know that. I saw things that just were not there, because drugs had frazzled my brain, or those things that I had seen, were just lost souls. To put it simply, they were so real to me at the time, more likely though that I was psychotic, from too many drugs and the no or little sleep. The mind is extremely sensitive, the voices after many months seemed to disappear, hopefully I was back on the road to recovery.

John Leman was sectioned a mad scientist in his late sixties, a thin man with enormous intelligence, but he was also crazy, but in a funny way to make people laugh with jokes and his mad way. He would say, "My name is John 007 licensed to thrill 'he said this to most of the ladies. He knew which plants to smoke to achieve the desired psychedelic effects, he had these plants in his garden that were from China. I smoked a leaf from this plant and the effect was very tense, a trippy effect it felt like my vision was blurry and it made me feel so sick, it I thought I was going to die. I gave John a game of chess, he told me that he never lost a game, I could play chess quite well but got destroyed by his intelligence.

After waiting for a while, I finally started going back to the gym and playing football again. I was on the verge of getting out again, when suddenly I was given a couple of hours of leave, the first stage of getting out. They do this as part of their process, a few hours' leave leads to five hours or more, all the time till eventually leading to freedom. Tom thought it was not right to call him Tom, as it was God and that was it. Tom was also on the open ward downstairs; he also had some leave; Shaun was back in hospital he had some leave, too. Phil, Shaun, Tom, and I made our way to my flat, which was about a twenty-minute walk to the other side of the woods. Mat was in the company of Mark and came to my flat friends from the estate.

Tom remarked on what a unique opportunity it would have been to share a joint with the Lord. He stated that the opportunity to have a joint with God is not one that arises every day. Everyone burst into laughter, I rolled a joint, Tom said that "it was only right because he was God, he should light the joint" Tom was having a good time, he kept insisting that he was the all-powerful God, that we were privileged to be in his company with him getting stoned. He told us that he could make thunder at any time, so we all asked him to make it thunder. "However, the medication had a negative side effect and reduced some of his abilities," Tom said. He stated that it was important for him to investigate the forest, trying to change the conversation. He said "let us go out to explore the woods" as he looked out my back-room window, it was an amazing view of the woods.

The most advantageous route for us was to walk back through the woods to Glenbourne, to keep Tom happy, we walked him through the Forrest, he kept laughing saying this was all his creation, listen to the sound of birds they talk to me he said we eventually got back. Tom was like he was an eccentric time traveller from the past.

A week later it was a sad day. Nicky was a close friend, especially in my youth I still used to visit from time to time, he was an addict who used heroin. It was a terrible irony that he died of a drug overdose, just after becoming a father for the first time, he was found with his cousin in a car on the moors. His cousin did wake up in hospital, the first time for him after that experience it was his last, I had the privilege of growing up with Nicky.

I was supposed to be released the next day; Phil had told me about the hallucinations produced by the crystal that he possessed. He assured me that it was the most potent crystal that could be found anywhere in this world, it was the same as taking an acid tab, I did not believe him, that it could make me hallucinate. He held it for the first two minutes, after which Phil started to laugh, I stupidly said, let me have a go on holding this magical crystal. We were sitting on a bench in the garden, he advised me not to hold it for longer than two minutes.

After I held it for two minutes I bolted with the crystal whilst Phil was chasing me around the garden. I managed to keep it in my hand for about five minutes, I handed it over to him again. We went back to the wooden bench and sat watching the trees which had transformed into elephants that waved at me. For a long time, I was hallucinating. I thought the nurses were flirting with me licking their lips, I went back to the garden and all the patients were getting off with each other in the garden. I honestly tripped out and thought we were in a porn movie.

I stupidly went to a woman manager as she was flirty with me, I hallucinated, but said with all the cameras everywhere that we were in a porn movie. The manager made a nurse give me a tablet, she could see I was tripping, I told her that I had held a crystal, and I was tripping my box off. They informed me that I was in no condition to leave the hospital, I was stuck there for yet another six-month section, I felt trapped and wished I had never touched the crystal, those crystals were dangerous, well the one he had certainly was.

A few days past I went to the cafe and bought a Kit-Kat, the wrapper said winner in gold writing inside the red wrapper, was gold instead of silver, it was a genuine winner, I won a holiday to Saint Lucia. I showed it to the ladies who worked in the café and asked them if it was a winner. They went as far as telling me that I had won but I could not go on holiday as I was stuck in Glenbourne, they offered me good money for the wrapper, I warned them not to disclose any information to anyone about this. They treated me well, I had no trouble with them, as they had told me they would not tell a soul, I knew I could trust them, it was my intention to escape and flee. Glenbourne at the time was close to an airport which was located a short distance up the road, a mile away.

I had some money, but I was not thinking straight but at the time, I devised a plan to flee to Saint Lucia by first flying to London, and then continuing by air. The building had two sets of doors which both had security locks to get through. I was able to have a good relationship with the security guard, we shared a lot of laughs together, he was in his later years, I was aware that I could run quicker than him. I was keeping an eye out for a visitor, one would eventually show up, he opened the door by pressing a button, I often went out and chatted to him, so he did not expect me to run. I legged it so fast while the security man pursued me, he was faster than I thought, but eventually he gave up, I made a mad dash for the airport I bought a ticket for the flight.

I sat in the waiting room remembering that I was terrified of flying, I got on the plane trembling, but they could tell that I was sick from the way I looked, the police arrived. I did not even have a passport, so there was no way I could go on the holiday, I would have needed a passport but back then, I was in a psychotic world and not in the real world at all, but it was a winning ticket.

 They took me to the local police station, I was put in a cell for a short while, I looked everywhere for the wrapper, but I could not find it. The police must have taken the wrapper and never given it back to me, the police eventually took me back to the hospital and back to the ward, I was quite shocked that I was not put downstairs in the secure unit. Even though going to the garden was out of the question for me, I was always being watched. Mel was engaged in a fight with another patient, so she was taken to a Secure Unit by the riot police when they arrived. I got along well with Terry, he had blonde hair, he was on the short side, but friendly he was addicted to heroin, and spoke with a London accent loud and proud. He was a good friend there over time, Terry did not scab anything, he was the decent sort, trying to kick the habit.

Hilary, the staff nurse, well she looked like a German scientist, she was so strict, always telling me that I looked ill. I was stoned too, but it always upset me the word you are ill, she was rude to me, I told Terry that I was going to grab the needle out of her hands, when she tried giving me the injection. I was serious, I was going to inject her, I wanted to see if Hilary would feel ill, after that lethal drug entered her bloodstream. I went to grab the injection; when Hilary came to inject me, Terry stopped me and grabbed my arms, lucky she thought we were messing around. Hilary was just being traditional in her strictness; I was finally able to have a good relationship with her. Hilary was right, my psychosis was bizarre, I started seeing sprits, just walking freely in the garden, walking through walls. The usual black souls seemed like they were the lost souls, they even sat in the TV room watching television. The atmosphere was scary I thought they had come to kill me, then the worst possible voice had returned Chopper saying I must pay for my sins, everything was getting too much for my brain, my hallucinations were out of this world. I told Jackie that I was hallucinating badly, with threats that I was going to be killed with Chopper, waving a gun. Jackie got me a blue pill to help me to calm down, it made me even more crazy. I was having a massive panic attack and was having the worst hallucinations. This poor British African lady just started her first shift, she stood by the door where it was the only way out of the ward. I could not breathe, I was getting locked muscles in my jaw, I desperately needed air, I asked whether it would be possible for me to do a roll-up on the balcony which was about ten steps past her in the green cage. She told me I had to stay, and I could not go for a roll up on the balcony. I looked at her, she had a pair of red boxing gloves on and transformed into Mike Tyson, I walked back down the hallway towards the TV room. Chopper commanded me to knock out Tyson as if he were holding a remote control over my head, I took a big run up, I punched her on the jaw, but it was the face of Mike Tyson in my psychotic episode. The unfortunate lady hit her head on the door, from the impact of my punch, and the poor lady passed out on the ground knocked out cold. I would never have done this, if it were not for the voice, who pushed me over the edge. The real cause and route of the problem being my use of drugs, the evil speed, no sleep this would never have happened if I had not used drugs. Unbeknown to me at the time, she had gone to the hospital with a broken jaw, and was on a life support machine, and in a coma for three months.

Loads of staff had to bundle me on the floor, to give me an injection, while the riot police then carried me downstairs, with cuffs to my legs and to my wrists to the Secure Unit. I was placed in what appeared to be a cell but was in fact a padded room, I was having some intense hallucinations at the time, so I was trapped. There was a laser gun with blue and red lights on the ceiling wall directly above me, the laser gun was moving up and down the ceiling, was out to kill me.

Chopper told me the rules, I had to make a pointed gun out of my hands, to stop the laser from relishing its fire onto me, if I did not keep my finger pointing at the laser to block it from firing, it would kill me, it was constantly on the move. Chopper was making fun of me and laughing, for twenty-four hours my arm was killing, as I constantly had my hands locked as a gun following the laser gun around, I had to keep an eye on it. It would move in a crosshatch pattern, across the ceiling, moving in various directions constantly, after three days the laser finally disappeared, like it had never been there. I was back to banging on the door, begging for a Roll-up, after five days in that padded room. They were trying to transfer me to Broadmoor, but there were no beds available, Broadmoor housed the most dangerous people in the country. I was so lucky that Broadmoor was full. They did not know what to do with me, they tried a place in London, a high security institution, but the beds were also full.

I very luckily snapped out of it and was so apologetic about what I had done, they knew I was not myself and it was out of my normal character, they went beyond for me and gave me one last chance. I was taken over by a malevolent power that is certainly what it seemed, it was bad psychosis, but to me at the time, it felt like I had been taken over by one hell of an evil spirit. They knew that if they had told me what I had done to the nurse, I would not have been able to cope with the information, so they withheld that from me, for two years. I had been responsible for that horrible deed, that poor lady had only been working for a single day. I had come very dangerously close to killing her, I would then have been a murderer.

It was a good thing that I did not end up in jail, like some of the other people there, for getting locked up for assaulting the staff, for much less than I had done.

The mind is so sensitive, hearing voices or hallucinating can be so difficult to control, although I am aware that the voice can take control of the situation, there was nothing I could do to stop it, when it chose to, it could exercise control at any time. Psychosis for that individual person is like a matrix world, illusions and hearing voices are very real to them, and them only. Almost six months passed while I was in that Secure Unit, I had no hope that the door would open for me this time, even though I was feeling down, I knew that I deserved everything that was coming my way.

There was a gipsy lady called Debbie from the hippy town of Totnes, she was kind to me despite her nomadic lifestyle, she only had one breast due to cancer. She was an amazingly talented painter; she would do lots of drawings to an extremely high standard. She told me that oak leaves acted the same way as amphetamines, she told me that she made leaf juice, which produced an extremely high buzz, but that only oak tree leaves had this effect, she told me to eat the leaves the next time that I saw an oak tree. She would frequently expose her breast to get a laugh out of me, in addition to that, she was a spiritual medium and could read palms.

Mel was also present in the Secure Unit. She was ill from the injection, she looked so tired and drained she was not the same person that I knew of before, it was like she had no energy whatsoever, it was hell for twelve months it seemed like ten years I was finally back on the open ward.

Jerry was the name of the key worker I had, he reminded me of Jerry Kyle, he even looked like Jerry Kyle. Jerry was an ex-police officer who worked in Exeter before he took on this job, he was a good guy and assisted me in getting back into shape after I severely injured my knee before, from having an old injury to my ACL, in my knee. I needed surgery, but I had chickened out of the operation, he assured me that he would help me to build up my knee to be stronger. I trusted him as he seemed quite sure that he could help me to build my knee up, without surgery. He took me swimming twice a week to the local swimming pool and told me that if I behaved myself and stopped getting into trouble, he would help me get back into shape, so that I could join the football team that played at the Civil Service Club in Plymouth. He helped me get into shape, and I really enjoyed playing five-a-side football, there was a man that came to play, he travelled all the way from Dawlish. He was incarcerated for the crime of murder in a secure unit, in Dawlish. Swilly, Plymouth, he said he had been attacked by several people, he hit someone with an exhaust pipe in self-defence, and then killed the person who attacked him. As he was so kind and pleasant, it was so exceedingly difficult to believe that he could cause harm to anyone. After being committed to the mental institution for the past fourteen years, he was getting remarkably close to being released.

We were going to have to take turns choosing our teams, as he was the captain of the opposing team. A few of the staff members who played as well believed that because I played so well, I could have still been at least a semi pro player, Jerry was a member of the Exmouth team. He played once down there, he was a skilful player, he helped me to get better and fit, I joined a snooker group, went fishing, and went to the gym, I would do anything to get out of that hospital.

Jason was admitted to the hospital with his ginger hair and bright yellow T-shirt on, he was about thirty-six stone, and twenty-one years old and high on loads of ecstasy. When he heard my CD player playing Trance music his mouth began to vibrate, and his eyes were massive. They began to wobble; he was dancing with his arms everywhere in the air. He then shouted, "easy groove is in the house." There was a huge bookshelf dangerously right in the middle of the TV room, Jason was jumping and dancing to the music, he then crashed into the bookshelf. Under the bookshelf, there was a young lady seated, I was successful in catching the huge unit. If I had not caught it would have knocked her out. He was shouting we are all spies in here, he said we are all grasses in here, he made me laugh my head off. He told me there was one big mafia family in here, he added that only the very select few were allowed in the mental hospital. We played football, for such a large young man, he was incredibly fast, we had a race from one end of the garden to the other end, the garden was huge. I only just managed to beat him, and I was fast. He was also a fast boxer, he showed me his moves, as I was sparring with him, he was so dangerously fast for a massive heavyweight. He loved KFC, his Mum always bought it in for him, it was his favourite, he was just a big teddy bear, as well as being someone who could look after himself, but was a big baby. He was nice to everyone, he was polite, he was so sensitive. When his Mum left, he started crying, please do not leave. "I will come back tomorrow," she used to have to say, the same thing every visit. He used to go into baby mode and made her promise that she would come back the following day.

After a few weeks passed, we sat and listened to some music, at the opposite end of the television room was a man who introduced himself as Ian, he thought that he was hard. Trance music by Paul van Dyke was playing on a little cd player, we danced to the beat, we were having an enjoyable time. While doing so, Ian was reading a book, he was there attempting to wean himself off heroin, and said, "Turn off that fucking annoying music, if you don't want me to be the one to silence you." After leaping from his seat and seizing his opportunity, Jason sprinted down to the other side of the room, he laid right and left hooks into Ian's face.

Ian tried to punch back but Jason was electrifyingly fast, with about twenty punches to his head, Jason picked up the big armchair which was so heavy and violently smacked him over the head about ten times with the chair. Ian just lay on the floor, the staff came running in, me and Jason, both told them that Ian had started the fight. Luckily for Jason, he did not get sent downstairs. If that had been me, I would have been placed there, in the Secure Unit in a flash. He did not receive any punishment, I was glad Jason had not get sent down there, as he was fun to be around.

We ordered two pizzas from a local Pizza King to be delivered, we did not have any money. Our devious plan was to grab the pizzas from the boy, as he got the pizza out of the bag at the entrance of our ward, we managed exactly as planned, we legged it to our room, we ate the large pizza's laughing our heads off, we had the munchies, but we knew only too well, that we would be in trouble. There was so much commotion, staff telling us the police would be called if we did not pay, we did not really care if the police came, but in the end, we got our parents to pay the bill. Jason stated that he was from Swilly, he told me that his mother dealt in firearms, he was ill if he made that up, or did deal in them, it was extremely hard to tell, if he was telling the truth? It made me extremely suspicious. Jason's Mum communicated with a different Shaun than whom I was familiar with, because of my heightened paranoia, I was convinced that she had given him a gun. I was under the impression that the gun was coming for me, I was not feeling well at all, and because of my irrational fears about things that did not exist, I was unable to fall asleep at night. This went on for an entire week, with me expecting him to shoot me, as I was so sure that he had a gun on his possession. One evening, as he sat opposite me, I said "Shaun come on then let us fucking have it," as I leaped up from my seat. He pleaded with me not to hit him, he was so terrified of me, I felt so bad for him, as he was such a nice lad. I explained to him that I thought he had a gun. But after speaking to him, I just knew that it was the psychosis that had gotten the better of me, he understood, I could tell he was not the fighting type of person, I had gotten it all wrong. I got on well with him, after that he did not say much, but most of us were quiet as the medication was designed to sedate us.

Maggie was certainly not quite, an elderly lady in her sixties who mumbled a million words in an hour, but I had a good relationship with her. She was fine for weeks with me, then one day I sat next to her, she suddenly punched me full pelt in the ear, right whilst we were in the middle of conversation. She yelled at the other people, that she would have Gypsy Joe shoot them, Gypsy Joe, was a man that Maggie claimed, she was having an affair with.

 This bird had a mental breakdown, she followed me everywhere, she was about ten years older, she was rich, a psychologist from Luton. She talked about her boyfriend in Luton, but he was a player, always going off with other women. She was insecure phoning him all the time, she was all over me, like a rash, she would not stop feeding me up with energy drinks, crisps and chocolates, I thought she was kind but annoying at the same time. I had some leave and so did she, she offered to buy me an ounce of hash, I took her to the woods by my Mum's house, we smoked hash together. I took her to see Mum, after we had a smoke, Mum said, she did not have any electricity left, she asked if I would go to the shop to get electric, for her top up key. We both walked to the shop, she grabbed the key from me, she put fifty pounds on the electric key. I said, "you cannot do that." She said that she had thousands in the bank. Mum said the same, "you cannot do that but thanks so much for your kindness."

Two weeks had past she would not leave me alone. She kissed me, she wanted to be more than just friends. I did not want what she wanted; she was starting to get on my nerves. She was just pouring Red Bull down my throat, she always tried to make me stay up late, I needed my rest, but she would not let me have it. I was attempting to rest; she would not allow me to go to sleep. She banged on my door, it lit my fuse, I exploded like a bomb, I booted the door without realizing that she was on the other side of it, I sent her flying in the air, smashing her head into the wall, she just laid on the floor, I ran and got a staff member. I walked past her room. The door was open with a doctor had a stethoscope listening to her stomach, she was carrying an unborn baby, but had failed to disclose her pregnancy to me, sadly, she lost the unborn baby. I was so sad that I kicked that door, I had to live with that guilt, it was not good, I apologized, she did not blame me as she knew, she should not have come in my room.

Then, the familiar terror voice of Chopper ringing through my ears again, he constantly managed to make me into a ticking bomb, with his devilish demands.

I heard from many people that Steve was one of the toughest men in Plymouth, even though he was a nice guy, was of big build, he played for the Bugle Football Team, the same team that I did, when I was a teenager, we got on well, he was known as a hard gentle giant, he was in his thirties but still lived with his Mum. Steve liked his beers too much, which caused depression and that is why he had been admitted to hospital. I had a hallucination that Mum was sitting next to him. The voice of Chopper told me to hit him, I ran down the corridor at full speed, and gave him the hardest punch I could muster, it was unbelievable, that his head did not even move at all, he was still wearing his glasses at the time. I really liked him. I would never have done something like that, if it were not for the terrorizing voice, it always had a hold on me. I was moved to the secure unit once more, hallucinating was the last thing that I wanted, when Chopper started to mess with my head, there was nothing in the world that I could do about it.

I had to stay there for three- four months before being allowed to move back onto the open ward, I expressed my total regret to Steve, as I had gotten along with him so well, he knew I had not been well, he was genuinely nice about it. He also said that it was a hell of a punch and told me that I had broken his jaw, but it was much better, now. I was able to regain my health and return to normal although I did not get put back down the secure unit again. I was on the open ward for another three months, before being released back into society.

After only a few weeks I was back to my sly ways, dealing hash, taking the awful amphetamine. I had sworn to myself that I would never steal anyone else's drugs again, as it had gotten me into so much trouble. Danny, a boy from my old school, was with another guy named Justin, a heroin user, who was frequently arrested for stealing, and burglary offences, in and out of jail, all his life. I ended up on the heroin for a while whilst hanging around with him. There was a young man selling hash who seemed quite vulnerable, and simple to steal from. I was getting hash for a good month he trusted me, I then asked to buy a bar of hash.

In the back of my car was Danny and Justin, I have never, and will never stab anyone, but for some reason, waved a knife, I told him that if he did not give me the hash. I just grabbed the hash and said "you have been taxed by the TCE" stupidly while he sat in my car, I told him to get out of my car, he left. I gave Justin and Danny both half of what I had stolen to share between themselves. Justin said that "no one had ever given me something for nothing." He was nice to me, but a ruthless thief, he went into superstores with a syringe full of heroin. If security tried to stop him and his girlfriend with a shopping trolley full of food, he would pull the syringe full of heroin, and threaten them with saying do you want catch aids. Then he would just run with his girlfriend to the car, he they well known for doing this at the time, eventually he went to prison, I never saw him again after that. I returned to my flat, when I was with Andy, John who was about three years younger than me, of big build, told us that he was the hardest in Plymouth for his age. I opened the door to my apartment, there were a bunch of meatheads standing behind me, around twenty of them, standing there, John and Andy ran away. A man tapped me on the shoulders, he was on some serious drugs, he had the biggest eyes and on angel dust or something, he punched me right in the jaw, I was knocked out and seeing stars, but on my feet. Everything went black with flashes of lightning in my head, it took me a few seconds to come around. Then I was dragged up the stairs to my front room, this older man had a knife to my throat, the one who punched me was asking me questions, he told me to return the hash, but I told them I had none left. This well-known older man was still holding a knife to my throat, I had sold it all and spent the money, I did have a few ounces left, but it was not worth saying I had any.

My front room was full of meatheads, about twenty in total, they told me I would be going for a drive on the moors, I had to think quickly, so I suggested that they took my car as payment. He said "no." I said, "Dad will give me the money if you let me phone him." He said, "go on phone your dad." I rang him about the money, I yelled down the phone to get up there quickly. I swiped the knife out of the meat head hands and said, "Come on then lets fucking have it" chasing all twenty men out of my flat. Fortunately for me, they had already escaped from the area, Andy and John went looking for weapons but came back with sticks, it was too late, they said otherwise we would have helped, some hard boy, you are John I thought. Dad waited in the car park all night with a baseball bat, just in case they returned during the night, I spent the night at Andy's place.

A few weeks later I still had not learnt from my mistakes, I was spending time together with Vinnie, he told me about a man named Henry who was addicted to speed, Henry was a bad person, he was a short, pudgy man and had no hair. Even though Shaun had been discharged from the hospital, he was with me when we met Henry, but Shaun chose to return home because he did not like Henry. He told me he never trusted him and got a bad vibe. Henry told me he could get some nice amphetamine, so I decided to go with him, he injected it, which is something I would never do, I would eat it or sniff it instead, but he was a hard-core user.

Henry was not a particularly good person, he had been in and out of prison for being a thief and he had been convicted of stealing, multiple times. He took advantage of me by buying some amphetamine, which led to my downfall, I ended up injecting it the first and last time I tried that. I spent the day chatting and hanging out with him. We went into town, and we each got a beer while we were there, he introduced me to his friend, who was with an extremely attractive woman. She was with a male friend, but she was single, she was the most stunningly beautiful person I had ever laid eyes on, she told me that my eyes were incredibly beautiful. We rode on a bus to Efford, she gave me an enthusiastic kiss. I fell instantly in love with her, she cuddled me, and we were completely close, we were like a boyfriend and a girlfriend instantly. I asked her if we could meet for a drink later in the evening, she said she would love that. I had no money but thought I could borrow from Mum; this was the woman of my dreams.

Henry came with me and waited at my flat, as I was planning to ask Mum to borrow the money, I simply could not believe my good fortune. She was so gorgeous, she had a mixture of Native Indian blood like I do, but she was the most beautiful girl that I had ever seen in Plymouth. I knew she was the one for me, Henry and I were both famished, so I went to see Mum. I explained that I was going out with a girl, but that I was short of cash, so I asked if I could get some food. Mum said, "What exactly are you doing"? I did not say anything, I sneaked away to get some food out of the fridge, she asked again, "what are you doing"? and informed me that I was not permitted to have anything. I was not able to go out with the woman of my dreams, so I went completely insane.

I kicked Mum's fridge, she threatened that she would call the police. After I had returned to my apartment, Henry would not stop talking. I kicked and punched the door to my bathroom, there was the largest hole, there was nothing left of the door. I ripped it to shreds. I told him that if he did not shut up, moaning, he would be getting it like the door, Henry got up and left. My Mum and sister had arrived at the scene, she implied that I was not feeling well, and threatened to call the authorities on me, I told them that were in my apartment, but I had complete freedom to do just as I please. "Can you leave"? I asked. She did not leave, I said "I am going to put my head through the window." Before I knew it, the police had arrived with a doctor who was an American.

His name was Dr Coco Cabana. I said, "you are taking the mick, which is not your real name." He told me it was, and he wanted me to return to the hospital. I said, "no way there is nothing wrong with me." The Dr left; the police told me that I had to go to the hospital. I said, " Can I have a few bongs, they had no choice in the matter, so they let me have my last smoke of Hash.

Those police personal was nice and kind to me, I pulled about three bongs in a row, in front of a room full of police, I got to the hospital and went straight to the secure unit. A man with a northern accent put some pills in my hand and told me to take the medication, I held the pills tightly in my hand, I was so extraordinarily strong. He was trying to open my hands, he was a big man, but I would not let him, he had been trying for at least half an hour of trying to get them back out of my hands, he must have called for assistance as I decided to take the pills, when loads of staff turned up. I thought about the woman of my dreams 24/7. I constantly had her beautiful face in my mind, I thought about what it could have been like together with her. It hurt like mad, like you would not believe, my soul was ripped apart, I would never get to meet anyone like that again.

I was in the Secure Unit for about four months, it was pure torture. This man called Brian, listened, and sang in his Yorkshire accent to Frank Sinatra, all the time in the smoking room. It did my nut in, he was a murderous person, which was all I knew about him, I did not like him he was rude. One day told he told me to fuck off after I had turned the radio on to the dance channel. I leapt right out of my seat and gave him an uppercut too, his nose split open. He legged it to his room, I went and told the staff that he had attacked me. He went to the nearby general hospital to have his nose stitched up. I did not get punished, I found out that he had killed a child in Yorkshire. Every day I looked at him, I thought about that poor girl, I could have strangled him. I did have that thought, but thought he is not worth doing time for. If I had killed him, it would have been an effortless way out for him, whereas I would be stuck in places like this for the rest of my life.

I managed to get back onto the open ward, there were some new faces, and some people had left. Jerry would take me to football every Tuesday, I liked doing this and enjoyed playing five a side, Thursday was snooker which I also liked to do. Phil had committed suicide by jumping off the Tamar Bridge, his dad had not wanted anything to do with him, he had often talked to me about it. I was upset as Phil was such a nice person. I met a man called Mark, he was on a different ward, he was up for a football game every day, we played every day. I went up for a header with him, he elbowed me on the head and nearly knocked me out. We had a little five-a-side match in the garden, and Mark looked like my dad, I kept on saying you are my dad's brother. He said "no, I live on the moors." He sure did look like him, I got on well with him and always sat next to him in the garden. He was an alcoholic but told me he so fancied a drink, but also told me he could not drink again and had to stay off it. He asked me to sneak some in, but then he changed his mind as he would be in serious trouble. He explained that he was badly on it before, although he was tempted, he knew that he had to stay clean.

There was a TCE lad in the garden, he was related to an Argyle player he was a quiet lad. I could not understand why Mark was in the hospital, there seemed to be nothing wrong with him. I asked him what his reason was for being placed in hospital as there seemed nothing wrong with him, apart from being a funny character to be around. He did not trust anyone, especially TCE, he told me that he had feared the football firm. He said he knew that I was in the football gang but had trust in me, he told me he felt safe with me. He said, there is one on the bench beside us, but the quiet TCE lad left the garden. I said just tell me he told me he could not tell anyone and said "no, I cannot say why I am in here." I said, "you can trust me, I am your friend I promise not to tell anyone." He told me that he had never told anyone, he said a woman and a man were fighting after drinking two big bottles of vodka in his flat. He told me that the woman went mad after she had a drink and would not leave the man alone with her mental abuse.

The lady had stabbed her boyfriend, a couple of weeks before this, nine times in the chest. Her boyfriend had lied saying that he had held the knife that she was holding and stabbed himself, to get her off all the charges because the boyfriend loved her. They were arguing about what had happened a few weeks prior to this evening, her boyfriend said "stay away, you are a dangerous person" she was in his face, there was blood everywhere as they were fighting yet again. Mark had tried to break the fight up by hitting the man with a frying pan, this had killed the man. He told me hitting the man with the frying pan was the only way they would stop. He told me that I was the only person that he had ever told me, and I could please not tell anyone. If the boyfriend pressed charges against her, she would have been in jail for stabbing him two weeks before this dreadful night, and none of this would have happened.

My Dad came knocking on the window from above the garden, he took me out on leave, I was only allowed out with my parents. I told Dad the story that Mark had just told me, he drove me onto the moors as far as Dartmoor Prison, he told me if I did not start to behave myself, I would end up in prison myself, Dad then returned me to the hospital.

A few weeks later, Michelle kept driving me mad she always called me by the name of Thomas, that we were great lovers. It drove me mad as the Thomas thing really did make me angry. She stunk because the staff never gave her or made her have a bath, all the time that I was there in hospital She would not let it rest, I heard the voice of Chopper telling me to kill her, and when he came into my head, I would explode. I picked her up in her wheelchair and tried to throw her out of the window. It was a significant drop to the garden; thank God her wheelchair and her bounced off the bullet proof window and did not go through it. Otherwise, she would have been dead, she was in pain on the floor lopsided in her a wheelchair, I snapped out of the psychotic episode, I said" oh no what have I done", I picked her up and went and told the staff member exactly what I had done.

Once more I was taken to the Stalford Ward, Mark was in the Secure Unit, I do not know why I shouted, "I am going to kill you," and I went to beat him up. He ran into his room and locked the door; they moved him onto another ward. I was in there for three months, then back up to the open ward, and I saw Mark again in the garden. I told him that I was not well and did not know what I was doing when I threatened to kill him. He understood, we were just like before, mates again. I apologized to Michelle, gave her a pouch of tobacco, and made her tea all the time. She was all right, and I spoilt her as I would never have hurt her intentionally.

I eventually got out after an exceptionally long time. I was out for a month, but I never ever learnt as I went to Darren's one New Year's Eve, he said he was having a party with lots of birds, but there were not any, it was just the two of us, he had tricked me into it. He said why don't we just do an ecstasy tablet, called Snow White I said, "no I can't take anything anymore as nothing agrees with me", I said. After a few drinks I asked him to get four ecstasy pills two each, Darren did not normally do drugs he was a big beer drinker. We done the two ecstasy pills, as he is blind in one eye, the working eye started spinning around, his face changed into the devil, his room started spinning, whilst he wanted to have a boxing match, he caught me in the jaw. He taught me some great fighting moves which did impress me. I was off my head all night, morning came, it was time to catch the taxi home. It was freezing cold, I looked up to a beautiful sky, there were red clouds everywhere, each cloud looked like a devil cloud. I went home, watching millions of red devil clouds for a few hours in the sky, every one of them had a body and face of different devils. I had loads of money on me, but I had run out of cannabis. I got a taxi to Andy's, he did not smoke it, but he could get it cheap he lived near Kingy. I was hallucinating in a bad way, it seemed like I was in hell, with an unbelievable insecure feeling. I saw devils everywhere even the taxi driver looked like Lucifer, I was very relieved to see Andy, he got me a nine bar of hash, He was trying to help me as he could see that I was in a right state from taking the ecstasy tablets, it was about eighteen hours since I had taken the pills, I was still flying. Andy was worried so he told me to stay with him till I felt ok, I told him I was going to go and knock Kingy out, for giving me the ecstasy tablets in the first place. I left Andy's and this girl was walking behind me. I started chucking money in the air, five hundred pounds for her to pick up as I thought I did not need money where I was going as I really wanted to beat Kingy up. I went banging on Kingy's door, he had an extraordinarily strong door, as he did not answer I told him I was going to kill him. I booted his door, I nearly got it open, but the old bill turned up with an ambulance. They took me to Glenbourne where loads of people who had taken the Snow-White ecstasy had all messed up, it had landed quite a few of us in hospital, as the ecstasy had been laced with acid.

I dashed to the toilet and put the nine- bar in the bin. The staff knew what I was doing and confiscated it. When I was in hospital Kingy was worried, he came to visit, I apologized for trying to kick his door down, but he had forgiven me. He told me that Andy was in prison, Kingy used to get fake designer clothes cheap, Andy got thousands of pounds worth on credit when he sold them, he had to pay the money back Kingy had helped him get the clothes from his friend. Andy had swindled it; it was three thousand pounds worth, he pretended that he was in prison, but he was not really, he was out so he didn't have to pay the money back. A good move because Kingy and his mate fell for it and they were always ripping people off, all the time, especially Kingy.

It took me another three months of being there and I agreed to go to Rehab to finally get off speed as it was the cause of all my wrongdoings. I was severely depressed, it was just a little place with four people there, but I stuck it out as drugs had made me do the evilest of acts. Jason came to the Rehab after a few months of me being there we walked over to a football field and smoked weed, Jason went nuts on it, a right mess it made him go crazy. Nick W was there well that is what he called himself, but that was his bogus name, Nick was into his hardcore music, time went so slow, but I managed to get through it. The building was ancient, it felt like it was haunted, we played football across the fields, I went fishing with a professional angler, I had never caught a fish before, but with his help, we caught about fifty fish in one day. He rubbed oil on his line, but he knew where to cast, I had never seen anything like it before, so many fish. We did chuck them back into the sea, I played snooker sometimes with the group and played five aside football every week.

Finally, I got out of Rehab after six months of being there. I went back to my flat, my brother, and his friend were staying with me, Mat would look out for me, we did get up to some mischief, though. Alan pinched a van from Marjon's University, it said Marjon on the side of the van. We went out pinching statues from people's gardens, my brother was not as bad as Alan was, always getting up to mischief, but he followed the crowd. Me and Alan were getting up to mischief one late evening, we looked up above us and these lights were in the sky spinning, like a huge UFO, not far above our heads, it stayed for a long time before disappearing at four in the morning, it was something out of the ordinary, I have never seen anything like it.

    Two days later I went out with my sister for a drink, I was shaking like a leaf from the medication, we went to a pub there was a lad called Paul, a brilliant lad who worked as a builder. He was a TCE lad but took heroin, he was kind, not a thief he was not your usual heroin addict, he worked hard for his money, he bought me a drink. I dropped the pint on the floor it smashed everywhere, it was not exceptionally long after this, a couple of weeks or so, that Paul died of a heroin overdose which was so sad, he was particularly good friends with my sister.

Chapter 19. The Devils Trap

My sister phoned a friend in a pub as my sister thought Tracey might come out for a drink. My sister thought she would match me, so I spoke to her on the phone. Tracey sounded sexy with her Husky voice, so I asked her if she wanted to go for a drink. She told me to come to her house during the week, so I did. I took some wine and chocolates. I got on well with her, I asked "do you know Cathy as you look like her?" I do not know why, I said that. She said, "how did you know that Cathy was my friend, I said I don't know. After that I said to Tracey you look like a roman gipsy. She told me that she had Italian Irish blood, her dad was an Irish gipsy, she had lost her Mum when she was fourteen. I felt so sorry for her, Tracey told me her sons, and everybody had accused her of murdering her ex-boyfriend, whom she had moved down from Essex with.

I should have had the sense to get out of there then, she was drunk, I spent the night there and all that a typical man would say was that she was easy. The following day Mum and my sister turned up, with one of the staff nurses from Glenbourne, they wanted me to go back to hospital for a brief time. I said "no, not again what have I done wrong"? and broke down. The nurse told me that I had cancer and needed to get treatment, so I went to the hospital in tears, thinking I had cancer. I did not want to leave Tracey, more mug me, but I stupidly felt like that at the time, I was not really that well when I met her. They told me that they had lied to get me back to the hospital, which was sick to lie saying that I had cancer, unbelievable, Mum and my sister heard those exact words.

While I was in hospital for a short stay, she cheated on me although she denied that I knew that she had I should have gotten out of that relationship, then. I told her it was over, and she begged me to go back with her. I sure wish I had not, but I did. She was much older than me, by twelve years with a son called Martin, who lived with his dad, the other son Stephen, lived with her, he did not like me at all. He was good at art and drew pictures of himself holding a knife, with me in the picture where he had stabbed me to death, I found that very disturbing he was quite an evil child. Tracey told me about the murder all the time, later I discovered that the person who murdered her ex-boyfriend was the man in the mental hospital. So, I am going out with another accused person, of the same murder, that was truly one in a million, that I had ended up with her, I was the only person in the world, who he had told.

I fell for her lies straight away, I was a fool getting with her, but she had helped me get off that evil drug, speed. Really though I had done it myself, she was one of those people who tried to take all the credit. I was in a hell's den, but I did not realize that until Tracey drank, then the hellish living nightmare began she went mad being accused of murder. I was there to tell her that she did not and put her at ease after a while. Tracey had a terrible temper on drink, she told me that she had stabbed Peter, a couple of weeks before the murder, and that she had stabbed him nine times in the chest. If Peter had not dropped the charges Peter would have still been alive today, her ex lied, he said he was holding the knife in his hands with her hands because he loved her so much. She repeated this every time she drank. She was lovely when she did not drink, that is what made me stay with her. She was very caring, but when she drank wine, she was like the devil had taken over her, she was violent, and her mouth was evil, it changed her into a different person. I took her out for drinks, she would start fights with men for no reason, I never had an enjoyable time when Tracey drank, I cannot recall it ever being a laugh, it was draining and embarrassing just doom and gloom, she was so erratic and unpredictable. She mentally abused her children and violently as wine bottles were thrown at their heads and glass ashtrays.

When I first got with her, she even took a knife out with her, when we returned home a women who lived a few houses away knocked on Tracey's door asked her to turn the music down, she went mad and five minutes later, Tracey knocked on the lady's house then had stabbed the neighbour, but the knife flew out of the girl's belly and did not penetrate her skin. The girl had not felt nor seen the knife; she was a large girl, and it bounced off her belly, onto the grass, as the police arrived, I kicked the knife, so the police did not see it.

I could understand now why her ex had died as she argued so much, she tried to kill me, or mentally abuse me every time that she drank, she was a binge drinker, she was like a ticking time bomb, with a bomb that would always go off. She never gave her motor mouth a rest, when that evil wine went down her bottomless pit, she drank three bottles of wine before going out. It was like she took a big bag full of amphetamine and would not give it a break about her ex-husband, telling one of her kids they were a mistake, slagging their dad off and all her ex-boyfriends. She phoned people and family ending up threatening to kill them by the end of the phone call.

 Her Mum was a Roman gypsy who died when she was fourteen years old it must have had a massive effect on her, I think. She only talked about them when she was drunk, she told the same old stories when she was drunk, from the previous time. She always went on about being accused of murder, and how she had gone to court, and found not guilty in the end. I married her a few years after getting with her, the nightmare then really started.

On our wedding night, I said "ok" to a female staff member in the hotel, she went crazy, holding a glass in her hand, telling me to get out and that we were over, it was crazy. She threatened to stab me with the wine glass, for just saying ok to someone, I should have walked then but I did not. I paid for a single room on my weeding night. The next day we ended up going to Newquay for a week, the worst honeymoon ever. After leaving the bar, I said goodbye to a couple that we had been talking with, she accused me of flirting with the lady whom I really was not. I was just being friendly; she was the one who would flirt with anyone. She began getting violent with her mouth, I just pretended to be asleep to shut her up. Nevertheless, it did not work because I was not listening to her, going on about her ex-husband or ex boyfriends, who had all done her wrong in the past. She lived in the past, on drink, she took a bite out of my stomach, I pushed her back restraining her, she had a chunk of my flesh in her mouth, with blood dripping from her teeth. I pushed her back, but she would not let go, so I pushed her harder off me she went flying off the bed, saying that it was all my fault, and that I had done her back in. She picked up the TV, and threw it towards me, smashing it up, people were shouting all night "can you please be quiet. The bathroom door came at me as she ripped it off, she had a lot of strength for a woman. She then threw a lamp shade, and a chair until I managed to get out of there, I felt so sorry for the poor man who owned the little hotel, the room looked like a bomb had hit it. He was stood outside, he said it all needs to be paid for in the morning, other guests said, "poor you" We have been listening to her all night, it was five in the morning, they said get out of the relationship while you can, she is evil, they didn't even know half of the story. The next day we pretended that we did not have any money, she gave him a ring, she had many that I had bought her.

Like an idiot she made me feel so sorry for her the next day, saying that I had broken her back, I was a pure mug. She always went on about when she got raped, well before I knew her, back in Essex, I could tell that she even lied about that, as the story always changed especially when she drank. She was someone who had slept around a lot, after three weeks of being with her, she and a friend at the time went out, she even got me to baby sit for one of her kids. She did not come home all night, something was not right, I think it was two in the afternoon, the next day she eventually came home. She was bruised all over her body, she had slept with her best friend's boyfriend, her friend had beaten her up for it. I found out years later, she had never spoken to her friend after that, she lied to me then, and lied that she had been raped. Her friend told me the truth years later, that she had slept with her boyfriend, I should have run a mile then, what was I doing. She had three kids, one with someone in Essex who lived in London, she was bad back then, her sister pretended to be his Mum, as her big family thought she was not capable of looking after him, they all knew about her violent ways on drink. The other one I got on well with, he lived with his dad luckily, the son that I lived with was gay. I have nothing against gays whatsoever, but I did not like him as he was pure evil. One night she had a few friends around, one of them was bisexual who I knew, the other lady I had only ever seen once before.

I was walking back from visiting my Mum, I had a gut feeling like my soul felt nervous, I knew that something was not right, I felt sick and felt like I was being cheated on, something was telling me. I walked into the house I went into the front room; Tracey was getting off with the lady who she only just got to know. I said to her bisexual friend "how long have they been like this"? She did not even see me, she said that they had been kissing for five minutes. They were gripped together, kissing each other passionately, they would not let go, their lips sealed together. I chucked the lady out, and I smashed her phone on the floor, she was well ugly, to just rub salt into the wound. It was just after that thank God, that I was seriously going off her especially after that, she stuck to the story that I was mad in the head, and I was making it all up, I could not forget nor forgive. There were loads more that went on, I mean it would take me another book to write it all. I tried for many years to draft a book, she did not like me writing, as it meant I needed my own space, and that she wouldn't get any attention. She drank every day, she often threatened me with knifes, or there would be a massive argument every time, she did it to all her ex-boyfriends I found out threaten to kill them or their places smashed up. I was just the next victim, I used to love a drink, but she put me right off that, as if I had, I might have ended up doing something to her, if she had pushed my buttons too hard. I would roar just like a lion at her, if she ever crossed the line with her knifes, I had to restrain her on many occasions, getting scratched, bitten, or punched, but not once did I ever hit her. I think many men would of, hit her but I never would, even though she lied so many times. If I had hit her, I would have known about it, I restrained her for her own safety, and for my own safety too, otherwise just like her ex before, I would have been dead.

She knew not to fuck with me, as I had a temper, especially after she had shouted for the whole night, which turned me into a complete nut. I had to shout at her to shut up, all night long the poor people next door had to live with the constant shouting. I had been trying to draft my book for about six months. I lived downstairs, we were living separately, she had met new friends. Some were males who went upstairs, she was a terrible flirt, she had a massive attention disorder, but she never went to the doctor about her mental illness, she always claimed that she was of sound mind. I had met thousands of people in my life, and even was in the cuckoo's nest where they housed the craziest people in my urban area, however she had to be the craziest person I had ever met in my whole life when she drank alcohol. Anyone ever around her would simply have more than a major headache, as she would just not let anyone speak a word, she must have had the biggest motor mouth in the UK that I have ever met. She never gave her gob a rest, from the moment she had a glass of wine, she was like the devil out to punish anyone who had to listen to her never-ending stories. But I felt sorry for her and could never leave as she was the nicest, caring person when she did not drink. I could not love her at this stage anymore, nor could I really understand how I could love being mentally abused with no sex life and being threatened to be killed every time the bitch drank. You would have thought she would have learnt from her bad drinking habit, after her ex died, through the drink that had made her turn into an evil devil. She had had thousands of fights with me, mentally and with knives in her hands, shouting for hours till the drink wore off, it was pure hell, as I knew it. She was the most dangerous person I have ever had a drink with, and I had met loads of hooligans, mental patients, however she was the most dangerous.

I did not get any sleep for weeks and weeks, as I was trying to draft this book, from quite a few years ago. I started playing music, as she would thump and bang on the ceiling with a stick, just to annoy me, whilst I was trying to write. She started getting violent whilst drinking again, I got chucked out of the house as I had gone to put the bins out, she closed the door on me and phoned the police. She told the police that I had been threatening to kill her, she got the domestic violence team against me, when it should have been the other way around. I wasted sixteen years of marriage but had a lucky escape. A local police officer who I grew up, with stopped me in the police car, then a riot van turned up, I said" I am not being arrested." The police officer said, "no but what are doing with that psycho"? "This is your opportunity to leave her and sort your life out."

Chapter 20. The Devils Maze

I lived in bed and breakfasts, hotels, for which my family helped to pay. The council could not help me at that time, although eventually they did. I could not sleep for a couple of weeks, and that is when psychosis came back, just as it was from twenty years before. I was in a hotel and started to hallucinate, I was watching Tyson Fury on one of his fights, and Tyson said if you ask God for anything, he will grant it to you if you believe that anything is possible. I was forty-six years old at the time, but I thought that if anyone in the world could beat him in a fight, it was me, it sent me over the edge, again. I believed that if you asked God for anything he would grant you that if you believed in yourself. I had been praying for about a year before, I do believe in the afterlife, even if those around me do not, I am not one for church as they have too many rules which is just not the way it should be. I believed that I could beat Tyson in a fight, so I trained hard. I was hoping for a date with

Tyson, I had never boxed before but I could fight. I had a weapon my right arm was as fast as a bullet; I trained my weaker arm to be as strong as my right arm. Getting a fight was going to be impossible but I texted him on social media quite a few times, but I never had a reply.

I was homeless, getting moved from one hotel to the other, the council sometimes paid the bill, but other days the council left me on the streets, and my family stepped in and paid. I was punching walls, windows, anything to build me up, I was so fast and even showed people how fast I really was. I am a diabetic type 1, I do not know if insulin makes you faster, but I was super-fast, I ran around Plymouth trying to get fit as I really thought I could get into a fight with Tyson.

I thought even being forty-six that I could beat him in a fight. Punching no stop to what would have been his head, so high, I worked on punching so high in the air, as he was much taller than me, I was doing this training for a long while. I was psychotic again, by simply not sleeping, doing my book, and training to fight Tyson Fury. I really thought I could do it as Tyson's words made me believe anything was possible. I was fifty times stronger, I was so fast, I trained all day, at night I was doing my book a little bit, as I was researching things what were in my book at the time. I was doing my research on free masons on the internet. It said the grandmaster was considered a brother of the royal family. I had totally lost the plot and thought that my Great Grandad was related to the royal family. By reading it wrongly I started thinking that I oversaw the freemasons, I thought I was like the Mafia. I was going up to people saying you are a freemason, thinking that the whole city consisted of spies, I even asked friends to join. I was in a matrix world, even the dance tunes I listened to were speaking to me through the music.

I even went to a bed and breakfast, I got a taxi from Mum's house, the taxi driver told me he was from Europe, and that he was a famous DJ, who played at Tomorrowland, he told me that he kept busy and was working for the freemasons. I thought that I was in charge after speaking to him, I thought that this must have been a code. We were not to speak about it, but he had spoken.

I was more convinced I was a freemason, and I was under a test to see if I could cope. I was not well and psychotic, it was so real and intense the taxi driver had told me he was worth over twenty million pounds when I asked him how much he was worth. I then believed even more what he said his name he did look like a DJ that I had seen on you tube. He told me to look him up on

Facebook and that I could play a set with him and meet him at Tomorrowland.

The bed and breakfast where I stayed, I thought, was being run by the Illuminati as it had a massive Illuminati flag outside the building. The big Chinese man had strict rules like being in by ten o'clock, I thought in the psychotic world I was under a test to become the new grandmaster of the freemasons, like my great-grandfather before me, I lost the plot for sure and all because of I had no sleep for a month.

A young girl was brutally murdered in Mum's neighbourhood; Mum worked at the school; she was terribly upset at what had happened; she knew the girl quite well. I cannot mention names, it would not be fair as I do not have permission. The poor girl was waiting at a bus stop to catch a bus to see her boyfriend, a car pulled up and this sick boy dragged her into the car, beat her, took her to the moors, and killed her, he left her body by a nearby beach. I was in bed and breakfast it was dark I was looking out to sea at the Hoe. My room turned into a pyramid like a temple with a window looking out to sea, with magical views over Plymouth Sound I was looking out from the Hoe, then it was like someone had spiked me with an acid tab. I could see the girl who had died as an angel, but in her favourite colour, she was a purple angel. There were two angels there, another purple one glowing like magical. Christmas lights, but breath-taking with massive red hearts, beside each of them, they were a few meters apart. They stayed outside of my window, next to a parking meter all night, every time I looked out, I could see the angel who I was convinced was her. Then it was so scary it sounded like a bomb had gone off in a nearby hotel, it made the whole building shake, my ears were ringing it was so loud. I looked up to the stars; each one had turned into all the star signs. They were all dancing with each other, it was beautiful, it looked like they were having a party in the sky. So many colours and angels of all sorts were lighting up the sky. The colours were out of this world, I could see heaven in the sky. The gold colour was a sight that only I seemed to see, I will never ever forget that it was real at the time looking through my eyes, either in my reality or through my psychosis. I prayed every day after what Tyson Fury had said, I thought God was showing me heaven, as only certain people could see this magical world, I had a sense there was really something else out there it was unbelievable, and I felt no fear.

I heard a lad talking to the Chinese man, he was put into the room next to me, I recognized his voice saying he just came from Glenbourne, I went out of my room to say hello, but he looked so evil, and had no response. A voice told me that he had killed the girl from the bus stop. On our wall it said no noise after midnight, he was off his head on drugs but not as off it as me, I told him to "shut the fuck up, it was one thirty." He shouted, "you are the one shouting not me," he just carried on being loud and talking to himself. I was not well, and tripping, the angel was outside telling me to kill him, "he killed me," said the angel. I started tapping the wall, he told me to shut up. I kept on tapping on it until four in the morning, driving him mad on purpose.

We all had to share the toilet, there were four rooms upstairs, you could hear when each person went to the toilet. I could hear that the lad had gone to use the toilet, I went out and said, "come on then," he looked like the devil, he had demon features and ran into his room. I went to his door and started booting it, he opened it, I beat the hell out of him, I thought that I had killed him. I went back to my room, I was going to inject him with my insulin, as I really thought that he had killed that poor girl. I was lucky that he was ok, and that he had not grassed me up for the beating, that I had given him, he was out of it, on whatever drugs that he had taken, which also helped me to not get arrested.

The next morning, I thought that I had passed the test, and that I was a grandmaster in charge of all the underground spies, even the Illuminati. I walked into town; the leaders of the illuminati were speaking through speakers. Cameras were everywhere, they could see what was going on, and even told me when to take my insulin, they were talking to me through my earphones. I constantly listened to dance music, I had a personal trainer through the music, telling me to punch, run and I was getting training for the Tyson fight. I was fit and fired up on a mad one to the max, I would have beaten Tyson, as I was one hundred times my normal strength, I was on fire, training non-stop.

My family thought I was crazy, which I clearly was, I questioned to whether I was part of the royal family, the whole thing about what I saw that night in the bed and breakfast. I felt on top of the world, flying with no care in the world, I thought I was going to be rich; I only had a thousand pounds on me, maybe more, it did not last very long as I went around and gave it away to all the homeless people in the City Centre. I bumped into a lady outside a refuge place for the homeless, she had nowhere to stay as the refuge was full up.

The lady gave me a story, she claimed to be William Wallace, Braveheart the film, was based on the life of

William Wallace, she was an elderly woman who claimed to remember everything from her past life. Some friends used to call me Braveheart, growing up because of my mixed blood, being a native American, and having Scottish and English blood, so it was strange hearing her story. She was on the streets, she had no help from the council, she told me that she had been dead and buried in the ground for an exceptionally long time. She was then re-born thousands of years later and claimed that the English had killed her. She had had the worst death anyone could ever imagine and told me that she had been tortured brutally before her death. She claimed to be William in her past life, she believed it so much so and she was not on drugs, like the majority who pretended to be on the streets. Some just begged for their drug habit, she was genuine about her situation. I knew the system, she was on the streets, freezing cold, her story touched me, she looked like a big man, but she was a woman raped by someone who she had lived with, she was about sixty years old. She was in the middle of drafting a book about her past life as William Wallace. It was cold, I took her for something to eat. She told the horror life that she had as William Wallace, the execution of him was something that she always remembered, she really believed that in her past she was William Wallace. William's heart was ripped out of his body, his head was put onto London Bridge, to show his head and all the insides had been ripped out, she told me the horror story. She was on the streets that night, we ate something nice to eat in Turtle Bay. She spoke to me about her present life, she hated drugs and did not do them she had a drink and said, "it's the first I've had for years," I believed her and her story of being on the streets, as she could hardly walk. I gave her two hundred pounds; she could not believe it she went to a hotel.

My brother picked me up, as he thought that I needed help, which I did, I stayed at Mums. My brother took me to be assessed by a psychiatrist, my family thought I would be locked up for my own benefit. Me and my brother were in the accident and emergency bit of the hospital, it was so busy, staff were run off their feet. I used to work in this hospital, me and my brother started to muck in, helping patients to get comfortable and seeing to their needs for hours. I did not get seen that night, but they did arrange for specialists to see me, the next day so I slept at Mums to return to the hospital the next morning.

I was incredibly lucky to have a good family, otherwise I would have been left on the streets. When I went into a room full of people, I was asked a lot of questions, one was about what I had seen, out the window that night in the bed and breakfast. I said, "I saw heaven in the sky, why are you going to lock up and every person who goes to church"? I played it cool; I did not go on one, I said, "What's wrong with training to fight Tyson Fury"? They all agreed I did not need to go into hospital, but I had to promise to take tablets otherwise, I would be sectioned. I did as I was told, a taxi was sent to whichever hotel I was in, to be taken to Mount Gould hospital for a few tablets at six o'clock every evening.

I was tripping every day in an effective way; I thought the tablets that they gave to me were to help me to fight Tyson. I kept taking them, I was still flying for a few months, training every minute of the day, until the tablets got a hold of me, it was like a plane crash to the ground. I was high not a care in the world, and now the tablets were controlling my mind.

My arms from the air boxing for sixteen hours a day were killing for months, I had pulled every muscle in my arm. Only when I stopped, I hit reality, with a huge bang and I gave up weed. I stayed in hotels, I was moved around to many unusual places, it got too much being a diabetic I found it hard I was totally in a zombie state with no energy, my depression was deep, after flying for such a long time, I would have crashed for even longer.

I went back to my Mum for whom is the best Mum I could ever wish. I lived there for a year on strong tablets. After the year the tablets that I were taking made me into a shell, I felt empty and brain dead, I needed to get through hell to fix my brain. I stayed in bed for most of my time living there, after having treatment from Livewell. Eventually I argued that I wanted my brain back and that the tablets were making me brain dead. They eventually agreed after a year or two of being on them, I no longer had to take them, otherwise I would just be a living zombie, now. I was not going to let them do that to me, as I wanted to be the author of my book.

When taking tablets and trying to draft a book it is impossible, as your mind becomes blank, and you suffer constant panic attacks. I was placed in a shared supported house, where I managed to draft my book and finally, I finished it. I have now moved into a stunning flat, I am traveling the country again supporting my favourite football team, Plymouth Argyle, it is a great feeling, catching up with old and new friends. I have faith, I would never preach, but it has gotten me this far. I know that I have done some unbelievably dreadful things, and it causes mayhem in the past because of drugs and my violent act I was punished in hell, in a deep depression. Now I am on the better side, trying to be a good person and so lucky and grateful to be out of that hell of a marriage.

The reason for my book is to show that when someone has psychosis to try to see it from their mindset. Sleep is so important the one thing that I learnt, the hard way I am much better now, life feels good I can just start again, and give people hope that I turned my life around with a saine mindset no longer a drug user and clean from drugs. I do apologize for any repeated sentences in this book. I might have got events such as football fights the wrong way around. Writing has been particularly challenging for me due to my dyslexia. Thank you for reading to the end.

Printed in Great Britain
by Amazon